Consolatio
Philosophiae
The Consolation of Philosophy

Consolatio
Philosophiae

The Consolation of Philosophy

written by Boethius
translated by H.R. James

Pluteo Pleno • Chicago, Illinois

ConsolationePhilosophiae: The Consolation of Philosophy
Boethius
translated by H.R. James
edited by Peter Sipes

Pluteo Pleno
5516 N Linder Avenue
Chicago, Illinois 60630

www.opensourceclassics.com
www.pluteopleno.com

Edition 1.0, February 2014

ISBN 978-1-937847-04-3

Contents

Introduction

The purpose of this book is to put an affordable edition of Boethius's *Consolation of Philosophy* into your hands, but with a difference. What distinguishes this book from other editions is that the original Latin text is placed alongside the English translation.

Beyond that, every part of this book was assembled from publicly available texts and open source software. The world's cultural legacy is deep and deserves to be brought to those who are interested in it. And the original language of the book is part of that legacy. Expensive editions, copyright and linguistic inexperience have largely kept the original language of many books from curious readers. No more.

Before now, projects like this book never made it to publication because of its limited audience. Technology, specifically on-demand printing and online sales channels, has mostly solved the problem of a limited audience. Since I do not have to keep hundreds of copies of a book on hand to sell you one, I can easily make specialized editions available for sale.

The other advantage to on-demand is the ability to correct mistakes. In any book mistakes creep in. As mistakes are found and collected, they can be corrected in future editions quickly and easily.

Because translation is not an exact science and languages have different structures, there are discrepancies between the Latin and English side of each page. The page breaks have also been made so that the English and Latin on each page correspond to each other. As a result, the spacing between the lines varies. To help you keep track of paragraphs, I have added a ⸿ mark wherever one language starts a new paragraph where the other does not. Where the paragraphs line up between the two languages, there is no mark. I have added these two items as signposts to help you see the relation between the original language and the translation.

Without trying to overstate matters, Boethius's work is one that stands with one foot squarely in pagan antiquity and the other just as squarely in the Christian middle ages. C.S. Lewis once said, "To acquire a taste for it is almost to become naturalised in the Middle Ages." The next page has a selection of resources to get you started.

Happy exploring,
Peter Sipes

Resources

Print

Boethius The Consolation of Philosophy. Penguin classics, 1969.

Marenbon, John, (ed.) 2009, *The Cambridge Companion to Boethius.* Cambridge: Cambridge University Press.

Online

Georgetown's Consolatio Philosophiae – http://bit.ly/1m201vr – An old HTML website with commentaries on the *Consolatio Philosophiae*, including German language materials.

Stanford Encyclopedia of Philosophy – http://stanford.io/1eFuX23 – An overview of Boethius's writings and thought.

Annotations on the Latin – http://bit.ly/JTsEPE – The Perseus Project has put Weinberger's annotations for the *Consolatio Philosophiae* online.

King Alfred's Anglo-Saxon de Consolatione Philosophiae – http://bit.ly/1cZeTFD – As noted on the title, a translation of Boethius's work into Old English. Almost too medieval to actually exist.

Vocabulary analysis of *Consolatio Philosophiae* – http://bit.ly/1eVt9Cn – Concordance, frequency lists and statistics.

About the texts

The Latin text of *Consolatio Philosophiae* is taken from the version at Wikisource, which appears to have a CC-BY-SA license (though the text should be public domain at this point). The original paper edition of that text is not indicated. I've made no additions to the text save for an Latin translation of the included Greek text. Per license, the text is available at http://bit.ly/1aRxhAf.

The English translation of *The Consolation of Philosphy* is the James translation, which is in the public domain. It was transcribed along with James's notes by Johathan Ingram, Karina Aleksandrove and others. I have left in all but a few notes. To match the Latin, the text is available at http://bit.ly/1h9Vw1L.

Consolatio Philosophiae

The Consolation of Philosophy

Book I

Song I – Boethius' Complaint

Who wrought my studious numbers
Smoothly once in happier days,
Now perforce in tears and sadness
Learn a mournful strain to raise.
Lo, the Muses, grief-dishevelled,
Guide my pen and voice my woe;
Down their cheeks unfeigned the tear drops
To my sad complainings flow!
These alone in danger's hour
Faithful found, have dared attend
On the footsteps of the exile
To his lonely journey's end.
These that were the pride and pleasure
Of my youth and high estate
Still remain the only solace
Of the old man's mournful fate.
Old? Ah yes; swift, ere I knew it,
By these sorrows on me pressed
Age hath come; lo, Grief hath bid me
Wear the garb that fits her best.
O'er my head untimely sprinkled
These white hairs my woes proclaim,
And the skin hangs loose and shrivelled
On this sorrow-shrunken frame.
Blest is death that intervenes not
In the sweet, sweet years of peace,
But unto the broken-hearted,
When they call him, brings release!
Yet Death passes by the wretched,
Shuts his ear and slumbers deep;
Will not heed the cry of anguish,
Will not close the eyes that weep.
For, while yet inconstant Fortune

Liber Primus

Metrum I

Carmina qui quondam studio florente peregi,
Flebilis heu maestos cogor inire modos.
Ecce mihi lacerae dictant scribenda Camenae
Et ueris elegi fletibus ora rigant.
Has saltem nullus potuit peruincere terror,
Ne nostrum comites prosequerentur iter.
Gloria felicis olim uiridisque iuuentae,
Solantur maesti nunc mea fata senis.
Venit enim properata malis inopina senectus
Et dolor aetatem iussit inesse suam.
Intempestiui funduntur uertice cani
Et tremit effeto corpore laxa cutis.
Mors hominum felix, quae se nec dulcibus annis
Inserit et maestis saepe uocata uenit.
Eheu, quam surda miseros auertitur aure
Et flentes oculos claudere saeua negat!

Poured her gifts and all was bright,
Death's dark hour had all but whelmed me
In the gloom of endless night.
Now, because misfortune's shadow
Hath o'erclouded that false face,
Cruel Life still halts and lingers,
Though I loathe his weary race.
Friends, why did ye once so lightly
Vaunt me happy among men?
Surely he who so hath fallen
Was not firmly founded then.

I

While I was thus mutely pondering within myself, and recording my sorrowful complainings with my pen, it seemed to me that there appeared above my head a woman of a countenance exceeding venerable. Her eyes were bright as fire, and of a more than human keenness; her complexion was lively, her vigour showed no trace of enfeeblement; and yet her years were right full, and she plainly seemed not of our age and time. Her stature was difficult to judge. At one moment it exceeded not the common height, at another her forehead seemed to strike the sky; and whenever she raised her head higher, she began to pierce within the very heavens, and to baffle the eyes of them that looked upon her. Her garments were of an imperishable fabric, wrought with the finest threads and of the most delicate workmanship; and these, as her own lips afterwards assured me, she had herself woven with her own hands. The beauty of this vesture had been somewhat tarnished by age and neglect, and wore that dingy look which marble contracts from exposure. On the lower-most edge was inwoven the Greek letter Π [Greek: P], on the topmost the letter θ [Greek: Th],[1] and between the two were to be seen steps, like a staircase, from the lower to the upper letter. This robe, moreover, had been torn by the hands of violent persons, who had each snatched away what he could clutch.[2] Her right hand held a note-book; in her left she bore a staff. ⟨And when she saw the Muses of Poesie standing by my bedside, dictating the words of my lamentations, she was moved awhile to wrath, and her eyes flashed sternly. 'Who,' said she, 'has allowed yon play-acting wantons to approach this sick man—these who, so far from giving medicine to heal his malady, even feed it with sweet poison? These it is who kill the rich crop of reason with the barren thorns of passion, who accustom men's minds to disease, instead of setting them free. Now, were it some common man whom your allurements were seducing, as is usually your way, I should be less indignant. On such a one I should not have spent my pains for naught. But this is one nurtured in the Eleatic and Academic philosophies. Nay, get ye gone, ye sirens, whose sweetness lasteth not; leave him for my muses to tend and heal!' At these words of upbraiding, the whole band, in deepened sadness, with downcast eyes, and blushes that confessed their shame, dolefully left the chamber.

---

1   Π (P) stands for the Political life, the life of action; θ (Th) for the Theoretical life, the life of thought.

2   The Stoic, Epicurean, and other philosophical sects, which Boethius regards as heterodox.

Dum leuibus male fida bonis fortuna faueret
Paene caput tristis merserat hora meum;
Nunc quia fallacem mutauit nubila uultum
Protrahit ingratas impia uita moras.
Quid me felicem totiens iactastis, amici?
Qui cecidit, stabili non erat ille gradu.

Prosa I

Haec dum me cum tacitus ipse reputarem querimoniamque lacrimabilem stili officio sig‑
narem astitisse mihi supra uerticem uisa est mulier reuerendi admodum uultus, oculis arden‑
tibus et ultra commumem hominum ualentiam perspicacibus, colore uiuido atque inexhausti
uigoris, quamuis ita aeui plena foret ut nullo modo nostrae crederetur aetatis, statura discre‑
tionis ambiguae. Nam nunc quidem ad communem sese hominum mensuram cohibebat,nunc
uero pulsare caelum summi uerticis cacumine uidebatur; quae cum altius caput extulisset
ipsum etiam caelum penetrabat respicientiumque hominum frustrabatur intuitum. Vestes
erant tenuissimis filis subtili artificio indissolubili materia perfectae, quas, uti post eadem
prodente cognoui, suis manibus ipsa texuerat; quarum speciem, ueluti fumosas imagines so‑
let, caligo quaedam neglectae uetustatis obduxerat. Harum in extremo margine π[1] graecum,
in supremo uero θ[2] legebatur intextum atque inter utrasque litteras in scalarum modum
gradus quidam insigniti uidebantur, quibus ab inferiore ad superius elementum esset as‑
census. Eandem tamen uestem uiolentorum quorundam sciderant manus et particulas quas
quisque potuit abstulerant. Et dextra quidem eius libellos, sceptrum uero sinistra gestabat.

Quae ubi poeticas Musas uidit nostro assistentes toro fletibusque meis uerba dictantes,
commota paulisper ac toruis inflammata luminibus: quis, inquit, has scenicas meretriculas ad
hunc aegrum permisit accedere, quae dolores eius non modo nullis remediis fouerent, uerum
dulcibus insuper alerent uenenis? Hae sunt enim quae infructuosis affectuum spinis uberem
fructibus rationis segetem necant hominumque mentes assuefaciunt morbo, non liberant. At
si quem profanum, uti uulgo solitum uobis, blanditiae uestrae detraherent, minus moleste fer‑
endum putarem — nihil quippe in eo nostrae operae laederentur — hunc uero Eleaticis
atque Academicis studiis innutritum? Sed abite potius, Sirenes usque in exitium dulces,
meisque eum Musis curandum sanandumque relinquite. His ille chorus increpitus deiecit

---

1   latine scrbitur p littera
2   latine scribuntur th litterae

But I, because my sight was dimmed with much weeping, and I could not tell who was this woman of authority so commanding—I was dumfoundered, and, with my gaze fastened on the earth, continued silently to await what she might do next. Then she drew near me and sat on the edge of my couch, and, looking into my face all heavy with grief and fixed in sadness on the ground, she bewailed in these words the disorder of my mind:

Song II – His Despondency.

Alas! in what abyss his mind
Is plunged, how wildly tossed!
Still, still towards the outer night
She sinks, her true light lost,
As oft as, lashed tumultuously
By earth-born blasts, care's waves rise high.

Yet once he ranged the open heavens,
The sun's bright pathway tracked;
Watched how the cold moon waxed and waned;
Nor rested, till there lacked
To his wide ken no star that steers
Amid the maze of circling spheres.

The causes why the blusterous winds
Vex ocean's tranquil face,
Whose hand doth turn the stable globe,
Or why his even race
From out the ruddy east the sun
Unto the western waves doth run:

What is it tempers cunningly
The placid hours of spring,
So that it blossoms with the rose
For earth's engarlanding:
Who loads the year's maturer prime
With clustered grapes in autumn time:

All this he knew—thus ever strove
Deep Nature's lore to guess.
Now, reft of reason's light, he lies,
And bonds his neck oppress;
While by the heavy load constrained,
His eyes to this dull earth are chained.

humi maestior uultum confessusque rubore uerecundiam limen tristis excessit. ⟨At ego, cuius acies lacrimis mersa caligaret nec dinoscere possem quaenam haec esset mulier tam imperiosae auctoritatis, obstupui uisuque in terram defixo quidnam deinceps esset actura exspectare tacitus coepi. Tum illa propius accedens in extrema lectuli mei parte consedit meumque intuens uultum luctu grauem atque in humum maerore deiectum his uersibus de nostrae mentis perturbatione conquesta est:

Metrum II

Heu, quam praecipiti mersa profundo
Mens hebet et propria luce relicta
Tendit in externas ire tenebras
Terrenis quotiens flatibus aucta
Crescit in immensum noxia cura!
Hic quondam caelo liber aperto
Suetus in aetherios ire meatus
Cernebat rosei lumina solis,
Visebat gelidae sidera lunae
Et quaecumque uagos stella recursus
Exercet uarios flexa per orbes
Comprensam numeris uictor habebat;
Quin etiam causas unde sonora
Flamina sollicitent aequora ponti,
Quis uolat stabilem spiritus orbem
Vel cur hesperias sidus in undas
Casurum rutilo surgat ab ortu,
Quid ueris placidas temperet horas
Vt terram roseis floribus ornet,
Quis dedit ut pleno fertilis anno
Autumnus grauidis influat uuis
Rimari solitus atque latentis
Naturae uarias reddere causas:
Nunc iacet effeto lumine mentis
Et pressus grauibus colla catenis
Decliuem que gerens pondere uultum
Cogitur, heu, stolidam cernere terram.

II.

'But the time,' said she, 'calls rather for healing than for lamentation.' Then, with her eyes bent full upon me, 'Art thou that man,' she cries, 'who, erstwhile fed with the milk and reared upon the nourishment which is mine to give, had grown up to the full vigour of a manly spirit? And yet I had bestowed such armour on thee as would have proved an invincible defence, hadst thou not first cast it away. Dost thou know me? Why art thou silent? Is it shame or amazement that hath struck thee dumb? Would it were shame; but, as I see, a stupor hath seized upon thee.' Then, when she saw me not only answering nothing, but mute and utterly incapable of speech, she gently touched my breast with her hand, and said: 'There is no danger; these are the symptoms of lethargy, the usual sickness of deluded minds. For awhile he has forgotten himself; he will easily recover his memory, if only he first recognises me. And that he may do so, let me now wipe his eyes that are clouded with a mist of mortal things.' Thereat, with a fold of her robe, she dried my eyes all swimming with tears.

Song III — The Mists dispelled

Then the gloom of night was scattered,
Sight returned unto mine eyes.
So, when haply rainy Caurus
Rolls the storm-clouds through the skies,
Hidden is the sun; all heaven
Is obscured in starless night.
But if, in wild onset sweeping,
Boreas frees day's prisoned light,
All suddenly the radiant god outstreams,
And strikes our dazzled eyesight with his beams.

III

Even so the clouds of my melancholy were broken up. I saw the clear sky, and regained the power to recognise the face of my physician. Accordingly, when I had lifted my eyes and fixed my gaze upon her, I beheld my nurse, Philosophy, whose halls I had frequented from my youth up.

'Ah! why,' I cried, 'mistress of all excellence, hast thou come down from on high, and entered the solitude of this my exile? Is it that thou, too, even as I, mayst be persecuted with false accusations?'

'Could I desert thee, child,' said she, 'and not lighten the burden which thou hast taken upon thee through the hatred of my name, by sharing this trouble? Even forgetting that it were not lawful for Philosophy to leave companionless the way of the innocent, should I, thinkest thou, fear to incur reproach, or shrink from it, as though some strange new thing had befallen? Thinkest thou that now, for the first time in an evil age, Wisdom hath been assailed by peril? Did I not often in days of old, before my servant Plato lived, wage stern warfare with the rashness of folly? In his lifetime, too, Socrates, his master, won with my aid the victory of an unjust death. And when, one after the other, the Epicurean herd, the Stoic, and the

Prosa II

Sed medicinae, inquit, tempus est quam querelae. Tum uero totis in me intenta lu‑
minibus: tune ille es, ait, qui nostro quondam lacte nutritus, nostris educatus alimentis in uir‑
ilis animi robur euaseras? Atqui talia contuleramus arma quae nisi prior abiecisses inuicta te
firmitate tuerentur. Agnoscisne me? Quid taces? Pudore an stupore siluisti? Mallem pudore,
sed te, ut uideo, stupor oppressit. Cumque me non modo tacitum sed elinguem prorsus mu‑
tumque uidisset, ammouit pectori meo leniter manum et: nihil, inquit, pericli est, lethargum
patitur, communem illusarum mentium morbum. Sui paulisper oblitus est. Recordabitur fa‑
cile, si quidem nos ante cognouerit; quod ut possit, paulisper lumina eius mortalium rerum
nube caligantia tergamus. Haec dixit oculosque meos fletibus undantes contracta in rugam
ueste siccauit.

Metrum III

Tunc me discussa liquerunt nocte tenebrae
Luminibusque prior rediit uigor,
Vt cum praecipiti glomerantur sidera Coro
Nimbosisque polus stetit imbribus
Sol latet ac nondum caelo uenientibus astris
Desuper in terram nox funditur;
Hanc si Threicio Boreas emissus ab antro
Verberet et clausum reseret diem
Emicat et subito uibratus lumine Phoebus
Mirantes oculos radiis ferit

Prosa III

Haud aliter tristitiae nebulis dissolutis hausi caelum et ad cognoscendam medicantis fa‑
ciem mentem recepi. Itaque ubi in eam deduxi oculos intuitumque defixi, respicio nutricem
meam, cuius ab adulescentia laribus obuersatus fueram, Philosophiam.

Et quid, inquam, tu in has exsilii nostri solitudines, o omnium magistra uirtutum, supero
cardine delapsa uenisti? An ut tu quoque me cum rea falsis criminationibus agiteris?

— An, inquit illa, te, alumne, desererem nec sarcinam quam mei nominis inuidia sus‑
tulisti communicato te cum labore partirer? Atqui Philosophiae fas non erat incomitatum re‑
linquere iter innocentis. Meam scilicet criminationem uererer et quasi nouum aliquid acci‑
deret perhorrescerem? Nunc enim primum censes apud improbos mores lacessitam periculis
esse sapientiam? Nonne apud ueteres quoque ante nostri Platonis aetatem magnum saepe cer‑
tamen cum stultitiae temeritate certauimus eodemque superstite praeceptor eius Socrates
iniustae uictoriam mortis me astante promeruit? Cuius hereditatem cum deinceps Epi‑
cureum uulgus ac Stoicum ceterique pro sua quisque parte raptum ire molirentur meque

rest, each of them as far as in them lay, went about to seize the heritage he left, and were dragging me off protesting and resisting, as their booty, they tore in pieces the garment which I had woven with my own hands, and, clutching the torn pieces, went off, believing that the whole of me had passed into their possession. And some of them, because some traces of my vesture were seen upon them, were destroyed through the mistake of the lewd multitude, who falsely deemed them to be my disciples. It may be thou knowest not of the banishment of Anaxagoras, of the poison draught of Socrates, nor of Zeno's torturing, because these things happened in a distant country; yet mightest thou have learnt the fate of Arrius, of Seneca, of Soranus, whose stories are neither old nor unknown to fame. These men were brought to destruction for no other reason than that, settled as they were in my principles, their lives were a manifest contrast to the ways of the wicked. So there is nothing thou shouldst wonder at, if on the seas of this life we are tossed by storm-blasts, seeing that we have made it our chiefest aim to refuse compliance with evil-doers. And though, maybe, the host of the wicked is many in number, yet is it contemptible, since it is under no leadership, but is hurried hither and thither at the blind driving of mad error. And if at times and seasons they set in array against us, and fall on in overwhelming strength, our leader draws off her forces into the citadel while they are busy plundering the useless baggage. But we from our vantage ground, safe from all this wild work, laugh to see them making prize of the most valueless of things, protected by a bulwark which aggressive folly may not aspire to reach.'

Song IV — *Nothing can subdue Virtue.*

Whoso calm, serene, sedate,
Sets his foot on haughty fate;
Firm and steadfast, come what will,
Keeps his mien unconquered still;
Him the rage of furious seas,
Tossing high wild menaces,
Nor the flames from smoky forges
That Vesuvius disgorges,
Nor the bolt that from the sky
Smites the tower, can terrify.
Why, then, shouldst thou feel affright
At the tyrant's weakling might?
Dread him not, nor fear no harm,
And thou shall his rage disarm;
But who to hope or fear gives way—
Lost his bosom's rightful sway—
He hath cast away his shield,
Like a coward fled the field;
He hath forged all unaware
Fetters his own neck must bear!

reclamantem renitentemque uelut in partem praedae traherent, uestem quam meis texueram manibus disciderunt abreptisque ab ea panniculis totam me sibi cessisse credentes abiere. In quibus quoniam quaedam nostri habitus uestigia uidebantur, meos esse familiares impruden-tia rata nonnullos eorum profanae multitudinis errore peruertit. Quodsi nec Anaxagorae fu-gam nec Socratis uenenum nec Zenonis tormenta, quoniam sunt peregrina, nouisti, at Canios, at Senecas, at Soranos, quorum nec peruetusta nec incelebris memoria est, scire potuisti. Quos nihil aliud in cladem detraxit nisi quod nostris moribus instituti studiis improborum dissimillimi uidebantur. Itaque nihil est quod ammirere si in hoc uitae salo circumflantibus agitemur procellis, quibus hoc maxime propositum est, pessimis displicere. Quorum quidem tametsi est numerosus exercitus spernendus tamen est, quoniam nullo duce regitur sed errore tantum temere ac passim lymphante raptatur. Qui si quando contra nos aciem struens ualenti-or incubuerit, nostra quidem dux copias suas in arcem contrahit, illi uero circa diripiendas inutiles sarcinulas occupantur. At nos desuper irridemus uilissima rerum quaeque rapientes securi totius furiosi tumultus eoque uallo muniti quo grassanti stultitiae aspirare fas non sit.

Metrum IV

Quisquis composito serenus aeuo
Fatum sub pedibus egit superbum
Fortunamque tuens utramque rectus
Inuictum potuit tenere uultum,
Non illum miniaeque ponti
Versum funditus exagitantis aestum
Nec ruptis quotiens uagus caminis
Torquet fumificos Vesaeuus ignes
Aut celsas soliti ferire turres
Ardentis uia fulminis mouebit.
Quid tantum miseri saeuos tyrannos
Mirantur sine uiribus furentes?
Nec speres aliquid nec extimescas,
Exarmaueris impotentis iram;
At quisquis trepidus pauet uel optat,
Quod non sit stabilis suique iuris,
Abiecit clipeum locoque motus
Nectit qua ualeat trahi catenam.

IV

'Dost thou understand?' she asks. Do my words sink into thy mind? Or art thou dull "as the ass to the sound of the lyre"? Why dost thou weep? Why do tears stream from thy eyes?

'"Speak out, hide it not in thy heart."

If thou lookest for the physician's help, thou must needs disclose thy wound.'

Then I, gathering together what strength I could, began: 'Is there still need of telling? Is not the cruelty of fortune against me plain enough? Doth not the very aspect of this place move thee? Is this the library, the room which thou hadst chosen as thy constant resort in my home, the place where we so often sat together and held discourse of all things in heaven and earth? Was my garb and mien like this when I explored with thee nature's hid secrets, and thou didst trace for me with thy wand the courses of the stars, moulding the while my char- acter and the whole conduct of my life after the pattern of the celestial order? Is this the re- compense of my obedience? Yet thou hast enjoined by Plato's mouth the maxim, "that states would be happy, either if philosophers ruled them, or if it should so befall that their rulers would turn philosophers." By his mouth likewise thou didst point out this imperative reason why philosophers should enter public life, to wit, lest, if the reins of government be left to unprincipled and profligate citizens, trouble and destruction should come upon the good. Following these precepts, I have tried to apply in the business of public administration the principles which I learnt from thee in leisured seclusion. Thou art my witness and that di- vinity who hath implanted thee in the hearts of the wise, that I brought to my duties no aim but zeal for the public good. For this cause I have become involved in bitter and irreconcil- able feuds, and, as happens inevitably, if a man holds fast to the independence of conscience, I have had to think nothing of giving offence to the powerful in the cause of justice. ⸿How of- ten have I encountered and balked Conigastus in his assaults on the fortunes of the weak? How often have I thwarted Trigguilla, steward of the king's household, even when his vil- lainous schemes were as good as accomplished? How often have I risked my position and in- fluence to protect poor wretches from the false charges innumerable with which they were for ever being harassed by the greed and license of the barbarians? No one has ever drawn me aside from justice to oppression. When ruin was overtaking the fortunes of the provin- cials through the combined pressure of private rapine and public taxation, I grieved no less than the sufferers. When at a season of grievous scarcity a forced sale, disastrous as it was un- justifiable, was proclaimed, and threatened to overwhelm Campania with starvation, I em- barked on a struggle with the prætorian prefect in the public interest, I fought the case at the king's judgment-seat, and succeeded in preventing the enforcement of the sale. I rescued the consular Paulinus from the gaping jaws of the court bloodhounds, who in their covetous hopes had already made short work of his wealth. To save Albinus, who was of the same ex- alted rank, from the penalties of a prejudged charge, I exposed myself to the hatred of Cypri- an, the informer.

'Thinkest thou I had laid up for myself store of enmities enough? Well, with the rest of my countrymen, at any rate, my safety should have been assured, since my love of justice had left me no hope of security at court. Yet who was it brought the charges by which I have been struck down? Why, one of my accusers is Basil, who, after being dismissed from the king's household, was driven by his debts to lodge an information against my name. There is

Prosa IV

Sentisne, inquit, haec atque animo illabuntur tuo? Esne ὄνος λύρας?[3] Quid fles, quid lacrimis manas?

ἐξαύδα, μὴ κεῦθε νόῳ.[4]

Si operam medicantis exspectas, oportet uulnus detegas.

Tum ego collecto in uires animo: anne adhuc eget ammonitione nec per se satis eminet fortunae in nos saeuientis asperitas? Nihilne te ipsa loci facies mouet? Haecine est bibliotheca, quam certissimam tibi sedem nostris in laribus ipsa delegeras, in qua me cum saepe de humanarum diuinarumque rerum scientia disserebas? Talis habitus talisque uultus erat, cum te cum naturae secreta rimarer, cum mihi siderum uias radio describeres, cum mores nostros totiusque uitae rationem ad caelestis ordinis exempla formares? Haecine praemia referimus tibi obsequentes? Atqui tu hanc sententiam Platonis ore sanxisti beatas fore res publicas si eas uel studiosi sapientiae regerent uel earum rectores studere sapientiae contigisset. Tu eiusdem uiri ore hanc sapientibus capessendae rei publicae necessariam causam esse monuisti, ne improbis flagitiosisque ciuibus urbium relicta gubernacula pestem bonis ac perniciem ferrent. Hanc igitur auctoritatem secutus quod a te inter secreta otia didiceram transferre in actum publicae amministrationis optaui. Tu mihi et qui te sapientium mentibus inseruit deus conscii nullum me ad magistratum nisi commune bonorum omnium studium detulisse. Inde cum improbis graues inexorabilesque discordiae et, quod conscientiae libertas habet, pro tuendo iure spreta potentiorum semper offensio.

Quotiens ego Conigastum in imbecilli cuiusque fortunas impetum facientem obuius excepi, quotiens Trigguillam regiae praepositum domus ab incepta, perpetrata iam prorsus iniuria deieci, quotiens miseros quos infinitis calumniis impunita barbarorum semper auaritia uexabat obiecta periculis auctoritate protexi! Numquam me ab iure quis ad iniurium quicquam detraxit. Prouincialium fortunas tum priuatis rapinis tum publicis uectigalibus pessumdari non aliter quam qui patiebantur indolui. Cum acerbae famis tempore grauis atque inexplicabilis indicta coemptio profligatura inopia Campaniam prouinciam uideretur, certamen aduersum praefectum praetorii communis commodi ratione suscepi, rege cognoscente contendi et ne coemptio exigeretur euici. Paulinum consularem uirum, cuius opes Palatinae canes iam spe atque ambitione deuorassent, ab ipsis hiantium faucibus traxi. Ne Albinum consularem uirum praeiudicatae accusationis poena corriperet, odiis me Cypriani delatoris opposui. ℂSatisne in me magnas uideor exacerbasse discordias? Sed esse apud ceteros tutior debui, qui mihi amore iustitiae nihil apud aulicos quo magis essem tutior reseruaui. Quibus autem deferentibus perculsi sumus? Quorum Basilius olim regio ministerio depulsus in delationem nostri nominis alieni aeris necessitate compulsus est. Opilionem uero atque

---

3   Asinus lyrae, ille qui musicam non intellegit.
4   Eloquere, ne cela animum.

Opilio, there is Gaudentius, men who for many and various offences the king's sentence had condemned to banishment; and when they declined to obey, and sought to save themselves by taking sanctuary, the king, as soon as he heard of it, decreed that, if they did not depart from the city of Ravenna within a prescribed time, they should be branded on the forehead and expelled. What would exceed the rigour of this severity? And yet on that same day these very men lodged an information against me, and the information was admitted. Just Heaven! had I deserved this by my way of life? Did it make them fit accusers that my con-demnation was a foregone conclusion? Has fortune no shame—if not at the accusation of the innocent, at least for the vileness of the accusers? ⟨Perhaps thou wonderest what is the sum of the charges laid against me? I wished, they say, to save the senate. But how? I am accused of hindering an informer from producing evidence to prove the senate guilty of treason. Tell me, then, what is thy counsel, O my mistress. Shall I deny the charge, lest I bring shame on thee? But I did wish it, and I shall never cease to wish it. Shall I admit it? Then the work of thwarting the informer will come to an end. Shall I call the wish for the preservation of that illustrious house a crime? Of a truth the senate, by its decrees concerning me, has made it such! But blind folly, though it deceive itself with false names, cannot alter the true merits of things, and, mindful of the precept of Socrates, I do not think it right either to keep the truth concealed or allow falsehood to pass. But this, however it may be, I leave to thy judgment and to the verdict of the discerning. Moreover, lest the course of events and the true facts should be hidden from posterity, I have myself committed to writing an account of the transaction.

'What need to speak of the forged letters by which an attempt is made to prove that I hoped for the freedom of Rome? Their falsity would have been manifest, if I had been al-lowed to use the confession of the informers themselves, evidence which has in all matters the most convincing force. Why, what hope of freedom is left to us? Would there were any! I should have answered with the epigram of Canius when Caligula declared him to have been cognisant of a conspiracy against him. "If I had known," said he, "thou shouldst never have known." Grief hath not so blunted my perceptions in this matter that I should complain be-cause impious wretches contrive their villainies against the virtuous, but at their achieve-ment of their hopes I do exceedingly marvel. For evil purposes are, perchance, due to the im-perfection of human nature; that it should be possible for scoundrels to carry out their worst schemes against the innocent, while God beholdeth, is verily monstrous. For this cause, not without reason, one of thy disciples asked, "If God exists, whence comes evil? Yet whence comes good, if He exists not?" However, it might well be that wretches who seek the blood of all honest men and of the whole senate should wish to destroy me also, whom they saw to be a bulwark of the senate and all honest men. But did I deserve such a fate from the Fathers also? Thou rememberest, methinks—since thou didst ever stand by my side to direct what I should do or say—thou rememberest, I say, how at Verona, when the king, eager for the gen-eral destruction, was bent on implicating the whole senatorial order in the charge of treason brought against Albinus, with what indifference to my own peril I maintained the innocence of its members, one and all. Thou knowest that what I say is the truth, and that I have never boasted of my good deeds in a spirit of self-praise. For whenever a man by proclaiming his good deeds receives the recompense of fame, he diminishes in a measure the secret reward of a good conscience. What issues have overtaken my innocency thou seest. Instead of reaping the rewards of true virtue, I undergo the penalties of a guilt falsely laid to my charge—nay,

Gaudentium cum ob innumeras multiplicesque fraudes ire in exsilium regia censura decreuisset cumque illi parere nolentes sacrarum sese aedium defensione tuerentur compertumque id regi foret, edixit uti ni intra praescriptum diem Rauenna urbe decederent notas insigniti frontibus pellerentur. Quid huic seueritati posse astrui uidetur? Atquin eo die deferentibus eisdem nominis nostri delatio suscepta est. Quid igitur, nostraene artes ita meruerunt an illos accusatores iustos fecit praemissa damnatio? Itane nihil fortunam puduit si minus accusatae innocentiae at accusantium uilitas?

At cuius criminis arguimur summam quaeres. Senatum dicimur saluum esse uoluisse. Modum desideras? Delatorem, ne documenta deferret quibus senatum maiestatis reum faceret, impedisse criminamur. Quid igitur, o magistra, censes? Infitiabimur crimen, ne tibi pudor simus? At uolui nec umquam uelle desistam. Fatebimur? Sed impediendi delatoris opera cessauit. An optasse illius ordinis salutem nefas uocabo? Ille quidem suis de me decretis uti hoc nefas esset effecerat. Sed sibi semper mentiens imprudentia rerum merita non potest immutare nec mihi Socratico decreto fas esse arbitror uel occuluisse ueritatem uel concessisse mendacium. Verum id quoquo modo sit, tuo sapientiumque iudicio aestimandum relinquo. Cuius rei seriem atque ueritatem, ne latere posteros queat, stilo etiam memoriaeque mandaui.

Nam de compositis falso litteris, quibus libertatem arguor sperasse Romanam, quid attinet dicere? Quarum fraus aperta patuisset si nobis ipsorum confessione delatorum, quod in omnibus negotiis maximas uires habet, uti licuisset. Nam quae sperari reliqua libertas potest? Atque utinam posset ulla! Respondissem Canii uerbo, qui cum a Gaio Caesare Germanici filio conscius contra se factae coniurationis fuisse diceretur: 'si ego', inquit, 'scissem, tu nescisses'. Qua in re non ita sensus nostros maeror hebetauit ut impios scelerata contra uirtutem querar molitos, sed quae sperauerint effecisse uehementer ammiror. Nam deteriora uelle nostri fuerit fortasse defectus, posse contra innocentiam quae sceleratus quisque conceperit inspectante deo monstri simile est. Vnde haud iniuria tuorum quidam familiarium quaesiuit: 'si quidem deus', inquit, 'est, unde mala? Bona uero unde, si non est?' Sed fas fuerit nefarios homines, qui bonorum omnium totiusque senatus sanguinem petunt, nos etiam, quos propugnare bonis senatuique uiderant, perditum ire uoluisse. Sed num idem de patribus quoque merebamur? Meministi, ut opinor, quoniam me dicturum quid facturumue praesens semper ipsa dirigebas, meministi, inquam, Veronae cum rex auidus exitii communis maiestatis crimen in Albinum delatae ad cunctum senatus ordinem transferre moliretur, uniuersi innocentiam senatus quanta mei periculi securitate defenderim. Scis me haec et uera proferre et in nulla umquam mei laude iactasse; minuit enim quodam modo se probantis conscientiae secretum, quotiens ostentando quis factum recipit famae pretium. Sed innocentiam nostram quis exceperit euentus uides; pro uerae uirtutis praemiis falsi sceleris poenas subimus.

more than this; never did an open confession of guilt cause such unanimous severity among the assessors, but that some consideration, either of the mere frailty of human nature, or of fortune's universal instability, availed to soften the verdict of some few. Had I been accused of a design to fire the temples, to slaughter the priests with impious sword, of plotting the massacre of all honest men, I should yet have been produced in court, and only punished on due confession or conviction. Now for my too great zeal towards the senate I have been condemned to outlawry and death, unheard and undefended, at a distance of near five hundred miles away.[3] Oh, my judges, well do ye deserve that no one should hereafter be convicted of a fault like mine!

'Yet even my very accusers saw how honourable was the charge they brought against me, and, in order to overlay it with some shadow of guilt, they falsely asserted that in the pursuit of my ambition I had stained my conscience with sacrilegious acts. And yet thy spirit, indwelling in me, had driven from the chamber of my soul all lust of earthly success, and with thine eye ever upon me, there could be no place left for sacrilege. For thou didst daily repeat in my ear and instil into my mind the Pythagorean maxim, "Follow after God." It was not likely, then, that I should covet the assistance of the vilest spirits, when thou wert moulding me to such an excellence as should conform me to the likeness of God. Again, the innocency of the inner sanctuary of my home, the company of friends of the highest probity, a father-in-law revered at once for his pure character and his active beneficence, shield me from the very suspicion of sacrilege. Yet—atrocious as it is—they even draw credence for this charge from thee; I am like to be thought implicated in wickedness on this very account, that I am imbued with thy teachings and stablished in thy ways. So it is not enough that my devotion to thee should profit me nothing, but thou also must be assailed by reason of the odium which I have incurred. Verily this is the very crown of my misfortunes, that men's opinions for the most part look not to real merit, but to the event; and only recognise foresight where Fortune has crowned the issue with her approval. Whereby it comes to pass that reputation is the first of all things to abandon the unfortunate. I remember with chagrin how perverse is popular report, how various and discordant men's judgments. This only will I say, that the most crushing of misfortune's burdens is, that as soon as a charge is fastened upon the unhappy, they are believed to have deserved their sufferings. I, for my part, who have been banished from all life's blessings, stripped of my honours, stained in repute, am punished for well-doing.

'And now methinks I see the villainous dens of the wicked surging with joy and gladness, all the most recklessly unscrupulous threatening a new crop of lying informations, the good prostrate with terror at my danger, every ruffian incited by impunity to new daring and to success by the profits of audacity, the guiltless not only robbed of their peace of mind, but even of all means of defence. Wherefore I would fain cry out:

Song V – Boethius' Prayer.

'Builder of yon starry dome,
Thou that whirlest, throned eternal,
Heaven's swift globe, and, as they roam,

---

3   The distance from Rome to Pavia, the place of Boethius' imprisonment, is 455 Roman miles.

Eccuius umquam facinoris manifesta confessio ita iudices habuit in seueritate concordes ut non aliquos uel ipse ingenii error humani uel fortunae condicio cunctis mortalibus incerta summitteret? Si inflammare sacras aedes uoluisse, si sacerdotes impio iugulare gladio, si bonis omnibus necem struxisse diceremur, praesentem tamen sententia, confessum tamen conuictumue punisset; nunc quingentis fere passuum milibus procul muti atque indefensi ob studium propensius in senatum morti proscriptionique damnamur. O meritos de simili crimine neminem posse conuinci!

Cuius dignitatem reatus ipsi etiam qui detulere uiderunt; quam uti alicuius sceleris am-mixtione fuscarent, ob ambitum dignitatis sacrilegio me conscientiam polluisse mentiti sunt. Atqui et tu insita nobis omnem rerum mortalium cupidinem de nostri animi sede pellebas et sub tuis oculis sacrilegio locum esse fas non erat. Instillabas enim auribus cogitationibusque cotidie meis pythagoricum illud ἔπου θεῷ. Nec conueniebat uilissimorum me spirituum praesidia captare, quem tu in hanc excellentiam componebas ut consimilem deo faceres. Praeterea penetral innocens domus, honestissimorum coetus amicorum, socer etiam sanctus et aeque ac tu ipsa reuerendus ab omni nos huius criminis suspicione defendunt. Sed — O nefas! Illi uero de te tanti criminis fidem capiunt atque hoc ipso uidebimur affines fuisse male-ficio quod tuis imbuti disciplinis, tuis instituti moribus sumus. Ita non est satis nihil mihi tuam profuisse reuerentiam nisi ultro tu mea potius offensione lacereris. At uero hic etiam nostris malis cumulus accedit quod existimatio plurimorum non rerum merita sed fortunae spectat euentum eaque tantum iudicat esse prouisa quae felicitas commendauerit; quo fit ut existimatio bona prima omnium deserat infelices. Qui nunc populi rumores, quam dissonae multiplicesque sententiae, piget reminisci; hoc tantum dixerim ultimam esse aduersae fortu-nae sarcinam quod, dum miseris aliquod crimen affingitur, quae perferunt meruisse credun-tur. Et ego quidem bonis omnibus pulsus, dignitatibus exutus, existimatione foedatus ob be-neficium supplicium tuli. Videre autem uideor nefarias sceleratorum officinas gaudio laeti-tiaque fluitantes, perditissimum quemque nouis delationum fraudibus imminentem, iacere bonos nostri discriminis terrore prostratos, flagitiosum quemque ad audendum quidem fa-cinus impunitate, ad efficiendum uero praemiis incitari, insontes autem non modo securitate uerum ipsa etiam defensione priuatos. Itaque libet exclamare:

Metrum V

O stelliferi conditor orbis,
Qui perpetuo nixus solio
Rapido caelum turbine uersas

Guid'st the stars by laws supernal:
So in full-sphered splendour dight
Cynthia dims the lamps of night,
But unto the orb fraternal
Closer drawn,[4] doth lose her light.

'Who at fall of eventide,
Hesper, his cold radiance showeth,
Lucifer his beams doth hide,
Paling as the sun's light groweth,
Brief, while winter's frost holds sway,
By thy will the space of day;
Swift, when summer's fervour gloweth,
Speed the hours of night away.

'Thou dost rule the changing year:
When rude Boreas oppresses,
Fall the leaves; they reappear,
Wooed by Zephyr's soft caresses.
Fields that Sirius burns deep grown
By Arcturus' watch were sown:
Each the reign of law confesses,
Keeps the place that is his own.

'Sovereign Ruler, Lord of all!
Can it be that Thou disdainest
Only man? 'Gainst him, poor thrall,
Wanton Fortune plays her vainest.
Guilt's deserved punishment
Falleth on the innocent;
High uplifted, the profanest
On the just their malice vent.

'Virtue cowers in dark retreats,
Crime's foul stain the righteous beareth,
Perjury and false deceits
Hurt not him the wrong who dareth;
But whene'er the wicked trust
In ill strength to work their lust,
Kings, whom nations' awe declareth
Mighty, grovel in the dust.

'Look, oh look upon this earth,
Thou who on law's sure foundation
Framedst all! Have we no worth,
We poor men, of all creation?
Sore we toss on fortune's tide;

---

4   The moon is regarded as farthest from the sun at the full, and, as she wanes, approaching gradually nearer.

Legemque pati sidera cogis,
Vt nunc pleno lucida cornu
Totis fratris obuia flammis
Condat stellas luna minores,
Nunc obscuro pallida cornu
Phoebo propior lumina perdat
Et qui primae tempore noctis
Agit algentes Hesperos ortus
Solitas iterum mutet habenas
Phoebi pallens Lucifer ortu.
Tu frondifluae frigore brumae
Stringis lucem breuiore mora,
Tu cum feruida uenerit aestas
Agiles nocti diuidis horas.
Tua uis uarium temperat annum,
Vt quas Boreae spiritus aufert
Reuehat mites Zephyrus frondes,
Quaeque Arcturus semina uidit
Sirius altas urat segetes:
Nihil antiqua lege solutum
Linquit propriae stationis opus.
Omnia certo fine gubernans
Hominum solos respuis actus
Merito rector cohibere modo.
Nam cur tantas lubrica uersat
Fortuna uices? Premit insontes
Debita sceleri noxia poena,
At peruersi resident celso
Mores solio sanctaque calcant
Iniusta uice colla nocentes .
Latet obscuris condita uirtus
Clara tenebris iustusque tulit
Crimen iniqui.
Nil periuria, nil nocet ipsis
Fraus mendaci compta colore.
Sed cum libuit uiribus uti,
Quos innumeri metuunt populi
Summos gaudent subdere reges.
O iam miseras respice terras,
Quisquis rerum foedera nectis!
Operis tanti pars non uilis
Homines quatimur fortunae salo.

Master, bid the waves subside!
And earth's ways with consummation
Of Thy heaven's order guide!'

V.

When I had poured out my griefs in this long and unbroken strain of lamentation, she, with calm countenance, and in no wise disturbed at my complainings, thus spake:

'When I saw thee sorrowful, in tears, I straightway knew thee wretched and an exile. But how far distant that exile I should not know, had not thine own speech revealed it. Yet how far indeed from thy country hast thou, not been banished, but rather hast strayed; or, if thou wilt have it banishment, hast banished thyself! For no one else could ever lawfully have had this power over thee. Now, if thou wilt call to mind from what country thou art sprung, it is not ruled, as once was the Athenian polity, by the sovereignty of the multitude, but "one is its Ruler, one its King," who takes delight in the number of His citizens, not in their banishment; to submit to whose governance and to obey whose ordinances is perfect freedom. Art thou ignorant of that most ancient law of this thy country, whereby it is decreed that no one whatsoever, who hath chosen to fix there his dwelling, may be sent into exile? For truly there is no fear that one who is encompassed by its ramparts and defences should deserve to be exiled. But he who has ceased to wish to dwell therein, he likewise ceases to deserve to do so. And so it is not so much the aspect of this place which moves me, as thy aspect; not so much the library walls set off with glass and ivory which I miss, as the chamber of thy mind, wherein I once placed, not books, but that which gives books their value, the doctrines which my books contain. Now, what thou hast said of thy services to the commonweal is true, only too little compared with the greatness of thy deservings. The things laid to thy charge whereof thou hast spoken, whether such as redound to thy credit, or mere false accusations, are publicly known. As for the crimes and deceits of the informers, thou hast rightly deemed it fitting to pass them over lightly, because the popular voice hath better and more fully pronounced upon them. ℭThou hast bitterly complained of the injustice of the senate. Thou hast grieved over my calumniation, and likewise hast lamented the damage to my good name. Finally, thine indignation blazed forth against fortune; thou hast complained of the unfairness with which thy merits have been recompensed. Last of all thy frantic muse framed a prayer that the peace which reigns in heaven might rule earth also. But since a throng of tumultuous passions hath assailed thy soul, since thou art distraught with anger, pain, and grief, strong remedies are not proper for thee in this thy present mood. And so for a time I will use milder methods, that the tumours which have grown hard through the influx of disturbing passion may be softened by gentle treatment, till they can bear the force of sharper remedies.'

Song VI — All Things have their Needful Order.

He who to th' unwilling furrows
Gives the generous grain,
When the Crab with baleful fervours
Scorches all the plain;

Rapidos, rector, comprime fluctus
Et quo caelum regis immemsum
Firma stabiles foedere terras.

Prosa V

Haec ubi continuato dolore delatraui, illa uultu placido nihilque meis questibus mota:

Cum te, inquit, maestum lacrimantemque uidissem ilico miserum exsulemque cognoui; sed quam id longinquum esset exsilium, nisi tua prodidisset oratio, nesciebam. Sed tu quam procul a patria non quidem pulsus es sed aberrasti ac, si te pulsum existimari mauis, te potius ipse pepulisti; nam id quidem de te numquam cuiquam fas fuisset. Si enim cuius oriundo sis patriae reminiscare, non uti atheniensium quondam multitudinis imperio regitur, sed eis koiranos estin, eis basileus, qui frequentia ciuium non depulsione laetetur, cuius agi frenis atque obtemperare iustitiae libertas est. An ignoras illam tuae ciuitatis antiquissimam legem qua sanctum est ei ius exsulare non esse quisquis in ea sedem fundare maluerit? Nam qui uallo eius ac munimine continetur, nullus metus est ne exsul esse mereatur; at quisquis inhabitare eam uelle desierit pariter desinit etiam mereri. Itaque non tam me loci huius quam tua facies mouet nec bibliothecae potius comptos ebore ac uitro parietes quam tuae mentis sedem requiro, in qua non libros sed id quod libris pretium facit, librorum quondam meorum sententias collocaui. Et tu quidem de tuis in commune bonum meritis uera quidem, sed pro multitudine gestorum tibi pauca dixisti. De obiectorum tibi uel honestate uel falsitate cunctis nota memorasti. De sceleribus fraudibusque delatorum recte tu quidem strictim attingendum putasti, quod ea melius uberiusque recognoscentis omnia uulgi ore celebrentur.

Increpuisti etiam uehementer iniusti factum senatus. De nostra etiam criminatione doluisti, laesae quoque opinionis damna fleuisti. Postremus aduersum fortunam dolor incanduit conquestusque non aequa meritis praemia pensari in extremo Musae saeuientis, uti quae caelum terras quoque pax regeret, uota posuisti. Sed quoniam plurimus tibi affectuum tumultus incubuit diuersumque te dolor ira maeror distrahunt, uti nunc mentis es, nondum te ualidiora remedia contingunt. Itaque lenioribus paulisper utemur, ut quae in tumorem perturbationibus influentibus induruerunt ad acrioris uim medicaminis recipiendam tactu blandiore mollescant.

Metrum VI

Cum Phoebi radiis graue
Cancri sidus inaestuat,
Tum qui larga negantibus

He shall find his garner bare,
Acorns for his scanty fare.
Go not forth to cull sweet violets
From the purpled steep,
While the furious blasts of winter
Through the valleys sweep;
Nor the grape o'erhasty bring
To the press in days of spring.
For to each thing God hath givenIts appointed time;
No perplexing change permits HeIn His plan sublime.
So who quits the order due
Shall a luckless issue rue.

VI.

'First, then, wilt thou suffer me by a few questions to make some attempt to test the state of thy mind, that I may learn in what way to set about thy cure?'

'Ask what thou wilt,' said I, 'for I will answer whatever questions thou choosest to put.'

Then said she: 'This world of ours—thinkest thou it is governed haphazard and fortuitously, or believest thou that there is in it any rational guidance?'

'Nay,' said I, 'in no wise may I deem that such fixed motions can be determined by random hazard, but I know that God, the Creator, presideth over His work, nor will the day ever come that shall drive me from holding fast the truth of this belief.'

'Yes,' said she; 'thou didst even but now affirm it in song, lamenting that men alone had no portion in the divine care. As to the rest, thou wert unshaken in the belief that they were ruled by reason. Yet I marvel exceedingly how, in spite of thy firm hold on this opinion, thou art fallen into sickness. But let us probe more deeply: something or other is missing, I think. Now, tell me, since thou doubtest not that God governs the world, dost thou perceive by what means He rules it?'

'I scarcely understand what thou meanest,' I said, 'much less can I answer thy question.'

'Did I not say truly that something is missing, whereby, as through a breach in the ramparts, disease hath crept in to disturb thy mind? But, tell me, dost thou remember the universal end towards which the aim of all nature is directed?'

'I once heard,' said I, 'but sorrow hath dulled my recollection.'

'And yet thou knowest whence all things have proceeded.'

'Yes, that I know,' said I, 'and have answered that it is from God.'

Sulcis semina credidit
Elusus Cereris fide
Quernas pergat ad arbores.
Numquam purpureum nemus
Lecturus uiolas petas
Cum saeuis Aquilonibus
Stridens campus inhorruit;
Nec quaeras auida manu
Vernos stringere palmites
Vuis si libeat frui;
Autumno potius sua
Bacchus munera contulit.
Signat tempora propriis
Aptans officiis deus
Nec quas ipse cohercuit
Misceri patitur uices.
Sic quod praecipiti uia
Certum deserit ordinem
Laetos non habet exitus.

Prosa VI

Primum igitur paterisne me pauculis rogationibus statum tuae mentis attingere atque, ut qui modus sit tuae curationis intellegam?

Tu uero arbitratu, inquam, tuo quae uoles ut responsurum rogato.

Tum illa: huncine, inquit, mundum temerariis agi fortuitisque casibus putas an ullum credis ei regimen inesse rationis?

Atqui, inquam, nullo existimauerim modo ut fortuita temeritate tam certa moueantur, uerum operi suo conditorem praesidere deum scio nec umquam fuerit dies qui me ab hac sententiae ueritate depellat.

Ita est, inquit nam id etiam paulo ante cecinisti hominesque tantum diuinae exsortes curae esse deplorasti; nam de ceteris quin ratione regerentur nihil mouebare. Papae autem, uehementer ammiror cur in tam salubri sententia locatus aegrotes. Verum altius perscrutemur; nescio quid abesse coniecto. Sed dic mihi, quoniam deo mundum regi non ambigis, quibus etiam gubernaculis regatur aduertis?

Vix, inquam, rogationis tuae sententiam nosco, nedum ad inquisita respondere queam.

Num me, inquit, fefellit abesse aliquid, per quod uelut hiante ualli robore in animum tuum perturbationum morbus inrepserit? Sed dic mihi, meministine quis sit rerum finis quoue totius naturae tendat intentio?

Audieram, inquam, sed memoriam maeror hebetauit.

Atqui scis unde cuncta processerint.

Noui, inquam, deumque esse respondi.

'Yet how is it possible that thou knowest not what is the end of existence, when thou dost understand its source and origin? However, these disturbances of mind have force to shake a man's position, but cannot pluck him up and root him altogether out of himself. But answer this also, I pray thee: rememberest thou that thou art a man?'

'How should I not?' said I.

'Then, canst thou say what man is?'

'Is this thy question: Whether I know myself for a being endowed with reason and subject to death? Surely I do acknowledge myself such.'

Then she: 'Dost know nothing else that thou art?'

'Nothing.'

'Now,' said she, 'I know another cause of thy disease, one, too, of grave moment. Thou hast ceased to know thy own nature. So, then, I have made full discovery both of the causes of thy sickness and the means of restoring thy health. It is because forgetfulness of thyself hath bewildered thy mind that thou hast bewailed thee as an exile, as one stripped of the blessings that were his; it is because thou knowest not the end of existence that thou deemest abominable and wicked men to be happy and powerful; while, because thou hast forgotten by what means the earth is governed, thou deemest that fortune's changes ebb and flow without the restraint of a guiding hand. These are serious enough to cause not sickness only, but even death; but, thanks be to the Author of our health, the light of nature hath not yet left thee utterly. In thy true judgment concerning the world's government, in that thou believest it subject, not to the random drift of chance, but to divine reason, we have the divine spark from which thy recovery may be hoped. Have, then, no fear; from these weak embers the vital heat shall once more be kindled within thee. But seeing that it is not yet time for strong remedies, and that the mind is manifestly so constituted that when it casts off true opinions it straightway puts on false, wherefrom arises a cloud of confusion that disturbs its true vision, I will now try and disperse these mists by mild and soothing application, that so the darkness of misleading passion may be scattered, and thou mayst come to discern the splendour of the true light.'

Song VII – The Perturbations of Passion.

Stars shed no light
Through the black night,
When the clouds hide;
And the lashed wave,
If the winds rave
O'er ocean's tide,—
Though once serene
As day's fair sheen,—
Soon fouled and spoiled
By the storm's spite,
Shows to the sight
Turbid and soiled.

Et qui fieri potest ut principio cognito quis sit rerum finis ignores? Verum hi perturba-tionum mores, ea ualentia est, ut mouere quidem loco hominem possint, conuellere autem sibique totum exstirpare non possint. Sed hoc quoque respondeas uelim: hominemne te esse meministi?

Quidni, inquam, meminerim?

Quid igitur homo sit poterisne proferre?

Hocine interrogas, an esse me sciam rationale animal atque mortale? Scio, et id me esse confiteor.

Et illa: nihilne aliud te esse nouisti?

Nihil.

Iam scio, inquit, morbi tui aliam uel maximam causam; quid ipse sis nosse desisti. Quare plenissime uel aegritudinis tuae rationem uel aditum reconciliandae sospitatis inueni. Nam quoniam tui obliuione confunderis et exsulem te et exspoliatum propriis bonis esse doluisti;quoniam uero quis sit rerum finis ignoras, nequam homines atque nefarios potentes felicesque arbitraris; quoniam uero quibus gubernaculis mundus regatur oblitus es, has fortu-narum uices aestimas sine rectore fluitare: magnae non ad morbum modo, uerum ad interitum quoque causae. Sed sospitatis auctori grates quod te nondum totum natura destituit. Habemus maximum tuae fomitem salutis ueram de mundi gubernatione sententiam, quod eam non casuum temeritati sed diuinae rationi subditam credis; nihil igitur pertimescas, iam tibi ex hac minima scintillula uitalis calor illuxerit. Sed quoniam firmioribus remediis non-dum tempus est, et eam mentium constat esse naturam ut quotiens abiecerint ueras, falsis opinionibus induantur, ex quibus orta perturbationum caligo uerum illum confundit intu-itum, hanc paulisper lenibus mediocribusque fomentis attenuare temptabo, ut dimotis fallaci-um affectionum tenebris splendorem uerae lucis possis agnoscere.

Metrum VII

Nubibus atris
Condita nullum
Fundere possunt
Sidera lumen.
Si mare uoluens
Turbidus Auster
Misceat aestum,
Vitrea dudum
Par que serenis
Vnda diebus
Mox resoluto
Sordida caeno
Visibus obstat,

Oft the fair rill,
Down the steep hill
Seaward that strays,
Some tumbled block
Of fallen rock
Hinders and stays.
Then art thou fain
Clear and most plain
Truth to discern,
In the right way
Firmly to stay,
Nor from it turn?
Joy, hope and fear
Suffer not near,
Drive grief away:
Shackled and blind
And lost is the mind
Where these have sway.

Quique uagatur
Montibus altis
Defluus amnis
Saepe resistit
Rupe soluti
Obice saxi
Tu quoque si uis
Lumine claro
Cernere uerum,
Tramite recto
Carpere callem:
Gaudia pelle,
Pelle timorem
Spemque fugato
Nec dolor adsit,
Nubila mens est
Vincta que frenis
Haec ubi regnant.

Book II
The Vanity of Fortune's Gifts

I.

Thereafter for awhile she remained silent; and when she had restored my flagging attention by a moderate pause in her discourse, she thus began: 'If I have thoroughly ascertained the character and causes of thy sickness, thou art pining with regretful longing for thy former fortune. It is the change, as thou deemest, of this fortune that hath so wrought upon thy mind. Well do I understand that Siren's manifold wiles, the fatal charm of the friendship she pretends for her victims, so long as she is scheming to entrap them—how she unexpectedly abandons them and leaves them overwhelmed with insupportable grief. Bethink thee of her nature, character, and deserts, and thou wilt soon acknowledge that in her thou hast neither possessed, nor hast thou lost, aught of any worth. Methinks I need not spend much pains in bringing this to thy mind, since, even when she was still with thee, even while she was caressing thee, thou usedst to assail her in manly terms, to rebuke her, with maxims drawn from my holy treasure-house. But all sudden changes of circumstances bring inevitably a certain commotion of spirit. Thus it hath come to pass that thou also for awhile hast been parted from thy mind's tranquillity. But it is time for thee to take and drain a draught, soft and pleasant to the taste, which, as it penetrates within, may prepare the way for stronger potions. Wherefore I call to my aid the sweet persuasiveness of Rhetoric, who then only walketh in the right way when she forsakes not my instructions, and Music, my handmaid, I bid to join with her singing, now in lighter, now in graver strain.

'What is it, then, poor mortal, that hath cast thee into lamentation and mourning? Some strange, unwonted sight, methinks, have thine eyes seen. Thou deemest Fortune to have changed towards thee; thou mistakest. Such ever were her ways, ever such her nature. Rather in her very mutability hath she preserved towards thee her true constancy. Such was she when she loaded thee with caresses, when she deluded thee with the allurements of a false happiness. Thou hast found out how changeful is the face of the blind goddess. She who still veils herself from others hath fully discovered to thee her whole character. If thou likest her, take her as she is, and do not complain. If thou abhorrest her perfidy, turn from her in disdain, renounce her, for baneful are her delusions. The very thing which is now the cause of thy great grief ought to have brought thee tranquillity. Thou hast been forsaken by one of whom no one can be sure that she will not forsake him. Or dost thou indeed set value on a happiness that is certain to depart? Again I ask, Is Fortune's presence dear to thee if she cannot be trusted to stay, and though she will bring sorrow when she is gone? Why, if she

Liber Secundus

Prosa I

Post haec paulisper obticuit atque ubi attentionem meam modesta taciturnitate collegit sic exorsa est: si penitus aegritudinis tuae causas habitumque cognoui, fortunae prioris affectu desiderioque tabescis; ea tantum animi tui sicuti tu tibi fingis mutata peruertit. Intellego multiformes illius prodigii fucos et eo usque cum his quos eludere nititur blandissimam familiaritatem, dum intolerabili dolore confundat quos insperata reliquerit. Cuius si naturam, mores ac meritum reminiscare, nec habuisse te in ea pulchrum aliquid nec amisisse cognosces; sed, ut arbitror, haud multum tibi haec in memoriam reuocare laborauerim. Solebas enim praesentem quoque, blandientem quoque uirilibus incessere uerbis eamque de nostro adyto prolatis insectabare sententiis. Verum omnis subita mutatio rerum non sine quodam quasi fluctu contingit animorum; sic factum est ut tu quoque paulisper a tua tranquillitate descisceres. Sed tempus est haurire te aliquid ac degustare molle atque iucundum, quod ad interiora transmissum ualidioribus haustibus uiam fecerit. Adsit igitur rhetoricae suadela dulcedinis, quae tum tantum recta calle procedit cum nostra instituta non deserit cumque hac musica laris nostri uernacula nunc leuiores nunc grauiores modos succinat.

Quid est igitur, o homo, quod te in maestitiam luctumque deiecit? Nouum, credo, aliquid inusitatumque uidisti. Tu fortunam putas erga te esse mutatam: erras. Hi semper eius mores sunt, ista natura. Seruauit circa te propriam potius in ipsa sui mutabilitate constantiam; talis erat cum blandiebatur, cum tibi falsae illecebris felicitatis alluderet. Deprehendisti caeci numinis ambiguos uultus. Quae sese adhuc uelat aliis, tota tibi prorsus innotuit. Si probas, utere moribus, ne queraris. Si perfidiam perhorrescis, sperne atque abice perniciosa ludentem; nam quae nunc tibi est tanti causa maeroris, haec eadem tranquillitatis esse debuisset. Reliquit enim te quam non relicturam nemo umquam poterit esse securus. An uero tu pretiosam aestimas abituram felicitatem et cara tibi est fortuna nec praesens manendi fida et cum

cannot be kept at pleasure, and if her flight overwhelms with calamity, what is this fleeting visitant but a token of coming trouble? Truly it is not enough to look only at what lies before the eyes; wisdom gauges the issues of things, and this same mutability, with its two aspects, makes the threats of Fortune void of terror, and her caresses little to be desired. Finally, thou oughtest to bear with whatever takes place within the boundaries of Fortune's demesne, when thou hast placed thy head beneath her yoke. But if thou wishest to impose a law of staying and departing on her whom thou hast of thine own accord chosen for thy mistress, art thou not acting wrongfully, art thou not embittering by impatience a lot which thou canst not alter? Didst thou commit thy sails to the winds, thou wouldst voyage not whither thy intention was to go, but whither the winds drave thee; didst thou entrust thy seed to the fields, thou wouldst set off the fruitful years against the barren. Thou hast resigned thyself to the sway of Fortune; thou must submit to thy mistress's caprices. What! art thou verily striving to stay the swing of the revolving wheel? Oh, stupidest of mortals, if it takes to standing still, it ceases to be the wheel of Fortune.'

Song I — Fortune's Malice.

Mad Fortune sweeps along in wanton pride,
Uncertain as Euripus' surging tide;
Now tramples mighty kings beneath her feet;
Now sets the conquered in the victor's seat.
She heedeth not the wail of hapless woe,
But mocks the griefs that from her mischief flow.
Such is her sport; so proveth she her power;
And great the marvel, when in one brief hour
She shows her darling lifted high in bliss,
Then headlong plunged in misery's abyss.

II.

'Now I would fain also reason with thee a little in Fortune's own words. Do thou observe whether her contentions be just. "Man," she might say, "why dost thou pursue me with thy daily complainings? What wrong have I done thee? What goods of thine have I taken from thee? Choose an thou wilt a judge, and let us dispute before him concerning the rightful ownership of wealth and rank. If thou succeedest in showing that any one of these things is the true property of mortal man, I freely grant those things to be thine which thou claimest. When nature brought thee forth out of thy mother's womb, I took thee, naked and destitute as thou wast, I cherished thee with my substance, and, in the partiality of my favour for thee, I brought thee up somewhat too indulgently, and this it is which now makes thee rebellious against me. I surrounded thee with a royal abundance of all those things that are in my power. Now it is my pleasure to draw back my hand. Thou hast reason to thank me for the use of what was not thine own; thou hast no right to complain, as if thou hadst lost what was wholly thine. Why, then, dost bemoan thyself? I have done thee no violence. Wealth, honour, and all such things are placed under my control. My handmaidens know their mistress; with me they come, and at my going they depart. I might boldly affirm that if those

discesserit allatura maerorem? Quodsi nec ex arbitrio retineri potest et calamitosos fugiens facit, quid est aliud quam futurae quoddam calamitatis indicium? Neque enim quod ante oculos situm est suffecerit intueri, rerum exitus prudentia metitur; eademque in alterutro mutabilitas nec formidandas fortunae minas nec exoptandas facit esse blanditias. Postremo aequo animo toleres oportet quicquid intra fortunae aream geritur cum semel iugo eius colla summiseris. Quodsi manendi abeundique scribere legem uelis ei quam tu tibi dominam sponte legisti, nonne iniurius fueris et impatientia sortem exacerbes quam permutare non possis? Si uentis uela committeres, non quo uoluntas peteret sed quo flatus impellerent promoueres; si aruis semina crederes, feraces inter se annos sterilesque pensares. Fortunae te regendum dedisti, dominae moribus oportet obtemperes. Tu uero uoluentis rotae impetum retinere conaris? At, omnium mortalium stolidissime, si manere incipit fors esse desistit.

Metrum I

Haec cum superba uerterit uices dextra
Et aestuantis more fertur Euripi,
Dudum tremendos saeua proterit reges
Humilemque uicti subleuat fallax uultum.
Non illa miseros audit aut curat fletus
Vltroque gemitus, dura quos fecit, ridet.
Sic illa ludit, sic suas probat uires
Magnumque su[ae v]is monstrat ostentum, si quis
Visatur una stratus ac felix hora.

Prosa II

Vellem autem pauca te cum Fortunae ipsius uerbis agitare; tu igitur an ius postulet an-imaduerte. 'Quid tu, homo, ream me cotidianis agis querelis? Quam tibi fecimus iniuriam? Quae tibi tua detraximus bona? Quouis iudice de opum dignitatumque me cum possessione contende et si cuiusquam mortalium proprium quid horum esse monstraueris ego iam tua fuisse quae repetis sponte concedam. Cum te matris utero produxit, nudum rebus omnibus inopemque suscepi, meis opibus foui et, quod te nunc impatientem nostri facit, fauore prona indulgentius educaui, omnium quae mei iuris sunt affluentia et splendore circumdedi. Nunc mihi retrahere manum libet: habes gratiam uelut usus alienis, non habes ius querelae tam-quam prorsus tua perdideris. Quid igitur ingemescis? Nulla tibi a nobis est allata uiolentia. Opes, honores ceteraque talium mei sunt iuris. Dominam famulae cognoscunt: me cum ueni-unt, me abeunte discedunt. Audacter adfirmem, si tua forent quae amissa conquereris, nullo

things the loss of which thou lamentest had been thine, thou couldst never have lost them. Am I alone to be forbidden to do what I will with my own? Unrebuked, the skies now reveal the brightness of day, now shroud the daylight in the darkness of night; the year may now engarland the face of the earth with flowers and fruits, now disfigure it with storms and cold. The sea is permitted to invite with smooth and tranquil surface to-day, to-morrow to roughen with wave and storm. Shall man's insatiate greed bind me to a constancy foreign to my character? This is my art, this the game I never cease to play. I turn the wheel that spins. I delight to see the high come down and the low ascend. Mount up, if thou wilt, but only on condition that thou wilt not think it a hardship to come down when the rules of my game require it. Wert thou ignorant of my character? Didst not know how Crœsus, King of the Lydians, erstwhile the dreaded rival of Cyrus, was afterwards pitiably consigned to the flame of the pyre, and only saved by a shower sent from heaven? Has it 'scaped thee how Paullus paid a meed of pious tears to the misfortunes of King Perseus, his prisoner? What else do tragedies make such woeful outcry over save the overthrow of kingdoms by the indiscriminate strokes of Fortune? Didst thou not learn in thy childhood how there stand at the threshold of Zeus 'two jars', 'the one full of blessings, the other of calamities'? How if thou hast drawn over-liberally from the good jar? What if not even now have I departed wholly from thee? What if this very mutability of mine is a just ground for hoping better things? But listen now, and cease to let thy heart consume away with fretfulness, nor expect to live on thine own terms in a realm that is common to all.'

Song II — Man's Covetousness

What though Plenty pour her gifts
With a lavish hand,
Numberless as are the stars,
Countless as the sand,
Will the race of man, content,
Cease to murmur and lament?
Nay, though God, all-bounteous, give
Gold at man's desire—
Honours, rank, and fame—content
Not a whit is nigher;
But an all-devouring greed
Yawns with ever-widening need.
Then what bounds can e'er restrain
This wild lust of having,
When with each new bounty fed
Grows the frantic craving?
He is never rich whose fear
Sees grim Want forever near.

modo perdidisses. An ego sola meum ius exercere prohibebor? Licet caelo proferre lucidos dies eosdemque tenebrosis noctibus condere, licet anno terrae uultum nunc floribus frugibusque redimire nunc nimbis frigoribusque confundere, ius est mari nunc strato aequore blandiri nunc procellis ac fluctibus inhorrescere: nos ad constantiam nostris moribus alienam inexpleta hominum cupiditas alligabit? Haec nostra uis est, hunc continuum ludum ludimus: rotam uolubili orbe uersamus, infima summis, summa infimis mutare gaudemus. Ascende si placet, sed ea lege, ne uti cum ludicri mei ratio poscet descendere iniuriam putes. An tu mores ignorabas meos? Nesciebas Croesum regem Lydorum Cyro paulo ante formidabilem mox deinde miserandum rogi flammis traditum misso caelitus imbre defensum? Num te praeterit Paulum Persi regis a se capti calamitatibus pias impendisse lacrimas? Quid tragoediarum clamor aliud deflet nisi indiscreto ictu fortunam felicia regna uertentem? Nonne adulescentulus duo pikous, ton men ena kakon ton de eteron eaon in Iouis limine iacere didicisti? Quid si uberius de bonorum parte sumpsisti, quid si a te non tota discessi, quid si haec ipsa mei mutabilitas iusta tibi causa est sperandi meliora, tamen ne animo contabescas et intra commune omnibus regnum locatus proprio uiuere iure desideres?'

Metrum II

Si quantas rapidis flatibus incitus
Pontus uersat harenas
Aut quot stelliferis edita noctibus
Caelo sidera fulgent
Tantas fundat opes nec retrahat manum
Pleno Copia cornu,
Humanum miseras haud ideo genus
Cesset flere querelas.
Quamuis uota libens excipiat deus
Multi prodigus auri
Et claris auidos ornet honoribus,
Nil iam parta uidentur,
Sed quaesita uorans saeua rapacitas
Alios pandit hiatus.
Quae iam praecipitem frena cupidinem
Certo fine retentent,
Largis cum potius muneribus fluens
Sitis ardescit habendi?
Numquam diues agit qui trepidus gemens
Sese credit egentem.

III

'If Fortune should plead thus against thee, assuredly thou wouldst not have one word to offer in reply; or, if thou canst find any justification of thy complainings, thou must show what it is. I will give thee space to speak.'

Then said I: 'Verily, thy pleas are plausible—yea, steeped in the honeyed sweetness of music and rhetoric. But their charm lasts only while they are sounding in the ear; the sense of his misfortunes lies deeper in the heart of the wretched. So, when the sound ceases to vibrate upon the air, the heart's indwelling sorrow is felt with renewed bitterness.'

Then said she: 'It is indeed as thou sayest, for we have not yet come to the curing of thy sickness; as yet these are but lenitives conducing to the treatment of a malady hitherto obstinate. The remedies which go deep I will apply in due season. Nevertheless, to deprecate thy determination to be thought wretched, I ask thee, Hast thou forgotten the extent and bounds of thy felicity? I say nothing of how, when orphaned and desolate, thou wast taken into the care of illustrious men; how thou wast chosen for alliance with the highest in the state—and even before thou wert bound to their house by marriage, wert already dear to their love—which is the most precious of all ties. Did not all pronounce thee most happy in the virtues of thy wife, the splendid honours of her father, and the blessing of male issue? I pass over—for I care not to speak of blessings in which others also have shared—the distinctions often denied to age which thou enjoyedst in thy youth. I choose rather to come to the unparalleled culmination of thy good fortune. If the fruition of any earthly success has weight in the scale of happiness, can the memory of that splendour be swept away by any rising flood of troubles? That day when thou didst see thy two sons ride forth from home joint consuls, followed by a train of senators, and welcomed by the good-will of the people; when these two sat in curule chairs in the Senate-house, and thou by thy panegyric on the king didst earn the fame of eloquence and ability; when in the Circus, seated between the two consuls, thou didst glut the multitude thronging around with the triumphal largesses for which they looked—methinks thou didst cozen Fortune while she caressed thee, and made thee her darling. Thou didst bear off a boon which she had never before granted to any private person. Art thou, then, minded to cast up a reckoning with Fortune? Now for the first time she has turned a jealous glance upon thee. If thou compare the extent and bounds of thy blessings and misfortunes, thou canst not deny that thou art still fortunate. Or if thou esteem not thyself favoured by Fortune in that thy then seeming prosperity hath departed, deem not thyself wretched, since what thou now believest to be calamitous passeth also. What! art thou but now come suddenly and a stranger to the scene of this life? Thinkest thou there is any stability in human affairs, when man himself vanishes away in the swift course of time? It is true that there is little trust that the gifts of chance will abide; yet the last day of life is in a manner the death of all remaining Fortune. What difference, then, thinkest thou, is there, whether thou leavest her by dying, or she leave thee by fleeing away?'

Song III – *All passes*

When, in rosy chariot drawn,
Phœbus 'gins to light the dawn,

Prosa III

His igitur si pro se te cum Fortuna loqueretur, quid profecto contra hisceres non haberes; aut si quid est quo querelam tuam iure tuearis, proferas oportet, dabimus dicendi locum.

Tum ego: speciosa quidem ista sunt, inquam, oblitaque rhetoricae ac musicae melle dulcedinis tum tantum cum audiuntur oblectant, sed miseris malorum altior sensus est; itaque cum haec auribus insonare desierint insitus animum maeror praegrauat.

Et illa: ita est, inquit; haec enim nondum morbi tui remedia, sed adhuc contumacis aduersum curationem doloris fomenta quaedam sunt. Nam quae in profundum sese penetrent cum tempestiuum fuerit ammouebo. Verumtamen ne te existimari miserum uelis; an numerum modumque tuae felicitatis oblitus es? Taceo quod desolatum parente summorum te uirorum cura suscepit delectusque in affinitatem principum ciuitatis, quod pretiosissimum propinquitatis genus est, prius carus quam proximus esse coepisti. Quis non te felicissimum cum tanto splendore socerorum cum coniugis pudore tum masculae quoque prolis oportunitate praedicauit? Praetereo — Libet enim praeterire communia — Sumptas in adulescentia negatas senibus dignitates; ad singularem felicitatis tuae cumulum uenire delectat. Si quis rerum mortalium fructus ullum beatitudinis pondus habet, poteritne illius memoria lucis quantalibet ingruentium malorum mole deleri cum duos pariter consules liberos tuos domo prouehi sub frequentia patrum sub plebis alacritate uidisti, cum eisdem in curia curules insidentibus tu regiae laudis orator ingenii gloriam facundiaeque meruisti, cum in circo duorum medius consulum circumfusae multitudinis exspectationem triumphali largitione satiasti? Dedisti, ut opinor, uerba Fortunae dum te illa demulcet, dum te ut delicias suas fouet. Munus quod nulli umquam priuato commodauerat abstulisti. Visne igitur cum Fortuna calculum ponere? Nunc te primum liuenti oculo praestrinxit. Si numerum modumque laetorum tristiumue considere, adhuc te felicem negare non possis. Quodsi idcirco te fortunatum esse non aestimas, quoniam quae tunc laeta uidebantur abierunt, non est quod te miserum putes, quoniam quae nunc creduntur maesta praetereunt. An tu in hanc uitae scenam nunc primum subitus hospesque uenisti? Vllamne humanis rebus inesse constantiam reris, cum ipsum saepe hominem uelox hora dissoluat? Nam etsi rara est fortuitis manendi fides, ultimus tamen uitae dies mors quaedam fortunae est etiam manentis. Quid igitur referre putas tune illam moriendo deseras an te illa fugiendo?

Metrum III

Cum polo Phoebus roseis quadrigis
Lucem spargere coeperit,

By his flaming beams assailed,
Every glimmering star is paled.
When the grove, by Zephyrs fed,
With rose-blossom blushes red;—
Doth rude Auster breathe thereon,
Bare it stands, its glory gone.
Smooth and tranquil lies the deep
While the winds are hushed in sleep.
Soon, when angry tempests lash,
Wild and high the billows dash.
Thus if Nature's changing face
Holds not still a moment's space,
Fleeting deem man's fortunes; deem
Bliss as transient as a dream.
One law only standeth fast:
Things created may not last.

IV.

Then said I: 'True are thine admonishings, thou nurse of all excellence; nor can I deny the wonder of my fortune's swift career. Yet it is this which chafes me the more cruelly in the recalling. For truly in adverse fortune the worst sting of misery is to have been happy.'

'Well,' said she, 'if thou art paying the penalty of a mistaken belief, thou canst not rightly impute the fault to circumstances. If it is the felicity which Fortune gives that moves thee— mere name though it be—come reckon up with me how rich thou art in the number and weightiness of thy blessings. Then if, by the blessing of Providence, thou hast still preserved unto thee safe and inviolate that which, howsoever thou mightest reckon thy fortune, thou wouldst have thought thy most precious possession, what right hast thou to talk of ill-for-tune whilst keeping all Fortune's better gifts? Yet Symmachus, thy wife's father—a man whose splendid character does honour to the human race—is safe and unharmed; and while he bewails thy wrongs, this rare nature, in whom wisdom and virtue are so nobly blended, is himself out of danger—a boon thou wouldst have been quick to purchase at the price of life itself. Thy wife yet lives, with her gentle disposition, her peerless modesty and virtue—this the epitome of all her graces, that she is the true daughter of her sire—she lives, I say, and for thy sake only preserves the breath of life, though she loathes it, and pines away in grief and tears for thy absence, wherein, if in naught else, I would allow some marring of thy felicity. What shall I say of thy sons and their consular dignity—how in them, so far as may be in youths of their age, the example of their father's and grandfather's character shines out? Since, then, the chief care of mortal man is to preserve his life, how happy art thou, couldst thou but recognise thy blessings, who possessest even now what no one doubts to be dearer than life! Wherefore, now dry thy tears. Fortune's hate hath not involved all thy dear ones; the stress of the storm that has assailed thee is not beyond measure intolerable, since there

Pallet albentes hebetata uultus

Flammis stella prementibus.

Cum nemus flatu Zephyri tepentis

Vernis inrubuit rosis,

Spiret insanum nebulosus Auster,

Iam spinis abeat decus.

Saepe tranquillo radiat sereno

Immotis mare fluctibus,

Saepe feruentes Aquilo procellas

Verso concitat aequore.

Rara si constat sua forma mundo,

Si tantas uariat uices,

Crede fortunis hominum caducis,

Bonis crede fugacibus!

Constat aeterna positumque lege est

Vt constet genitum nihil.

Prosa IV

Tum ego: uera, inquam, commemoras, o uirtutum omnium nutrix, nec infitiari possum prosperitatis meae uelocissimum cursum. Sed hoc est quod recolentem uehementius coquit; nam in omni aduersitate fortunae infelicissimum est genus infortunii fuisse felicem.

Sed quod tu, inquit, falsae opinionis supplicium luas, id rebus iure imputare non possis. Nam si te hoc inane nomen fortuitae felicitatis mouet, quam pluribus maximisque abundes me cum reputes licet. Igitur si quod in omni fortunae tuae censu pretiosissimum possidebas id tibi diuinitus inlaesum adhuc inuiolatumque seruatur, poterisne meliora quaeque retinens de infortunio iure causari? Atqui uiget incolumis illud pretiosissimum generis humani decus Symmachus socer et, quod uitae pretio non segnis emeres, uir totus ex sapientia uirtuti‑ busque factus: suarum securus tuis ingemescit iniuriis. Viuit uxor ingenio modesta, pudicitia pudore praecellens et, ut omnes eius dotes breuiter includam, patri similis; uiuit, inquam, tibique tantum uitae huius exosa spiritum seruat, quoque uno felicitatem minui tuam uel ipsa concesserim, tui desiderio lacrimis ac dolore tabescit. Quid dicam liberos consulares, quor‑ um iam ut in id aetatis pueris uel paterni uel auiti specimen elucet ingenii? Cum igitur prae‑ cipua sit mortalibus uitae cura retinendae, o te, si tua bona cognoscas, felicem, cui suppetunt etiam nunc quae uita nemo dubitat esse cariora. Quare sicca iam lacrimas; nondum est ad

are anchors still holding firm which suffer thee not to lack either consolation in the present or hope for the future.'

'I pray that they still may hold. For while they still remain, however things may go, I shall ride out the storm. Yet thou seest how much is shorn of the splendour of my fortunes.'

'We are gaining a little ground,' said she, 'if there is something in thy lot wherewith thou art not yet altogether discontented. But I cannot stomach thy daintiness when thou complainest with such violence of grief and anxiety because thy happiness falls short of completeness. Why, who enjoys such settled felicity as not to have some quarrel with the circumstances of his lot? A troublous matter are the conditions of human bliss; either they are never realized in full, or never stay permanently. One has abundant riches, but is shamed by his ignoble birth. Another is conspicuous for his nobility,but through the embarrassments of poverty would prefer to be obscure. A third, richly endowed with both, laments the loneliness of an unwedded life. Another, though happily married, is doomed to childlessness, and nurses his wealth for a stranger to inherit. Yet another, blest with children, mournfully bewails the misdeeds of son or daughter. Wherefore, it is not easy for anyone to be at perfect peace with the circumstances of his lot. There lurks in each several portion something which they who experience it not know nothing of, but which makes the sufferer wince. Besides, the more favoured a man is by Fortune, the more fastidiously sensitive is he; and, unless all things answer to his whim, he is overwhelmed by the most trifling misfortunes, because utterly unschooled in adversity. So petty are the trifles which rob the most fortunate of perfect happiness! How many are there, dost thou imagine, who would think themselves nigh heaven, if but a small portion from the wreck of thy fortune should fall to them? This very place which thou callest exile is to them thatdwell therein their native land. So true is it that nothing is wretched, but thinking makes it so, and conversely every lot is happy if borne with equanimity. Who is so blest by Fortune as not to wish to change his state, if once he gives rein to a rebellious spirit? With how many bitternesses is the sweetness of human felicity blent! And even if that sweetness seem to him to bring delight in the enjoying, yet he cannot keep it from departing when it will. How manifestly wretched, then, is the bliss of earthly fortune, which lasts not for ever with those whose temper is equable, and can give no perfect satisfaction to the anxious-minded!

'Why, then, ye children of mortality, seek ye from without that happiness whose seat is only within us? Error and ignorance bewilder you. I will show thee, in brief, the hinge on which perfect happiness turns. Is there anything more precious to thee than thyself? Nothing, thou wilt say. If, then, thou art master of thyself, thou wilt possess that which thou wilt never be willing to lose, and which Fortune cannot take from thee. And that thou mayst see that happiness cannot possibly consist in these things which are the sport of chance, reflect that, if happiness is the highest good of a creature living in accordance with reason, and if a thing which can in any wise be reft away is not the highest good, since that which cannot be taken away is better than it, it is plain that Fortune cannot aspire to bestow happiness by reason of its instability. And, besides, a man borne along by this transitory felicity must either know or not know its unstability. If he knows not, how poor is a happiness which depends on the blindness of ignorance! If he knows it, he needs must fear to lose a happiness whose loss he believes to be possible. Wherefore, a never-ceasing fear suffers him not to be happy. Or does he count the possibility of this loss a trifling matter? Insignificant, then, must

unum omnes exosa fortuna nec tibi nimium ualida tempestas incubuit quando tenaces haerent ancorae quae nec praesentis solamen nec futuri spem temporis abesse patiantur.

Et haereant, inquam, precor; illis namque manentibus, utcumque se res habeant, enat‐ abimus. Sed quantum ornamentis nostris decesserit uides.

Et illa: promouimus, inquit, aliquantum si te non iam totius tuae sortis piget. Sed deli‐ cias tuas ferre non possum, qui abesse aliquid tuae beatitudini tam luctuosus atque anxius conqueraris. Quis est enim tam compositae felicitatis ut non aliqua ex parte cum status sui qualitate rixetur? Anxia enim res est humanorum condicio bonorum et quae uel numquam tota proueniat uel numquam perpetua subsistat. Huic census exuberat, sed est pudori degen‐ er sanguis; hunc nobilitas notum facit, sed angustia rei familiaris inclusus esse mallet ignotus. Ille utroque circumfluus uitam caelibem deflet; ille nuptiis felix orbus liberis alieno censum nutrit heredi; alius prole laetatus filii filiaeue delictis maestus illacrimat. Idcirco nemo facile cum fortunae suae condicione concordat; inest enim singulis quod inexpertus ignoret, ex‐ pertus exhorreat. Adde quod felicissimi cuiusque delicatissimus sensus est, et nisi ad nutum cuncta suppetant omnis aduersitatis insolens minimis quibusque prosternitur: adeo per‐ exigua sunt quae fortunatissimis beatitudinis summam detrahunt. Quam multos esse coniectas qui sese caelo proximos arbitrentur si de fortunae tuae reliquiis pars eis minima contingat? Hic ipse locus, quem tu exsilium uocas, incolentibus patria est. Adeo nihil est miserum nisi cum putes, contraque beata sors omnis est aequanimitate tolerantis. Quis est ille tam felix, qui cum dederit impatientiae manus statum suum mutare non optet? Quam multis amaritudinibus humanae felicitatis dulcedo respersa est! Quae si etiam fruenti iucunda esse uideatur, tamen quominus cum uelit abeat retineri non possit. Liquet igitur quam sit mortalium rerum misera beatitudo, quae nec apud aequanimos perpetua perdurat nec anxios tota delectat.

Quid igitur, o mortales, extra petitis intra uos positam felicitatem? Error uos in‐ scitiaque confundit. Ostendam breuiter tibi summae cardinem felicitatis. Estne aliquid tibi te ipso pretiosius? Nihil, inquies. Igitur si tui compos fueris, possidebis quod nec tu amittere umquam uelis nec fortuna possit auferre. Atque ut agnoscas in his fortuitis rebus beatitud‐ inem constare non posse, sic collige. Si beatitudo est summum naturae bonum ratione degen‐ tis nec est summum bonum quod eripi ullo modo potest, quoniam praecellit id quod nequeat auferri, manifestum est quin ad beatitudinem percipiendam fortunae instabilitas aspirare non possit. Ad haec, quem caduca ista felicitas uehit uel scit eam uel nescit esse mutabilem. Si nescit, quaenam beata sors esse potest ignorantiae caecitate? Si scit, metuat necesse est ne amittat quod amitti posse non dubitat; quare continuus timor non sinit esse felicem. An uel si

be the good whose loss can be borne so equably. And, further, I know thee to be one settled in the belief that the souls of men certainly die not with them, and convinced thereof by numerous proofs; it is clear also that the felicity which Fortune bestows is brought to an end with the death of the body: therefore, it cannot be doubted but that, if happiness is conferred in this way, the whole human race sinks into misery when death brings the close of all. But if we know that many have sought the joy of happiness not through death only, but also through pain and suffering, how can life make men happy by its presence when it makes them not wretched by its loss?'

Song IV – The Golden Mean.

Who founded firm and sure
Would ever live secure,
In spite of storm and blast
Immovable and fast;
Whoso would fain deride
The ocean's threatening tide;—
His dwelling should not seek
On sands or mountain-peak.
Upon the mountain's height
The storm-winds wreak their spite:
The shifting sands disdain
Their burden to sustain.
Do thou these perils flee,
Fair though the prospect be,
And fix thy resting-place
On some low rock's sure base.
Then, though the tempests roar,
Seas thunder on the shore,
Thou in thy stronghold blest
And undisturbed shalt rest;
Live all thy days serene,
And mock the heavens' spleen.

V.

'But since my reasonings begin to work a soothing effect within thy mind, methinks I may resort to remedies somewhat stronger. Come, suppose, now, the gifts of Fortune were not fleeting and transitory, what is there in them capable of ever becoming truly thine, or which does not lose value when looked at steadily and fairly weighed in the balance? Are riches, I pray thee, precious either through thy nature or in their own? What are they but mere gold and heaps of money? Yet these fine things show their quality better in the

amiserit neglegendum putat? Sic quoque perexile bonum est quod aequo animo feratur amis-
sum. Et quoniam tu idem es cui persuasum atque insitum permultis demonstrationibus scio
mentes hominum nullo modo esse mortales, cumque clarum sit fortuitam felicitatem corporis
morte finiri, dubitari nequit, si haec afferre beatitudinem potest, quin omne mortalium genus
in miseriam mortis fine labatur. Quodsi multos scimus beatitudinis fructum non morte solum
uerum etiam doloribus suppliciisque quaesisse, quonam modo praesens facere beatos potest
quae miseros transacta non efficit?

Metrum IV

Quisquis uolet perennem
Cautus ponere sedem
Stabilisque nec sonori
Sterni flatibus Euri
Et fluctibus minantem
Curat spernere pontum,
Montis cacumen alti,
Bibulas uitet harenas;
Illud proteruus Auster
Totis uiribus urguet,
Hae pendulum solutae
Pondus ferre recusant.
Fugiens periculosam
Sortem sedis amoenae
Humili domum memento
Certus figere saxo.
Quamuis tonet ruinis
Miscens aequora uentus,
Tu conditus quieti
Felix robore ualli
Duces serenus aeuum
Ridens aetheris iras.

Prosa V

Sed quoniam rationum iam in te mearum fomenta descendunt, paulo ualidioribus uten-
dum puto. Age enim, si iam caduca et momentaria fortunae dona non essent, quid in eis est
quod aut uestrum umquam fieri queat aut non perspectum consideratumque uilescat? Diuiti-
aene uel uestrae uel sui natura pretiosae sunt? Quid earum potius? Aurumne ac uis congesta
pecuniae? Atqui haec effundendo magis quam coaceruando melius nitent, si quidem auaritia

spending than in the hoarding; for I suppose 'tis plain that greed Alva's makes men hateful, while liberality brings fame. But that which is transferred to another cannot remain in one's own possession; and if that be so, then money is only precious when it is given away, and, by being transferred to others, ceases to be one's own. Again, if all the money in the world were heaped up in one man's possession, all others would be made poor. Sound fills the ears of many at the same time without being broken into parts, but your riches cannot pass to many without being lessened in the process. And when this happens, they must needs impoverish those whom they leave. How poor and cramped a thing, then, is riches, which more than one cannot possess as an unbroken whole, which falls not to any one man's lot without the impoverishment of everyone else! ❲Or is it the glitter of gems that allures the eye? Yet, how rarely excellent soever may be their splendour, remember the flashing light is in the jewels, not in the man. Indeed, I greatly marvel at men's admiration of them; for what can rightly seem beautiful to a being endowed with life and reason, if it lack the movement and structure of life? And although such things do in the end take on them more beauty from their Maker's care and their own brilliancy, still they in no wise merit your admiration since their excellence is set at a lower grade than your own.

'Does the beauty of the fields delight you? Surely, yes; it is a beautiful part of a right beautiful whole. Fitly indeed do we at times enjoy the serene calm of the sea, admire the sky, the stars, the moon, the sun. Yet is any of these thy concern? Dost thou venture to boast thyself of the beauty of any one of them? Art thou decked with spring's flowers? is it thy fertility that swelleth in the fruits of autumn? Why art thou moved with empty transports? why embracest thou an alien excellence as thine own? Never will fortune make thine that which the nature of things has excluded from thy ownership. Doubtless the fruits of the earth are given for the sustenance of living creatures. But if thou art content to supply thy wants so far as suffices nature, there is no need to resort to fortune's bounty. Nature is content with few things, and with a very little of these. If thou art minded to force superfluities upon her when she is satisfied, that which thou addest will prove either unpleasant or harmful. But, now, thou thinkest it fine to shine in raiment of divers colours; yet—if, indeed, there is any pleasure in the sight of such things—it is the texture or the artist's skill which I shall admire.

'Or perhaps it is a long train of servants that makes thee happy? Why, if they behave viciously, they are a ruinous burden to thy house, and exceeding dangerous to their own master; while if they are honest, how canst thou count other men's virtue in the sum of thy possessions? From all which 'tis plainly proved that not one of these things which thou reckonest in the number of thy possessions is really thine. And if there is in them no beauty to be desired, why shouldst thou either grieve for their loss or find joy in their continued possession? While if they are beautiful in their own nature, what is that to thee? They would have been not less pleasing in themselves, though never included among thy possessions. For they derive not their preciousness from being counted in thy riches, but rather thou hast chosen to count them in thy riches because they seemed to thee precious.

'Then, what seek ye by all this noisy outcry about fortune? To chase away poverty, I ween, by means of abundance. And yet ye find the result just contrary. Why, this varied array of precious furniture needs more accessories for its protection; it is a true saying that they want most who possess most, and, conversely, they want very little who measure their abundance by nature's requirements, not by the superfluity of vain display. Have ye no good

semper odiosos, claros largitas facit. Quodsi manere apud quemque non potest quod transfertur in alterum, tunc est pretiosa pecunia cum translata in alios largiendi usu desinit possideri. At eadem, si apud unum quanta est ubique gentium congeratur, ceteros sui inopes fecerit. Et uox quidem tota pariter multorum replet auditum, uestrae uero diuitiae nisi comminutae in plures transire non possunt; quod cum factum est, pauperes necesse est faciant quos relinquunt. O igitur angustas inopesque diuitias, quas nec habere totas pluribus licet et ad quemlibet sine ceterorum paupertate non ueniunt.

An gemmarum fulgor oculos trahit? Sed si quid est in hoc splendore praecipui, gemmarum est lux illa, non hominum; quas quidem mirari homines uehementer ammiror. Quid est enim carens animae motu atque compage quod animatae rationabilique naturae pulchrum esse iure uideatur? Quae tametsi conditoris opera suique distinctione postremae aliquid pulchritudinis trahunt, infra uestram tamen excellentiam collocatae ammirationem uestram nullo modo mereantur.

An uos agrorum pulchritudo delectat? Quidni? Est enim pulcherrimi operis pulchra portio. Sic quondam sereni maris facie gaudemus, sic caelum, sidera, lunam solemque miramur. Num te horum aliquid attingit, num audes alicuius talium splendore gloriari? An uernis floribus ipse distingueris aut tua in aestiuos fructus intumescit ubertas? Quid inanibus gaudiis raperis, quid externa bona pro tuis amplexaris? Numquam tua faciet esse fortuna quae a te natura rerum fecit aliena. Terrarum quidem fructus animantium procul dubio debentur alimentis; sed si, quod naturae satis est, replere indigentiam uelis, nihil est quod fortunae affluentiam petas. Paucis enim minimisque natura contenta est; cuius satietatem si superfluis urguere uelis, aut iniucundum quod infuderis fiet aut noxium. Iam uero pulchrum uariis fulgere uestibus putas. Quarum si grata intuitu species est, aut materiae naturam aut ingenium mirabor artificis. ₵An uero te longus ordo famulorum facit esse felicem? Qui si uitiosi moribus sint, perniciosa domus sarcina et ipsi domino uehementer inimica; sin uero probi, quonam modo in tuis opibus aliena probitas numerabitur? Ex quibus omnibus nihil horum quae tu in tuis computas bonis tuum esse bonum liquido monstratur. Quibus si nihil inest appetendae pulchritudinis, quid est quod uel amissis doleas uel laeteris retentis? Quodsi natura pulchra sunt, quid id tua refert? Nam haec per se a tuis quoque opibus sequestrata placuissent. Neque enim idcirco sunt pretiosa quod in tuas uenere diuitias, sed quoniam pretiosa uidebantur tuis ea diuitiis annumerare maluisti.

Quid autem tanto fortunae strepitu desideratis? Fugare, credo, indigentiam copia quaeritis. Atqui hoc uobis in contrarium cedit; pluribus quippe amminiculis opus est ad tuendam pretiosae supellectilis uarietatem, uerumque illud est permultis eos indigere qui permulta possideant, contraque minimum qui abundantiam suam naturae necessitate non ambitus superfluitate metiantur. Itane autem nullum est proprium uobis atque insitum bonum ut in

of your own implanted within you, that ye seek your good in things external and separate? Is the nature of things so reversed that a creature divine by right of reason can in no other way be splendid in his own eyes save by the possession of lifeless chattels? Yet, while other things are content with their own, ye who in your intellect are God-like seek from the lowest of things adornment for a nature of supreme excellence, and perceive not how great a wrong ye do your Maker. His will was that mankind should excel all things on earth. Ye thrust down your worth beneath the lowest of things. For if that in which each thing finds its good is plainly more precious than that whose good it is, by your own estimation ye put yourselves below the vilest of things, when ye deem these vile things to be your good: nor does this fall out undeservedly. Indeed, man is so constituted that he then only excels other things when he knows himself; but he is brought lower than the beasts if he lose this self-knowledge. For that other creatures should be ignorant of themselves is natural; in man it shows as a defect. How extravagant, then, is this error of yours, in thinking that anything can be embellished by adornments not its own. It cannot be. For if such accessories add any lustre, it is the accessories that get the praise, while that which they veil and cover remains in its pristine ugliness. And again I say, That is no good, which injures its possessor. Is this untrue? No, quite true, thou sayest. And yet riches have often hurt those that possessed them, since the worst of men, who are all the more covetous by reason of their wickedness, think none but themselves worthy to possess all the gold and gems the world contains. So thou, who now dreadest pike and sword, mightest have trolled a carol "in the robber's face," hadst thou entered the road of life with empty pockets. Oh, wondrous blessedness of perishable wealth, whose acquisition robs thee of security!'

Song V – The Former Age.

Too blest the former age, their life
Who in the fields contented led,
And still, by luxury unspoiled,
On frugal acorns sparely fed.
No skill was theirs the luscious grape
With honey's sweetness to confuse;
Nor China's soft and sheeny silks
T' empurple with brave Tyrian hues.
The grass their wholesome couch, their drink
The stream, their roof the pine's tall shade;
Not theirs to cleave the deep, nor seek
In strange far lands the spoils of trade.
The trump of war was heard not yet,
Nor soiled the fields by bloodshed's stain;
For why should war's fierce madness arm
When strife brought wound, but brought not gain?

externis ac sepositis rebus bona uestra quaeratis? Sic rerum uersa condicio est ut diuinum merito rationis animal non aliter sibi splendere nisi inanimatae supellectilis possessione uideatur? Et alia quidem suis contenta sunt, uos autem deo mente consimiles ab rebus infimis excellentis naturae ornamenta captatis nec intellegitis quantam conditori uestro faciatis iniuriam. Ille genus humanum terrenis omnibus praestare uoluit, uos dignitatem uestram infra infima quaeque detruditis. Nam si omne cuiusque bonum eo cuius est constat esse pretiosius, cum uilissima rerum uestra bona esse iudicatis eisdem uosmet ipsos uestra existimatione summittitis. Quod quidem haud immerito cadit. Humanae quippe naturae ista condicio est ut tum tantum ceteris rebus cum se cognoscit excellat, eadem tamen infra bestias redigatur si se nosse desierit; nam ceteris animantibus sese ignorare naturae est, hominibus uitio uenit. Quam uero late patet uester hic error, qui ornari posse aliquid ornamentis existimatis alienis! At id fieri nequit; nam si quid ex appositis luceat, ipsa quidem quae sunt apposita laudantur, illud uero his tectum atque uelatum in sua nihilo minus foeditate perdurat. Ego uero nego ullum esse bonum quod noceat habenti num id mentior? Minime, inquis. Atqui diuitiae possidentibus persaepe nocuerunt, cum pessimus quisque eoque alieni magis auidus quicquid usquam auri gemmarumque est se solum qui habeat dignissimum putat. Tu igitur, qui nunc contum gladiumque sollicitus pertimescis, si uitae huius callem uacuus uiator intrasses coram latrone cantares. O praeclara opum mortalium beatitudo, quam cum adeptus fueris securus esse desistis!

Metrum V

Felix nimium prior aetas
Contenta fidelibus aruis
Nec inerti perdita luxu,
Facili quae sera solebat
Ieiunia soluere glande.
Non Bacchica munera norant
Liquido confundere melle
Nec lucida uellera Serum
Tyrio miscere ueneno.
Somnos dabat herba salubres,
Potum quoque lubricus amnis,
Vmbras altissima pinus.
Nondum maris alta secabat
Nec mercibus undique lectis
Noua litora uiderat hospes.
Tunc classica saeua tacebant
Odiis neque fusus acerbis
Cruor horrida tinxerat arua.
Quid enim furor hosticus ulla
Vellet prior arma mouere,
Cum uulnera saeua uiderent
Nec praemia sanguinis ulla?

Ah! would our hearts might still return
To following in those ancient ways.
Alas! the greed of getting glows
More fierce than Etna's fiery blaze.

Woe, woe for him, whoe'er it was,
Who first gold's hidden store revealed,
And—perilous treasure-trove—dug out
The gems that fain would be concealed!

VI.

'What now shall I say of rank and power, whereby, because ye know not true power and dignity, ye hope to reach the sky? Yet, when rank and power have fallen to the worst of men, did ever an Etna, belching forth flame and fiery deluge, work such mischief? Verily, as I think, thou dost remember how thine ancestors sought to abolish the consular power, which had been the foundation of their liberties, on account of the overweening pride of the consuls, and how for that self-same pride they had already abolished the kingly title! And if, as happens but rarely, these prerogatives are conferred on virtuous men, it is only the virtue of those who exercise them that pleases. So it appears that honour cometh not to virtue from rank, but to rank from virtue. Look, too, at the nature of that power which ye find so attractive and glorious! Do ye never consider, ye creatures of earth, what ye are, and over whom ye exercise your fancied lordship? Suppose, now, that in the mouse tribe there should rise up one claiming rights and powers for himself above the rest, would ye not laugh consumedly? Yet if thou lookest to his body alone, what creature canst thou find more feeble than man, who oftentimes is killed by the bite of a fly, or by some insect creeping into the inner passage of his system! Yet what rights can one exercise over another, save only as regards the body, and that which is lower than the body—I mean fortune? What! wilt thou bind with thy mandates the free spirit? Canst thou force from its due tranquillity the mind that is firmly composed by reason? A tyrant thought to drive a man of free birth to reveal his accomplices in a conspiracy, but the prisoner bit off his tongue and threw it into the furious tyrant's face; thus, the tortures which the tyrant thought the instrument of his cruelty the sage made an opportunity for heroism. Moreover, what is there that one man can do to another which he himself may not have to undergo in his turn? We are told that Busiris, who used to kill his guests, was himself slain by his guest, Hercules. Regulus had thrown into bonds many of the Carthaginians whom he had taken in war; soon after he himself submitted his hands to the chains of the vanquished. Then, thinkest thou that man hath any power who cannot prevent another's being able to do to him what he himself can do to others?

'Besides, if there were any element of natural and proper good in rank and power, they would never come to the utterly bad, since opposites are not wont to be associated. Nature brooks not the union of contraries. So, seeing there is no doubt that wicked wretches are oftentimes set in high places, it is also clear that things which suffer association with the worst of men cannot be good in their own nature. Indeed, this judgment may with some reason be passed concerning all the gifts of fortune which fall so plentifully to all the most wicked. This ought also to be considered here, I think: No one doubts a man to be brave in whom he

Vtinam modo nostra redirent
In mores tempora priscos!
Sed saeuior ignibus Aetnae
Feruens amor ardet habendi.
Heu, primus quis fuit ille
Auri qui pondera tecti
Gemmasque latere uolentes
Pretiosa pericula fodit?

Prosa VI

Quid autem de dignitatibus potentiaque disseram, qua uos uerae dignitatis ac potestatis inscii caelo exaequatis? Quae si in improbissimum quemque ceciderunt, quae flammis aetnae eructantibus, quod diluuium tantas strages dederint? Certe, uti meminisse te arbitror, consulare imperium, quod libertatis principium fuerat, ob superbiam consulum uestri ueteres abolere cupiuerunt, qui ob eandem superbiam prius regium de ciuitate nomen abstulerant. At si quando, quod perrarum est, probis deferantur, quid in eis aliud quam probitas utentium placet? Ita fit ut non uirtutibus ex dignitate sed ex uirtute dignitatibus honor accedat. Quae uero est ista uestra expetibilis ac praeclara potentia? Nonne, o terrena animalia, consideratis quibus qui praesidere uideamini? Nunc si inter mures uideres unum aliquem ius sibi ac potestatem prae ceteris uindicantem, quanto mouereris cachinno! Quid uero, si corpus spectes, imbecillius homine repperire queas, quos saepe muscularum quoque uel morsus uel in secreta quaeque reptantium necat introitus? Quo uero quisquam ius aliquod in quempiam nisi in solum corpus et quod infra corpus est — Fortunam loquor — Possit exserere? Num quicquam libero imperabis animo? Num mentem firma sibi ratione cohaerentem de statu propriae quietis amouebis? Cum liberum quendam uirum suppliciis se tyrannus adacturum putaret ut aduersum se factae coniurationis conscios proderet, linguam ille momordit atque abscidit et in os tyranni saeuientis abiecit; ita cruciatus, quos putabat tyrannus materiam crudelitatis, uir sapiens fecit esse uirtutis. Quid autem est quod in alium facere quisque possit, quod sustinere ab alio ipse non possit? Busiridem accepimus necare hospites solitum ab Hercule hospite fuisse mactatum. Regulus plures Poenorum bello captos in uincla coniecerat, sed mox ipse uictorum catenis manus praebuit. Vllamne igitur eius hominis potentiam putas qui quod ipse in alio potestne id in se alter ualeat efficere non possit?

Ad haec, si ipsis dignitatibus ac potestatibus inesset aliquid naturalis ac proprii boni, numquam pessimis prouenirent. Neque enim sibi solent aduersa sociari; natura respuit ut contraria quaeque iungantur. Ita cum pessimos plerumque dignitatibus fungi dubium non sit, illud etiam liquet natura sui bona non esse quae se pessimis haerere patiantur. Quod quidem de cunctis fortunae muneribus dignius existimari potest, quae ad improbissimum quemque uberiora perueniunt. De quibus illud etiam considerandum puto quod nemo dubitat esse

has observed a brave spirit residing. It is plain that one who is endowed with speed is swift-footed. So also music makes men musical, the healing art physicians, rhetoric public speakers. For each of these has naturally its own proper working; there is no confusion with the effects of contrary things—nay, even of itself it rejects what is incompatible. And yet wealth cannot extinguish insatiable greed, nor has power ever made him master of himself whom vicious lusts kept bound in indissoluble fetters; dignity conferred on the wicked not only fails to make them worthy, but contrarily reveals and displays their unworthiness. Why does it so happen? Because ye take pleasure in calling by false names things whose nature is quite incongruous thereto—by names which are easily proved false by the very effects of the things themselves; even so it is; these riches, that power, this dignity, are none of them rightly so called. Finally, we may draw the same conclusion concerning the whole sphere of Fortune, within which there is plainly nothing to be truly desired, nothing of intrinsic excellence; for she neither always joins herself to the good, nor does she make good men of those to whom she is united.'

Song VI – Neros' Infamy

We know what mischief dire he wrought—
Rome fired, the Fathers slain—
Whose hand with brother's slaughter wet
A mother's blood did stain.
No pitying tear his cheek bedewed,
As on the corse he gazed;
That mother's beauty, once so fair,
A critic's voice appraised.
Yet far and wide, from East to West,
His sway the nations own;
And scorching South and icy North
Obey his will alone.
Did, then, high power a curb impose
On Nero's phrenzied will?
Ah, woe when to the evil heart
Is joined the sword to kill!

VII.

Then said I: 'Thou knowest thyself that ambition for worldly success hath but little swayed me. Yet I have desired opportunity for action, lest virtue, in default of exercise, should languish away.'

Then she: 'This is that "last infirmity" which is able to allure minds which, though of noble quality, have not yet been moulded to any exquisite refinement by the perfecting of the virtues—I mean, the love of glory—and fame for high services rendered to the commonweal. And yet consider with me how poor and unsubstantial a thing this glory is! The whole of this earth's globe, as thou hast learnt from the demonstration of astronomy, compared with

fortem cui fortitudinem inesse conspexerit et cuicumque uelocitas adest manifestum est esse uelocem. Sic musica quidem musicos, medicina medicos, rhetorica rhetores facit: agit enim cuiusque rei natura quod proprium est nec contrariarum rerum miscetur effectibus et ultro quae sunt aduersa depellit. Atqui nec opes inexpletam restinguere auaritiam queunt, nec potestas sui compotem fecerit quem uitiosae libidines insolubilibus adstrictum retinent catenis, et collata improbis dignitas non modo non effecit dignos sed prodit potius et ostentat indignos. Cur ita prouenit? Gaudetis enim res sese aliter habentes falsis compellare nominibus, quae facile ipsarum rerum redarguuntur effectu; itaque nec illae diuitiae nec illa potentia nec haec dignitas iure appellari potest. Postremo idem de tota concludere fortuna licet, in qua nihil expetendum, nihil natiuae bonitatis inesse manifestum est, quae nec se bonis semper adiungit et bonos quibus fuerit adiuncta non efficit.

Metrum VI

Nouimus quantas dederit ruinas
Vrbe flammata patribusque caesis
Fratre qui quondam ferus interempto
Matris effuso maduit cruore
Corpus et uisu gelidum pererrans
Ora non tinxit lacrimis, sed esse
Censor exstincti potuit decoris.
Hic tamen sceptro populos regebat
Quos uidet condens radios sub undas
Phoebus, extremo ueniens ab ortu,
Quos premunt septem gelidi triones,
Quos Notus sicco uiolentus aestu
Torret ardentes recoquens harenas.
Celsa num tandem ualuit potestas
Vertere praui rabiem Neronis?
Heu grauem sortem, quotiens iniquus
Additur saeuo gladius ueneno!

Prosa VII

Tum ego: scis, inquam, ipsa minimum nobis ambitionem mortalium rerum fuisse dominatam; sed materiam gerendis rebus optauimus, quo ne uirtus tacita consenesceret.

Et illa: atqui hoc unum est quod praestantes quidem natura mentes sed nondum ad extremam manum uirtutum perfectione perductas allicere possit, gloriae scilicet cupido et optimorum in rem publicam fama meritorum. Quae quam sit exilis et totius uacua ponderis sic considera. Omnem terrae ambitum, sicuti astrologicis demonstrationibus accepisti, ad caeli

the expanse of heaven, is found no bigger than a point; that is to say, if measured by the vast-ness of heaven's sphere, it is held to occupy absolutely no space at all. Now, of this so insigni-ficant portion of the universe, it is about a fourth part, as Ptolemy's proofs have taught us, which is inhabited by living creatures known to us. If from this fourth part you take away in thought all that is usurped by seas and marshes, or lies a vast waste of waterless desert, barely is an exceeding narrow area left for human habitation. You, then, who are shut in and prisoned in this merest fraction of a point's space, do ye take thought for the blazoning of your fame, for the spreading abroad of your renown? Why, what amplitude or magnificence has glory when confined to such narrow and petty limits?

'Besides, the straitened bounds of this scant dwelling-place are inhabited by many na-tions differing widely in speech, in usages, in mode of life; to many of these, from the diffi-culty of travel, from diversities of speech, from want of commercial intercourse, the fame not only of individual men, but even of cities, is unable to reach. Why, in Cicero's days, as he himself somewhere points out, the fame of the Roman Republic had not yet crossed the Cau-casus, and yet by that time her name had grown formidable to the Parthians and other nations of those parts. Seest thou, then, how narrow, how confined, is the glory ye take pains to spread abroad and extend! Can the fame of a single Roman penetrate where the glory of the Roman name fails to pass? Moreover, the customs and institutions of different races agree not together, so that what is deemed praise worthy in one country is thought punishable in an-other. Wherefore, if any love the applause of fame, it shall not profit him to publish his name among many peoples. Then, each must be content to have the range of his glory limited to his own people; the splendid immortality of fame must be confined within the bounds of a single race.

'Once more, how many of high renown in their own times have been lost in oblivion for want of a record! Indeed, of what avail are written records even, which, with their authors, are overtaken by the dimness of age after a somewhat longer time? But ye, when ye think on future fame, fancy it an immortality that ye are begetting for yourselves. Why, if thou scan-nest the infinite spaces of eternity, what room hast thou left for rejoicing in the durability of thy name? Verily, if a single moment's space be compared with ten thousand years, it has a certain relative duration, however little, since each period is definite. But this same number of years—ay, and a number many times as great—cannot even be compared with endless duration; for, indeed, finite periods may in a sort be compared one with another, but a finite and an infinite never. So it comes to pass that fame, though it extend to ever so wide a space of years, if it be compared to never-lessening eternity, seems not short-lived merely, but alto-gether nothing. But as for you, ye know not how to act aright, unless it be to court the popu-lar breeze, and win the empty applause of the multitude—nay, ye abandon the superlative worth of conscience and virtue, and ask a recompense from the poor words of others. Let me tell thee how wittily one did mock the shallowness of this sort of arrogance. A certain man assailed one who had put on the name of philosopher as a cloak to pride and vain-glory, not for the practice of real virtue, and added: "Now shall I know if thou art a philosopher if thou bearest reproaches calmly and patiently." The other for awhile affected to be patient, and, having endured to be abused, cried out derisively: "Now, do you see that I am a philosopher?" The other, with biting sarcasm, retorted: "I should have hadst thou held thy peace." Moreover, what concern have choice spirits—for it is of such men we speak, men

spatium puncti constat obtinere rationem, id est, ut, si ad caelestis globi magnitudinem conferatur, nihil spatii prorsus habere iudicetur. Huius igitur tam exiguae in mundo regionis quarta fere portio est, sicut Ptolomaeo probante didicisti, quae nobis cognitis animantibus incolatur. Huic quartae si quantum maria paludesque premunt quantumque siti uasta regio distenditur cogitatione subtraxeris, uix angustissima inhabitandi hominibus area relinquetur. In hoc igitur minimo puncti quodam puncto circumsaepti atque conclusi de peruulganda fama, de proferendo nomine cogitatis, ut quid habeat amplum magnificumque gloria tam angustis exiguisque limitibus artata?

Adde quod hoc ipsum breuis habitaculi saeptum plures incolunt nationes lingua, moribus, totius uitae distantes, ad quas tum difficultate itinerum tum loquendi diuersitate tum commercii insolentia non modo fama hominum singulorum sed ne urbium quidem peruenire queat. Aetate denique M. Tullii, sicut ipse quodam loco significat, nondum Caucasum montem Romanae rei publicae fama transcenderat et erat tunc adulta Parthis etiam ceterisque id locorum gentibus formidolosa. Videsne igitur quam sit angusta, quam compressa gloria, quam dilatare ac propagare laboratis? An ubi Romani nominis transire fama nequit Romani hominis gloria progredietur? Quid quod diuersarum gentium mores inter se atque instituta discordant, ut quod apud alios laude apud alios supplicio dignum iudicetur? Quo fit ut si quem famae praedicatio delectat huic in plurimos populos nomen proferre nullo modo conducat. Erit igitur peruagata inter suos gloria quisque contentus et intra unius gentis terminos praeclara illa famae immortalitas coartabitur.

Sed quam multos clarissimos suis temporibus uiros scriptorum inops deleuit obliuio! Quamquam quid ipsa scripta proficiant, quae cum suis auctoribus premit longior atque obscura uetustas? Vos uero immortalitatem uobis propagare uidemini cum futuri famam temporis cogitatis. Quod si ad aeternitatis infinita spatia pertractes, quid habes quod de nominis tui diuturnitate laeteris? Vnius etenim mora momenti si decem milibus conferatur annis, quoniam utrumque spatium definitum est, minimam licet habet tamen aliquam portionem; at hic ipse numerus annorum eiusque quamlibet multiplex ad interminabilem diuturnitatem ne comparari quidem potest. Etenim finitis ad se inuicem fuerit quaedam, infiniti uero atque finiti nulla umquam poterit esse collatio. Ita fit, ut quamlibet prolixi temporis fama, si cum inexhausta aeternitate cogitetur, non parua sed plane nulla esse uideatur. Vos autem nisi ad populares auras inanesque rumores recte facere nescitis et relicta conscientiae uirtutisque praestantia de alienis praemia sermunculis postulatis. Accipe in huius modi arrogantiae leuitate quam festiue aliquis illuserit. Nam cum quidam adortus esset hominem contumeliis, qui non ad uerae uirtutis usum ad superbam gloriam falsum sibi philosophi nomen induerat, adiecissetque iam se sciturum an ille philosophus esset si quidem inlatas iniurias leniter patienterque tolerasset, ille patientiam paulisper assumpsit acceptaque contumelia uelut insultans: 'iam tandem', inquit, 'intellegis me esse philosophum?' tum ille nimium mordaciter: 'intellexeram', inquit, 'si tacuisses'. Quid autem est quod ad praecipuos uiros de his enim

who seek glory by virtue—what concern, I say, have these with fame after the dissolution of the body in death's last hour? For if men die wholly—which our reasonings forbid us to believe—there is no such thing as glory at all, since he to whom the glory is said to belong is altogether non-existent. But if the mind, conscious of its own rectitude, is released from its earthly prison, and seeks heaven in free flight, doth it not despise all earthly things when it rejoices in its deliverance from earthly bonds, and enters upon the joys of heaven?'

Song VII – Glory may not last.

Oh, let him, who pants for glory's guerdon,
Deeming glory all in all,
Look and see how wide the heaven expandeth,
Earth's enclosing bounds how small!
Shame it is, if your proud-swelling glory
May not fill this narrow room!
Why, then, strive so vainly, oh, ye proud ones!
To escape your mortal doom?
Though your name, to distant regions bruited,
O'er the earth be widely spread,
Though full many a lofty-sounding title
On your house its lustre shed,
Death at all this pomp and glory spurneth
When his hour draweth nigh,
Shrouds alike th' exalted and the humble,
Levels lowest and most high.
Where are now the bones of stanch Fabricius?
Brutus, Cato—where are they?
Lingering fame, with a few graven letters,
Doth their empty name display.
But to know the great dead is not given
From a gilded name alone;
Nay, ye all alike must lie forgotten,
'Tis not you that fame makes known.
Fondly do ye deem life's little hour
Lengthened by fame's mortal breath;
There but waits you—when this, too, is taken—
At the last a second death.

VIII.

'But that thou mayst not think that I wage implacable warfare against Fortune, I own there is a time when the deceitful goddess serves men well—I mean when she reveals herself, uncovers her face, and confesses her true character. Perhaps thou dost not yet grasp my meaning. Strange is the thing I am trying to express, and for this cause I can scarce find

sermo est, qui uirtute gloriam petunt, quid, inquam, est quod ad hos de fama post resolutum morte suprema corpus attineat? Nam si, quod nostrae rationes credi uetant, toti moriuntur homines, nulla est omnino gloria, cum is cuius ea esse dicitur non exstet omnino. Sin uero bene sibi mens conscia terreno carcere resoluta caelum libera petit, nonne omne terrenum negotium spernat, quae se caelo fruens terrenis gaudet exemptam?

Metrum VII

Quicumque solam mente praecipiti petit
Summumque credit gloriam,
Late patentes aetheris cernat plagas
Artumque terrarum situm;
Breuem replere non ualentis ambitum
Pudebit aucti nominis.
Quid, o superbi, colla mortali iugo
Frustra leuari gestiunt?
Licet remotos fama per populos means
Diffusa linguas explicet
Et magna titulis fulgeat claris domus,
Mors spernit altam gloriam,
Inuoluit humile pariter et celsum caput
Aequatque summis infima.
Vbi nunc fidelis ossa Fabricii manent,
Quid Brutus aut rigidus Cato?
Signat superstes fama tenuis pauculis
Inane nomen litteris.
Sed quod decora nouimus uocabula
Num scire consumptos datur?
Iacetis ergo prorsus ignorabiles
Nec fama notos efficit.
Quodsi putatis longius uitam trahi
Mortalis aura nominis,
Cum sera uobis rapiet hoc etiam dies
Iam uos secunda mors manet.

Prosa VIII

Sed ne me inexorabile contra fortunam gerere bellum putes: est aliquando cum de hominibus fallax illa nihil bene mereatur, tum scilicet cum se aperit, cum frontem detegit moresque profitetur. Nondum forte quid loquar intellegis; mirum est quod dicere gestio, eoque sententiam uerbis explicare uix queo. Etenim plus hominibus reor aduersam quam

words to make clear my thought. For truly I believe that Ill Fortune is of more use to men than Good Fortune. For Good Fortune, when she wears the guise of happiness, and most seems to caress, is always lying; Ill Fortune is always truthful, since, in changing, she shows her inconstancy. The one deceives, the other teaches; the one enchains the minds of those who enjoy her favour by the semblance of delusive good, the other delivers them by the knowledge of the frail nature of happiness. Accordingly, thou mayst see the one fickle, shifting as the breeze, and ever self-deceived; the other sober-minded, alert, and wary, by reason of the very discipline of adversity. Finally, Good Fortune, by her allurements, draws men far from the true good; Ill Fortune ofttimes draws men back to true good with grappling-irons. Again, should it be esteemed a trifling boon, thinkest thou, that this cruel, this odious Fortune hath discovered to thee the hearts of thy faithful friends—that other hid from thee alike the faces of the true friends and of the false, but in departing she hath taken away her friends, and left thee thine? What price wouldst thou not have given for this service in the fulness of thy prosperity when thou seemedst to thyself fortunate? Cease, then, to seek the wealth thou hast lost, since in true friends thou hast found the most precious of all riches.'

Song VIII – Love is Lord of all.

Why are Nature's changes bound
To a fixed and ordered round?
What to leaguèd peace hath bent
Every warring element?
Wherefore doth the rosy morn
Rise on Phœbus' car upborne?
Why should Phœbe rule the night,
Led by Hesper's guiding light?
What the power that doth restrain
In his place the restless main,
That within fixed bounds he keeps,
Nor o'er earth in deluge sweeps?
Love it is that holds the chains,
Love o'er sea and earth that reigns;
Love—whom else but sovereign Love?—
Love, high lord in heaven above!
Yet should he his care remit,
All that now so close is knit
In sweet love and holy peace,
Would no more from conflict cease,
But with strife's rude shock and jar
All the world's fair fabric mar.
Tribes and nations Love unites
By just treaty's sacred rites;
Wedlock's bonds he sanctifies
By affection's softest ties.

prosperam prodesse fortunam; illa enim semper specie felicitatis, cum uidetur blanda, mentitur, haec semper uera est, cum se instabilem mutatione demonstrat. Illa fallit, haec instruit; illa mendacium specie bonorum mentes fruentium ligat, haec cognitione fragilis, felicitatis absoluit; itaque illam uideas uentosam fluentem suique semper ignaram, hanc sobriam succinctamque et ipsius aduersitatis exercitatione prudentem. Postremo felix a uero bono deuios blanditiis trahit, aduersa plerumque ad uera bona reduces unco retrahit. An hoc inter minima aestimandum putas quod amicorum tibi fidelium mentes haec aspera, haec horribilis fortuna detexit? Haec tibi certos sodalium uultus ambiguosque secreuit, discedens suos abstulit, tuos reliquit. Quanti hoc integer et, ut uidebaris tibi, fortunatus emisses? Nunc amissas opes querere: quod pretiosissimum diuitiarum genus est, amicos inuenisti.

Metrum VIII

Quod mundus stabili fide
Concordes uariat uices,
Quod pugnantia semina
Foedus perpetuum tenent,
Quod Phoebus roseum diem
Curru prouehit aureo,
Vt quas duxerit Hesperos
Phoebe noctibus imperet,
Vt fluctus auidum mare
Certo fine coherceat,
Ne terris liceat uagis
Latos tendere terminos,
Hanc rerum seriem ligat
Terras ac pelagus regens
Et caelo imperitans amor.
Hic si frena remiserit,
Quicquid nunc amat inuicem
Bellum continuo geret
Et quam nunc socia fide
Pulchris motibus incitant
Certent soluere machinam.
Hic sancto populos quoque
Iunctos foedere continet,
Hic et coniugii sacrum
Castis nectit amoribus,

Love appointeth, as is due,
Faithful laws to comrades true—
Love, all-sovereign Love!—oh, then,
Ye are blest, ye sons of men,
If the love that rules the sky
In your hearts is throned on high!

Hic fidis etiam sua
Dictat iura sodalibus.
O felix hominum genus,
Si uestros animos amor
Quo caelum regitur regat!

Book III – True Happiness and False

I.

She ceased, but I stood fixed by the sweetness of the song in wonderment and eager ex‑
pectation, my ears still strained to listen. And then after a little I said: 'Thou sovereign solace
of the stricken soul, what refreshment hast thou brought me, no less by the sweetness of thy
singing than by the weightiness of thy discourse! Verily, I think not that I shall hereafter be
unequal to the blows of Fortune. Wherefore, I no longer dread the remedies which thou
saidst were something too severe for my strength; nay, rather, I am eager to hear of them and
call for them with all vehemence.'

Then said she: 'I marked thee fastening upon my words silently and intently, and I ex‑
pected, or—to speak more truly—I myself brought about in thee, this state of mind. What
now remains is of such sort that to the taste indeed it is biting, but when received within it
turns to sweetness. But whereas thou dost profess thyself desirous of hearing, with what ar‑
dour wouldst thou not burn didst thou but perceive whither it is my task to lead thee!'

'Whither?' said I.

'To true felicity,' said she, 'which even now thy spirit sees in dreams, but cannot behold
in very truth, while thine eyes are engrossed with semblances.'

Then said I: 'I beseech thee, do thou show to me her true shape without a moment's
loss.'

'Gladly will I, for thy sake,' said she. 'But first I will try to sketch in words, and de‑
scribe a cause which is more familiar to thee, that, when thou hast viewed this carefully, thou
mayst turn thy eyes the other way, and recognise the beauty of true happiness.'

Song I – The Thorns of Error.

Who fain would sow the fallow field,
And see the growing corn,
Must first remove the useless weeds,
The bramble and the thorn.
After ill savour, honey's taste
Is to the mouth more sweet;
After the storm, the twinkling stars
The eyes more cheerly greet.

Liber Tertius

Prosa I

Iam cantum illa finiuerat, cum me audiendi auidum stupentemque arrectis adhuc auribus carminis mulcedo defixerat. Itaque paulo post: o, inquam, summum lassorum solamen animorum, quam tu me uel sententiarum pondere uel canendi etiam iucunditate refouisti, adeo ut iam me posthac imparem fortunae ictibus esse non arbitrer! Itaque remedia quae paulo acriora esse dicebas non modo non perhorresco, sed audiendi auidus uehementer efflagito.

Tum illa: sensi, inquit, cum uerba nostra tacitus attentusque rapiebas, eumque tuae mentis habitum uel exspectaui uel, quod est uerius, ipsa perfeci; talia sunt quippe quae restant ut degustata quidem mordeant, interius autem recepta dulcescant. Sed quod tu te audiendi cupidum dicis, quanto ardore flagrares si quonam te ducere aggrediamur agnosceres!

Quonam? Inquam.

Ad ueram, inquit, felicitatem, quam tuus quoque somniat animus, sed occupato ad imagines uisu ipsam illam non potest intueri.

Tum ego: fac, obsecro, et quae illa uera sit sine cunctatione demonstra.

Faciam, inquit illa, tui causa libenter; sed quae tibi [causa] notior est, eam prius designare uerbis atque informare conabor, ut ea perspecta cum in contrariam partem flexeris oculos uerae specimen beatitudinis possis agnoscere.

Metrum I

Qui serere ingenuum uolet agrum
Liberat arua prius fruticibus,
Falce rubos filicemque resecat,
Vt noua fruge grauis Ceres eat.
Dulcior est apium mage labor
Si malus ora prius sapor edat.
Gratius astra nitent ubi Notus
Desinit imbriferos dare sonos.
Lucifer ut tenebras pepulerit
Pulchra dies roseos agit equos.

When night hath past, the bright dawn comes
In car of rosy hue;
So drive the false bliss from thy mind,
And thou shall see the true.

II.

For a little space she remained in a fixed gaze, withdrawn, as it were, into the august chamber of her mind; then she thus began:

'All mortal creatures in those anxious aims which find employment in so many varied pursuits, though they take many paths, yet strive to reach one goal—the goal of happiness. Now, the good is that which, when a man hath got, he can lack nothing further. This it is which is the supreme good of all, containing within itself all particular good; so that if anything is still wanting thereto, this cannot be the supreme good, since something would be left outside which might be desired. 'Tis clear, then, that happiness is a state perfected by the assembling together of all good things. To this state, as we have said, all men try to attain, but by different paths. For the desire of the true good is naturally implanted in the minds of men; only error leads them aside out of the way in pursuit of the false. Some, deeming it the highest good to want for nothing, spare no pains to attain affluence; others, judging the good to be that to which respect is most worthily paid, strive to win the reverence of their fellow-citizens by the attainment of official dignity. Some there are who fix the chief good in supreme power; these either wish themselves to enjoy sovereignty, or try to attach themselves to those who have it. Those, again, who think renown to be something of supreme excellence are in haste to spread abroad the glory of their name either through the arts of war or of peace. A great many measure the attainment of good by joy and gladness of heart; these think it the height of happiness to give themselves over to pleasure. Others there are, again, who interchange the ends and means one with the other in their aims; for instance, some want riches for the sake of pleasure and power, some covet power either for the sake of money or in order to bring renown to their name. So it is on these ends, then, that the aim of human acts and wishes is centred, and on others like to these—for instance, noble birth and popularity, which seem to compass a certain renown; wife and children, which are sought for the sweetness of their possession; while as for friendship, the most sacred kind indeed is counted in the category of virtue, not of fortune; but other kinds are entered upon for the sake of power or of enjoyment. And as for bodily excellences, it is obvious that they are to be ranged with the above. For strength and stature surely manifest power; beauty and fleetness of foot bring celebrity; health brings pleasure. It is plain, then, that the only object sought for in all these ways is happiness. For that which each seeks in preference to all else, that is in his judgment the supreme good. And we have defined the supreme good to be happiness. Therefore, that state which each wishes in preference to all others is in his judgment happy.

'Thou hast, then, set before thine eyes something like a scheme of human happiness—wealth, rank, power, glory, pleasure. Now Epicurus, from a sole regard to these considerations, with some consistency concluded the highest good to be pleasure, because all the other objects seem to bring some delight to the soul. But to return to human pursuits and aims: man's mind seeks to recover its proper good, in spite of the mistiness of its recollection, but,

Tu quoque falsa tuens bona prius
Incipe colla iugo retrahere:
Vera dehinc animum subierint.

Prosa II

Tum defixo paululum uisu et uelut in augustam suae mentis sedem recepta sic coepit:

Omnis mortalium cura quam multiplicium studiorum labor exercet diuerso quidem calle procedit, sed ad unum tamen beatitudinis finem nititur peruenire. Id autem est bonum quo quis adepto nihil ulterius desiderare queat. Quod quidem est omnium summum bonorum cunctaque intra se bona continens; cui si quid aforet summum esse non posset, quoniam relinqueretur extrinsecus quod posset optari. Liquet igitur esse beatitudinem statum bonorum omnium congregatione perfectum. Hunc, uti diximus, diuerso tramite omnes conantur adipisci: est enim mentibus hominum ueri boni naturaliter inserta cupiditas, sed ad falsa deuius error abducit. Quorum quidem alii summum bonum esse nihilo indigere credentes, ut diuitiis affluant elaborant, alii uero bonum quod sit dignissimum ueneratione iudicantes adeptis honoribus reuerendi ciuibus suis esse nituntur. Sunt qui summum bonum in summa potentia esse constituant; hi uel regnare ipsi uolunt uel regnantibus adhaerere conantur. At quibus optimum quiddam claritas uidetur, hi uel belli uel pacis artibus gloriosum nomen propagare festinant. Plurimi uero boni fructum gaudio laetitiaque metiuntur; hi felicissimum putant uoluptate diffluere. Sunt etiam qui horum fines causasque alterutro permutent, ut qui diuitias ob potentiam uoluptatesque desiderant uel qui potentiam seu pecuniae causa seu proferendi nominis petunt. In his igitur ceterisque talibus humanorum actuum uotorumque uersatur intentio ueluti nobilitas fauorque popularis, quae uidentur quandam claritudinem comparare, uxor ac liberi, quae iucunditatis gratia petuntur; amicorum uero quod sanctissimum quidem genus est non in fortuna sed in uirtute numeratur, reliquum uero uel potentiae causa uel delectationis assumitur. Iam uero corporis bona promptum est ut ad superiora referantur; robur enim magnitudoque uidetur praestare ualentiam, pulchritudo atque uelocitas celebritatem, salubritas uoluptatem. Quibus omnibus solam beatitudinem desiderari liquet; nam quod quisque prae ceteris petit id summum esse iudicat bonum. Sed summum bonum beatitudinem esse definiuimus; quare beatum esse iudicat statum quem prae ceteris quisque desiderat.

Habes igitur ante oculos propositam fere formam felicitatis humanae: opes, honores, potentiam, gloriam, uoluptates. Quae quidem sola considerans Epicurus consequenter sibi summum bonum uoluptatem esse constituit, quod cetera omnia iucunditatem animo uideantur afferre. Sed ad hominum studia reuertor, quorum animus etsi caligante memoria tamen bonum suum repetit, sed uelut ebrius domum quo tramite reuertatur ignorat. Num enim uidentur errare hi qui nihilo indigere nituntur? Atqui non est aliud quod aeque perficere beatitudinem possit quam copiosus bonorum omnium status nec alieni egens sed sibi ipse sufficiens. Num uero labuntur hi qui quod sit optimum id etiam reuerentiae cultu dignissimum putent? Minime; neque enim uile quiddam contemnendumque est quod adipisci omnium

like a drunken man, knows not by what path to return home. Think you they are wrong who strive to escape want? Nay, truly there is nothing which can so well complete happiness as a state abounding in all good things, needing nothing from outside, but wholly self-sufficing. Do they fall into error who deem that which is best to be also best deserving to receive the homage of reverence? Not at all. That cannot possibly be vile and contemptible, to attain which the endeavours of nearly all mankind are directed. Then, is power not to be reckoned in the category of good? Why, can that which is plainly more efficacious than anything else be esteemed a thing feeble and void of strength? Or is renown to be thought of no account? Nay, it cannot be ignored that the highest renown is constantly associated with the highest excellence. And what need is there to say that happiness is not haunted by care and gloom, nor exposed to trouble and vexation, since that is a condition we ask of the very least of things, from the possession and enjoyment of which we expect delight? So, then, these are the blessings men wish to win; they want riches, rank, sovereignty, glory, pleasure, because they believe that by these means they will secure independence, reverence, power, renown, and joy of heart. Therefore, it is the good which men seek by such divers courses; and herein is easily shown the might of Nature's power, since, although opinions are so various and dis-cordant, yet they agree in cherishing good as the end.'

Song II — The Bent of Nature.

How the might of Nature sways
All the world in ordered ways,
How resistless laws control
Each least portion of the whole—
Fain would I in sounding verse
On my pliant strings rehearse.
Lo, the lion captive ta'en
Meekly wears his gilded chain;
Yet though he by hand be fed,
Though a master's whip he dread,
If but once the taste of gore
Whet his cruel lips once more,
Straight his slumbering fierceness wakes,
With one roar his bonds he breaks,
And first wreaks his vengeful force
On his trainer's mangled corse.
And the woodland songster, pent
In forlorn imprisonment,
Though a mistress' lavish care
Store of honeyed sweets prepare;
Yet, if in his narrow cage,
As he hops from bar to bar,
He should spy the woods afar,
Cool with sheltering foliage,

fere mortalium laborat intentio. An in bonis non est numeranda potentia? Quid igitur, num imbecillum ac sine uiribus aestimandum est quod omnibus rebus constat esse praestantius? An claritudo nihili pendenda est? Sed sequestrari nequit quin omne quod excellentissimum sit id etiam uideatur esse clarissimum. Nam non esse anxiam tristemque beatitudinem nec doloribus molestiisque subiectam quid attinet dicere, quando in minimis quoque rebus id ap-petitur quod habere fruique delectet? Atqui haec sunt quae adipisci homines uolunt eaque de causa diuitias, dignitates, regna, gloriam uoluptatesque desiderant quod per haec sibi suffi-cientiam, reuerentiam, potentiam, celebritatem, laetitiam credunt esse uenturam. Bonum est igitur quod tam diuersis studiis homines petunt; in quo quanta sit naturae uis facile monstrat-ur, cum licet uariae dissidentesque sententiae tamen in diligendo boni fine consentiunt.

Metrum II

Quantas rerum flectat habenas
Natura potens, quibus immensum
Legibus orbem prouida seruet
Stringatque ligans inresoluto
Singula nexu, placet arguto
Fidibus lentis promere cantu.
Quamuis Poeni pulchra leones
Vincula gestent manibusque datas
Captent escas metuantque trucem
Soliti uerbera ferre magistrum,
Si cruor horrida tinxerit ora,
Resides olim redeunt animi
Fremituque graui meminere sui,
Laxant nodis colla solutis
Primusque lacer dente cruento
Domitor rabidas imbuit iras.
Quae canit altis garrula ramis
Ales caueae clauditur antro;
Huic licet inlita pocula melle
Largasque dapes dulci studio
Ludens hominum cura ministret,
Si tamen arto saliens texto
Nemorum gratas uiderit umbras,

All these dainties he will spurn,
To the woods his heart will turn;
Only for the woods he longs,
Pipes the woods in all his songs.
To rude force the sapling bends,
While the hand its pressure lends;
If the hand its pressure slack,
Straight the supple wood springs back.
Phœbus in the western main
Sinks; but swift his car again
By a secret path is borne
To the wonted gates of morn.
Thus are all things seen to yearn
In due time for due return;
And no order fixed may stay,
Save which in th' appointed way
Joins the end to the beginning
In a steady cycle spinning.

III.

'Ye, too, creatures of earth, have some glimmering of your origin, however faint, and though in a vision dim and clouded, yet in some wise, notwithstanding, ye discern the true end of happiness, and so the aim of nature leads you thither—to that true good—while error in many forms leads you astray therefrom. For reflect whether men are able to win happiness by those means through which they think to reach the proposed end. Truly, if either wealth, rank, or any of the rest, bring with them anything of such sort as seems to have nothing wanting to it that is good, we, too, acknowledge that some are made happy by the acquisition of these things. But if they are not able to fulfil their promises, and, moreover, lack many good things, is not the happiness men seek in them clearly discovered to be a false show? Therefore do I first ask thee thyself, who but lately wert living in affluence, amid all that abundance of wealth, was thy mind never troubled in consequence of some wrong done to thee?'

'Nay,' said I, 'I cannot ever remember a time when my mind was so completely at peace as not to feel the pang of some uneasiness.'

'Was it not because either something was absent which thou wouldst not have absent, or present which thou wouldst have away?'

'Yes,' said I.

'Then, thou didst want the presence of the one, the absence of the other?'

'Admitted.'

'But a man lacks that of which he is in want?'

'He does.'

'And he who lacks something is not in all points self-sufficing?'

'No; certainly not,' said I.

Sparsas pedibus proterit escas,
Siluas tantum maesta requirit,
Siluas dulci uoce susurrat.
Validis quondam uiribus acta
Pronum flectit uirga cacumen;
Hanc si curuans dextra remisit,
Recto spectat uertice caelum.
Cadit Hesperias Phoebus in undas,
Sed secreto tramite rursus
Currum solitos uertit ad ortus.
Repetunt proprios quaeque recursus
Redituque suo singula gaudent
Nec manet ulli traditus ordo
Nisi quod fini iunxerit ortum
Stabilemque sui fecerit orbem.

Prosa III

Vos quoque, o terrena animalia, tenui licet imagine uestrum tamen principium somniatis uerumque illum beatitudinis finem licet minime perspicaci qualicumque tamen cogitatione prospicitis, eoque uos et ad uerum bonum naturalis ducit intentio et ab eodem multiplex error abducit. Considera namque an per ea quibus se homines adepturos beatitudinem putant ad destinatum finem ualeant peruenire. Si enim uel pecunia uel honores ceteraque tale quid afferunt cui nihil bonorum abesse uideatur, nos quoque fateamur fieri aliquos horum adeptione felices. Quodsi neque id ualent efficere quod promittunt bonisque pluribus carent, nonne liquido falsa in eis beatitudinis species deprehenditur? Primum igitur te ipsum, qui paulo ante diuitiis affluebas, interrogo: inter illas abundantissimas opes numquamne animum tuum concepta ex qualibet iniuria confudit anxietas?

Atqui, inquam, libero me fuisse animo quin aliquid semper angerer reminisci non queo.

Nonne quia uel aberat quod abesse non uelles uel aderat quod adesse noluisses?

Ita est, inquam.

Illius igitur praesentiam, huius absentiam desiderabas?

Confiteor, inquam.

Eget uero, inquit, eo quod quisque desiderat?

Eget, inquam.

Qui uero eget aliquo non est usquequaque sibi ipse sufficiens.

Minime, inquam.

'So wert thou, then, in the plenitude of thy wealth, supporting this insufficiency?'

'I must have been.'

'Wealth, then, cannot make its possessor independent and free from all want, yet this was what it seemed to promise. Moreover, I think this also well deserves to be considered —that there is nothing in the special nature of money to hinder its being taken away from those who possess it against their will.'

'I admit it.'

'Why, of course, when every day the stronger wrests it from the weaker without his consent. Else, whence come lawsuits, except in seeking to recover moneys which have been taken away against their owner's will by force or fraud?'

'True,' said I.

'Then, everyone will need some extraneous means of protection to keep his money safe.'

'Who can venture to deny it?'

'Yet he would not, unless he possessed the money which it is possible to lose.'

'No; he certainly would not.'

'Then, we have worked round to an opposite conclusion: the wealth which was thought to make a man independent rather puts him in need of further protection. How in the world, then, can want be driven away by riches? Cannot the rich feel hunger? Cannot they thirst? Are not the limbs of the wealthy sensitive to the winter's cold? "But," thou wilt say, "the rich have the wherewithal to sate their hunger, the means to get rid of thirst and cold." True enough; want can thus be soothed by riches, wholly removed it cannot be. For if this ever-gaping, ever-craving want is glutted by wealth, it needs must be that the want itself which can be so glutted still remains. I do not speak of how very little suffices for nature, and how for avarice nothing is enough. Wherefore, if wealth cannot get rid of want, and makes new wants of its own, how can ye believe that it bestows independence?'

Song III – The Insatiableness of Avarice.

Though the covetous grown wealthy
See his piles of gold rise high;
Though he gather store of treasure
That can never satisfy;
Though with pearls his gorget blazes,
Rarest that the ocean yields;
Though a hundred head of oxen
Travail in his ample fields;
Ne'er shall carking care forsake him
While he draws this vital breath,
And his riches go not with him,
When his eyes are closed in death.

Tu itaque hanc insufficientiam plenus, inquit, opibus sustinebas?

Quidni? Inquam.

Opes igitur nihilo indigentem sufficientemque sibi facere nequeunt, et hoc erat quod promittere uidebantur. Atqui hoc quoque maxime considerandum puto quod nihil habeat suapte natura pecunia ut his quibus possidetur inuitis nequeat auferri.

Fateor, inquam.

Quidni fateare, cum eam cotidie ualentior aliquis eripiat inuito? Vnde enim forenses querimoniae, nisi quod uel ui uel fraude nolentibus pecuniae repetuntur ereptae?

Ita est, inquam.

Egebit igitur, inquit, extrinsecus petito praesidio quo suam pecuniam quisque tueatur.

Quis id, inquam, neget?

Atqui non egeret eo nisi possideret pecuniam, quam possit amittere.

Dubitari, inquam, nequit.

In contrarium igitur relapsa res est; nam quae sufficientes sibi facere putabantur opes alieno potius praesidio faciunt indigentes. Quis autem modus est quo pellatur diuitiis indigentia? Num enim diuites esurire nequeunt, num sitire non possunt, num frigus hibernum peculiosorum membra non sentiunt? Sed adest, inquies, opulentis quo famem satient, quo sitim frigusque depellant. Sed hoc modo consolari quidem diuitiis indigentia potest, auferri penitus non potest; nam si haec hians semper atque aliquid poscens opibus expletur, maneat necesse est quae possit expleri. Taceo, quod naturae minimum, quod auaritiae nihil satis est. Quare si opes nec summouere indigentiam possunt et ipsae suam faciunt, quid est quod eas sufficientiam praestare credatis?

Metrum III

Quamuis fluente diues auri gurgite
Non expleturas cogat auarus opes
Oneretque bacis colla rubri litoris
Ruraque centeno scindat opima boue,
Nec cura mordax deserit superstitem
Defunctumque leues non comitantur opes.

IV.

'Well, but official dignity clothes him to whom it comes with honour and reverence! Have, then, offices of state such power as to plant virtue in the minds of their possessors, and drive out vice? Nay, they are rather wont to signalize iniquity than to chase it away, and hence arises our indignation that honours so often fall to the most iniquitous of men. Accordingly, Catullus calls Nonius an "ulcer-spot," though "sitting in the curule chair." Dost not see what infamy high position brings upon the bad? Surely their unworthiness will be less conspicuous if their rank does not draw upon them the public notice! In thy own case, wouldst thou ever have been induced by all these perils to think of sharing office with Decoratus, since thou hast discerned in him the spirit of a rascally parasite and informer? No; we cannot deem men worthy of reverence on account of their office, whom we deem unworthy of the office itself. But didst thou see a man endued with wisdom, couldst thou suppose him not worthy of reverence, nor of that wisdom with which he was endued?'

'No; certainly not.'

'There is in Virtue a dignity of her own which she forthwith passes over to those to whom she is united. And since public honours cannot do this, it is clear that they do not possess the true beauty of dignity. And here this well deserves to be noticed—that if a man is the more scorned in proportion as he is despised by a greater number, high position not only fails to win reverence for the wicked, but even loads them the more with contempt by drawing more attention to them. But not without retribution; for the wicked pay back a return in kind to the dignities they put on by the pollution of their touch. Perhaps, too, another consideration may teach thee to confess that true reverence cannot come through these counterfeit dignities. It is this: If one who had been many times consul chanced to visit barbaric lands, would his office win him the reverence of the barbarians? And yet if reverence were the natural effect of dignities, they would not forego their proper function in any part of the world, even as fire never anywhere fails to give forth heat. But since this effect is not due to their own efficacy, but is attached to them by the mistaken opinion of mankind, they disappear straightway when they are set before those who do not esteem them dignities. Thus the case stands with foreign peoples. But does their repute last for ever, even in the land of their origin? Why, the prefecture, which was once a great power, is now an empty name—a burden merely on the senator's fortune; the commissioner of the public corn supply was once a personage—now what is more contemptible than this office? For, as we said just now, that which hath no true comeliness of its own now receives, now loses, lustre at the caprice of those who have to do with it. So, then, if dignities cannot win men reverence, if they are actually sullied by the contamination of the wicked, if they lose their splendour through time's changes, if they come into contempt merely for lack of public estimation, what precious beauty have they in themselves, much less to give to others?'

Prosa IV

Sed dignitates honorabilem reuerendumque cui prouenerint reddunt. Num uis ea est magistratibus ut utentium mentibus uirtutes inserant, uitia depellant? Atqui non fugare, sed inlustrare potius nequitiam solent. Quo fit ut indignemur eas saepe nequissimis hominibus contigisse; unde Catullus licet in curuli Nonium sedentem strumam tamen appellat. Videsne quantum malis dedecus adiciant dignitates? Atqui minus eorum patebit indignitas si nullis honoribus inclarescant. Tu quoque num tandem tot periculis adduci potuisti ut cum Decorato gerere magistratum putares, cum in eo mentem nequissimi scurrae delatorisque respiceres? Non enim possumus ob honores reuerentia dignos iudicare quos ipsis honoribus iudicamus indignos. At si quem sapientia praeditum uideres, num posses eum uel reuerentia uel ea qua est praeditus sapientia non dignum putare?

Minime.

Inest enim dignitas propria uirtuti, quam protinus in eos quibus fuerit adiuncta transfundit. Quod quia populares facere nequeunt honores, liquet eos propriam dignitatis pulchritudinem non habere. In quo illud est animaduertendum magis: nam si eo abiectior est quo magis a pluribus quisque contemnitur, cum reuerendos facere nequeat quos pluribus ostentat, despectiores potius improbos dignitas facit. Verum non impune; reddunt namque improbi parem dignitatibus uicem, quas sua contagione commaculant. Atque ut agnoscas ueram illam reuerentiam per has umbratiles dignitates non posse contingere: si qui multiplici consulatu functus in barbaras nationes forte deuenerit, uenerandumne barbaris honor faciet? Atqui si hoc naturale munus dignitatibus foret, ab officio suo quoquo gentium nullo modo cessarent, sicut ignis ubique terrarum numquam tamen calere destitit. Sed quoniam id eis non propria uis sed hominum fallax adnectit opinio, uanescunt ilico cum ad eos uenerint qui dignitates eas esse non aestimant. Sed hoc apud exteras nationes: inter eos uero apud quos ortae sunt num perpetuo perdurant? Atqui praetura magna olim potestas, nunc inane nomen et senatorii census grauis sarcina; si quis quondam populi curasset annonam magnus habebatur, nunc ea praefectura quid abiectius? Vt enim paulo ante diximus, quod nihil habet proprii decoris, opinione utentium nunc splendorem accipit, nunc amittit. Si igitur reuerendos facere nequeunt dignitates, si ultro improborum contagione sordescunt, si mutatione temporum splendere desinunt, si gentium aestimatione uilescunt, quid est quod in se expetendae pulchritudinis habeant, nedum aliis praestent?

Song IV — *Disgrace of Honours conferred by a Tyrant.*

Though royal purple soothes his pride,
And snowy pearls his neck adorn,
Nero in all his riot lives
The mark of universal scorn.
    Yet he on reverend heads conferred
Th' inglorious honours of the state.
Shall we, then, deem them truly blessed
Whom such preferment hath made great?

V.

'Well, then, does sovereignty and the intimacy of kings prove able to confer power? Why, surely does not the happiness of kings endure for ever? And yet antiquity is full of examples, and these days also, of kings whose happiness has turned into calamity. How glorious a power, which is not even found effectual for its own preservation! But if happiness has its source in sovereign power, is not happiness diminished, and misery inflicted in its stead, in so far as that power falls short of completeness? Yet, however widely human sovereignty be extended, there must still be more peoples left, over whom each several king holds no sway. Now, at whatever point the power on which happiness depends ceases, here powerlessness steals in and makes wretchedness; so, by this way of reckoning, there must needs be a balance of wretchedness in the lot of the king. The tyrant who had made trial of the perils of his condition figured the fears that haunt a throne under the image of a sword hanging over a man's head.[5] What sort of power, then, is this which cannot drive away the gnawings of anxiety, or shun the stings of terror? Fain would they themselves have lived secure, but they cannot; then they boast about their power! Dost thou count him to possess power whom thou seest to wish what he cannot bring to pass? Dost thou count him to possess power who encompasses himself with a body-guard, who fears those he terrifies more than they fear him, who, to keep up the semblance of power, is himself at the mercy of his slaves? Need I say anything of the friends of kings, when I show royal dominion itself so utterly and miserably weak—why ofttimes the royal power in its plenitude brings them low, ofttimes involves them in its fall? Nero drove his friend and preceptor, Seneca, to the choice of the manner of his death. Antoninus exposed Papinianus, who was long powerful at court, to the swords of the soldiery. Yet each of these was willing to renounce his power. Seneca tried to surrender his wealth also to Nero, and go into retirement; but neither achieved his purpose. When they tottered, their very greatness dragged them down. What manner of thing, then, is this power which keeps men in fear while they possess it—which when thou art fain to keep, thou art not safe, and when thou desirest to lay it aside thou canst not rid thyself of? Are friends any protection who have been attached by fortune, not by virtue? Nay; him whom good fortune has made a friend, ill fortune will make an enemy. And what plague is more effectual to do hurt than a foe of one's own household?'

---

5   The sword of Damocles.

Metrum IV

Quamuis se Tyrio superbus ostro
Comeret et niueis lapillis,
Inuisus tamen omnibus uigebat
Luxuriae Nero saeuientis;
Sed quondam dabat improbus uerendis
Patribus indecores curules.
Quis illos igitur putet beatos
Quos miseri tribuunt honores?

Prosa V

An uero regna regumque familiaritas efficere potentem ualet? Quidni, quando eorum fe‑
licitas perpetuo perdurat? Atqui plena est exemplorum uetustas, plena etiam praesens aetas,
qui reges felicitatem calamitate mutauerint. O praeclara potentia, quae ne ad conseruationem
quidem sui satis efficax inuenitur! Quodsi haec regnorum potestas beatitudinis auctor est,
nonne, si qua parte defuerit, felicitatem minuat, miseriam importet? Sed quamuis late humana
tendantur imperia, plures necesse est gentes relinqui quibus regum quisque non imperet.
Qua uero parte beatos faciens desinit potestas hac impotentia subintrat, quae miseros facit;
hoc igitur modo maiorem regibus inesse necesse est miseriae portionem. Expertus sortis suae
periculorum tyrannus regni metus pendentis supra uerticem gladii terrore simulauit. Quae
est igitur haec potestas, quae sollicitudinum morsus expellere, quae formidinum aculeos uit‑
are nequit? Atqui uellent ipsi uixisse securi, sed nequeunt; dehinc de potestate gloriantur.
An tu potentem censes quem uideas uelle quod non possit efficere, potentem censes qui satel‑
lite latus ambit, qui quos terret ipse plus metuit, qui ut potens esse uideatur in seruientium
manu situm est? Nam quid ego de regum familiaribus disseram — Cum regna ipsa tantae im‑
becillitatis plena demonstrem — Quos quidem regia potestas saepe incolumis, saepe autem
lapsa prosternit? Nero Senecam familiarem praeceptoremque suum ad eligendae mortis coe‑
git arbitrium, Papinianum diu inter aulicos potentem militum gladiis Antoninus obiecit.
Atqui uterque potentiae suae renuntiare uoluerunt, quorum Seneca opes etiam suas tradere
Neroni seque in otium conferre conatus est; sed dum ruituros moles ipsa trahit, neuter quod
uoluit effecit. Quae est igitur ista potentia, quam pertimescunt habentes, quam nec cum
habere uelis tutus sis et cum deponere cupias uitare non possis? An praesidio sunt amici quos
non uirtus sed fortuna conciliat? Sed quem felicitas amicum fecit infortunium faciet inimic‑
um. Quae uero pestis efficacior ad nocendum quam familiaris inimicus?

Song V — Self-mastery.

Who on power sets his aim,
First must his own spirit tame;
He must shun his neck to thrust
'Neath th' unholy yoke of lust.
For, though India's far-off land
Bow before his wide command,
Utmost Thule homage pay—
If he cannot drive away
Haunting care and black distress,
In his power, he's powerless.

VI.

'Again, how misleading, how base, a thing ofttimes is glory! Well does the tragic poet exclaim:

'"Oh, fond Repute, how many a time and oft
Hast them raised high in pride the base-born churl!"

For many have won a great name through the mistaken beliefs of the multitude—and what can be imagined more shameful than that? Nay, they who are praised falsely must needs themselves blush at their own praises! And even when praise is won by merit, still, how does it add to the good conscience of the wise man who measures his good not by popular repute, but by the truth of inner conviction? And if at all it does seem a fair thing to get this same renown spread abroad, it follows that any failure so to spread it is held foul. But if, as I set forth but now, there must needs be many tribes and peoples whom the fame of any single man cannot reach, it follows that he whom thou esteemest glorious seems all inglorious in a neighbouring quarter of the globe. As to popular favour, I do not think it even worthy of mention in this place, since it never cometh of judgment, and never lasteth steadily.

'Then, again, who does not see how empty, how foolish, is the fame of noble birth? Why, if the nobility is based on renown, the renown is another's! For, truly, nobility seems to be a sort of reputation coming from the merits of ancestors. But if it is the praise which brings renown, of necessity it is they who are praised that are famous. Wherefore, the fame of another clothes thee not with splendour if thou hast none of thine own. So, if there is any excellence in nobility of birth, methinks it is this alone—that it would seem to impose upon the nobly born the obligation not to degenerate from the virtue of their ancestors.'

Song VI — True Nobility.

All men are of one kindred stock, though scattered far and wide;
For one is Father of us all—one doth for all provide.
He gave the sun his golden beams, the moon her silver horn;
He set mankind upon the earth, as stars the heavens adorn.
He shut a soul—a heaven-born soul—within the body's frame;

Metrum V

Qui se uolet esse potentem,
Animos domet ille feroces
Nec uicta libidine colla
Foedis summittat habenis;
Etenim licet Indica longe
Tellus tua iura tremescat
Et seruiat ultima thyle,
Tamen atras pellere curas
Miserasque fugare querelas
Non posse potentia non est.

Prosa VI

Gloria uero quam fallax saepe, quam turpis est! Vnde non iniuria tragicus exclamat:

Ὦ δόξα, δόξα, μυρίοισι δὴ βρότων,
Οὐδέν γεγῶσι βίοτον ὤγκωσασ μέγαν.[5]

Plures enim magnum saepe nomen falsis uulgi opinionibus abstulerunt. Quo quid turpius. Excogitari potest? Nam qui falso praedicantur suis ipsi necesse est laudibus erubescant. Quae si etiam meritis conquisitae sint, quid tamen sapientis adiecerint conscientiae, qui bonum suum non populari rumore sed conscientiae ueritate metitur? Quodsi hoc ipsum propagasse nomen pulchrum uidetur, consequens est ut foedum non extendisse iudicetur. Sed cum, uti paulo ante disserui, plures gentes esse necesse sit ad quas unius fama hominis nequeat peruenire, fit ut quem tu aestimas esse gloriosum proxima parte terrarum uideatur inglorius. Inter haec uero popularem gratiam ne commemoratione quidem dignam puto, quae nec iudicio prouenit nec umquam firma perdurat.

Iam uero quam sit inane, quam futtile nobilitatis nomen, quis non uideat? Quae si ad claritudinem refertur, aliena est; uidetur namque esse nobilitas quaedam de meritis ueniens laus parentum. Quodsi claritudinem praedicatio facit, illi sint clari necesse est qui praedicantur; quare splendidum te, si tuam non habes, aliena claritudo non efficit. Quodsi quid est in nobilitate bonum, id esse arbitror solum, ut imposita nobilibus necessitudo uideatur ne a maiorum uirtute degeneret.

Metrum VI

Omne hominum genus in terris simili surgit ab ortu;
Vnus enim rerum pater est, unus cuncta ministrat.
Ille dedit Phoebo radios, dedit et cornua lunae,
Ille homines etiam terris dedit ut sidera caelo;
Hic clausit membris animos celsa sede petitos;

---

5   O Gloria, Gloria, multis verum mortalium,
inanem hominibus vitam sustulisti magnam.

The noble origin he gave each mortal wight may claim.
Why boast ye, then, so loud of race and high ancestral line?
If ye behold your being's source, and God's supreme design,
None is degenerate, none base, unless by taint of sin
And cherished vice he foully stain his heavenly origin.

VII.

'Then, what shall I say of the pleasures of the body? The lust thereof is full of uneasiness; the sating, of repentance. What sicknesses, what intolerable pains, are they wont to
bring on the bodies of those who enjoy them—the fruits of iniquity, as it were! Now, what
sweetness the stimulus of pleasure may have I do not know. But that the issues of pleasure are
painful everyone may understand who chooses to recall the memory of his own fleshly lusts.
Nay, if these can make happiness, there is no reason why the beasts also should not be happy,
since all their efforts are eagerly set upon satisfying the bodily wants. I know, indeed, that
the sweetness of wife and children should be right comely, yet only too true to nature is
what was said of one—that he found in his sons his tormentors. And how galling such a con-
tingency would be, I must needs put thee in mind, since thou hast never in any wise suffered
such experiences, nor art thou now under any uneasiness. In such a case, I agree with my servant Euripides, who said that a man without children was fortunate in his misfortune.'[6]

Song VII – Pleasure's Sting.

This is the way of Pleasure:
She stings them that despoil her;
And, like the wingéd toiler
Who's lost her honeyed treasure,
She flies, but leaves her smart
Deep-rankling in the heart.

VIII.

'It is beyond doubt, then, that these paths do not lead to happiness; they cannot guide
anyone to the promised goal. Now, I will very briefly show what serious evils are involved
in following them. Just consider. Is it thy endeavour to heap up money? Why, thou must
wrest it from its present possessor! Art thou minded to put on the splendour of official dignity? Thou must beg from those who have the giving of it; thou who covetest to outvie others in honour must lower thyself to the humble posture of petition. Dost thou long for
power? Thou must face perils, for thou wilt be at the mercy of thy subjects' plots. Is glory
thy aim? Thou art lured on through all manner of hardships, and there is an end to thy peace
of mind. Art fain to lead a life of pleasure? Yet who does not scorn and contemn one who is
the slave of the weakest and vilest of things—the body? Again, on how slight and perishable

---

6   Paley translates the lines in Euripides' 'Andromache': "They [the childless] are indeed spared from much pain
     and sorrow, but their supposed happiness is after all but wretchedness." Euripides' meaning is therefore
     really just the reverse of that which Boethius makes it. See Euripides, 'Andromache', ll. 418–420.

Mortales igitur cunctos edit nobile germen.
Quid genus et proauos strepitis? Si primordia uestra
Auctoremque deum spectes, nullus degener exstat,
Ni uitiis peiora fouens proprium deserat ortum.

Prosa VII

Quid autem de corporis uoluptatibus loquar, quarum appetentia quidem plena est anxi-
etatis, satietas uero paenitentiae? Quantos illae morbos, quam intolerabiles dolores quasi
quendam fructum nequitiae fruentium solent referre corporibus! Quarum motus quid habeat
iucunditatis ignoro; tristes uero esse uoluptatum exitus, quisquis reminisci libidinum suarum
uolet intelleget. Quae si beatos explicare possunt, nihil causae est quin pecudes quoque
beatae esse dicantur, quarum omnis ad explendam corporalem lacunam festinat intentio.
Honestissima quidem coniugis foret liberorumque iucunditas; sed nimis e natura dictum est
nescio quem filios inuenisse tortores. Quorum quam sit mordax quaecumque condicio neque
alias expertum te neque nunc anxium necesse est ammonere. In quo euripidis mei sententiam
probo, qui carentem liberis infortunio dixit esse felicem.

Metrum VII

Habet hoc uoluptas omnis,
Stimulis agit fruentes
Apiumque par uolantum,
Vbi grata mella fudit,
Fugit et nimis tenaci
Ferit icta corda morsu.

Prosa VIII

Nihil igitur dubium est quin hae ad beatitudinem uiae deuia quaedam sint nec per-
ducere quemquam eo ualeant ad quod se perducturas esse promittunt. Quantis uero implicit-
ae malis sint breuissime monstrabo. Quid enim? Pecuniamne congregare conaberis? Sed eri-
pies habenti. Dignitatibus fulgere uelis? Danti supplicabis et qui praeire ceteros honore cu-
pis poscendi humilitate uilesces. Potentiamne desideras? Subiectorum insidiis obnoxius
periculis subiacebis. Gloriam petas? Sed per aspera quaeque distractus securus esse desistis.
Voluptariam uitam degas? Sed quis non spernat atque abiciat uilissimae fragilissimaeque rei,

a possession do they rely who set before themselves bodily excellences! Can ye ever surpass the elephant in bulk or the bull in strength? Can ye excel the tiger in swiftness? Look upon the infinitude, the solidity, the swift motion, of the heavens, and for once cease to admire things mean and worthless. And yet the heavens are not so much to be admired on this ac-count as for the reason which guides them. Then, how transient is the lustre of beauty! how soon gone!—more fleeting than the fading bloom of spring flowers. And yet if, as Aristotle says, men should see with the eyes of Lynceus, so that their sight might pierce through ob-structions, would not that body of Alcibiades, so gloriously fair in outward seeming, appear altogether loathsome when all its inward parts lay open to the view? Therefore, it is not thy own nature that makes thee seem beautiful, but the weakness of the eyes that see thee. Yet prize as unduly as ye will that body's excellences; so long as ye know that this that ye ad-mire, whatever its worth, can be dissolved away by the feeble flame of a three days' fever. From all which considerations we may conclude as a whole, that these things which cannot make good the advantages they promise, which are never made perfect by the assemblage of all good things—these neither lead as by-ways to happiness, nor themselves make men com-pletely happy.'

Song VIII – Human Folly.

Alas! how wide astray
Doth Ignorance these wretched mortals lead
From Truth's own way!
For not on leafy stems
Do ye within the green wood look for gold,
Nor strip the vine for gems;
Your nets ye do not spread
Upon the hill-tops, that the groaning board
With fish be furnishèd;
If ye are fain to chase
The bounding goat, ye sweep not in vain search
The ocean's ruffled face.
The sea's far depths they know,
Each hidden nook, wherein the waves o'erwash
The pearl as white as snow;
Where lurks the Tyrian shell,
Where fish and prickly urchins do abound,
All this they know full well.
But not to know or care
Where hidden lies the good all hearts desire—
This blindness they can bear;
With gaze on earth low-bent,
They seek for that which reacheth far beyond
The starry firmament.

corporis, seruum? Iam uero qui bona prae se corporis ferunt, quam exigua, quam fragili pos-sessione nituntur! Num enim elephantos mole, tauros robore superare poteritis, num tigres uelocitate praeibitis? Respicite caeli spatium, firmitudinem, celeritatem et aliquando desin-ite uilia mirari. Quod quidem caelum non his potius est quam sua qua regitur ratione mir-andum. Formae uero nitor ut rapidus est, ut uelox et uernalium florum mutabilitate fugacior! Quodsi, ut Aristoteles ait, Lyncei oculis homines uterentur, ut eorum uisus obstantia penet-raret, nonne introspectis uisceribus illud Alcibiadis superficie pulcherrimum corpus turp-issimum uideretur? Igitur te pulchrum uideri non tua natura, sed oculorum spectantium red-dit infirmitas. Sed aestimate quam uultis nimio corporis bona, dum sciatis hoc quodcumque miramini triduanae febris igniculo posse dissolui. Ex quibus omnibus illud redigere in summam licet quod haec quae nec praestare quae pollicentur bona possunt nec omnium bonorum congregatione perfecta sunt, ea nec ad beatitudinem quasi quidam calles ferunt nec beatos ipsa perficiunt.

Metrum VIII

Eheu, quae miseros tramite deuios
Abducit ignorantia!
Non aurum in uiridi quaeritis arbore
Nec uite gemmas carpitis,
Non altis laqueos montibus abditis
Vt pisce ditetis dapes
Nec uobis capreas si libeat sequi
Tyrrhena captatis uada;
Ipsos quin etiam fluctibus abditos
Norunt recessus aequoris,
Quae gemmis niueis unda feracior
Vel quae rubentis purpurae
Nec non quae tenero pisce uel asperis
Praestent echinis litora.
Sed quonam lateat quod cupiunt bonum
Nescire caeci sustinent
Et quod stelliferum transabiit polum
Tellure demersi petunt.

What curse shall I call down
On hearts so dull?
May they the race still run
For wealth and high renown!
And when with much ado
The false good they have grasped—ah, then too late!—
May they discern the true!

IX.

'This much may well suffice to set forth the form of false happiness; if this is now clear to thine eyes, the next step is to show what true happiness is.'

'Indeed,' said I, 'I see clearly enough that neither is independence to be found in wealth, nor power in sovereignty, nor reverence in dignities, nor fame in glory, nor true joy in pleasures.'

'Hast thou discerned also the causes why this is so?'

'I seem to have some inkling, but I should like to learn more at large from thee.'

'Why, truly the reason is hard at hand. That which is simple and indivisible by nature human error separates, and transforms from the true and perfect to the false and imperfect. Dost thou imagine that which lacketh nothing can want power?'

'Certainly not.'

'Right; for if there is any feebleness of strength in anything, in this there must necessarily be need of external protection.'

'That is so.'

'Accordingly, the nature of independence and power is one and the same.'

'It seems so.'

'Well, but dost think that anything of such a nature as this can be looked upon with contempt, or is it rather of all things most worthy of veneration?'

'Nay; there can be no doubt as to that.'

'Let us, then, add reverence to independence and power, and conclude these three to be one.'

'We must if we will acknowledge the truth.'

'Thinkest thou, then, this combination of qualities to be obscure and without distinction, or rather famous in all renown? Just consider: can that want renown which has been agreed to be lacking in nothing, to be supreme in power, and right worthy of honour, for the reason that it cannot bestow this upon itself, and so comes to appear somewhat poor in esteem?'

'I cannot but acknowledge that, being what it is, this union of qualities is also right famous.'

'It follows, then, that we must admit that renown is not different from the other three.'

'It does,' said I.

Quid dignum stolidis mentibus imprecer?

Opes honores ambiant

Et cum falsa graui mole parauerint

Tum uera cognoscant bona.

Prosa IX

Hactenus mendacis formam felicitatis ostendisse suffecerit; quam si perspicaciter intueris, ordo est deinceps quae sit uera monstrare.

Atqui uideo, inquam, nec opibus sufficientiam nec regnis potentiam nec reuerentiam dignitatibus nec celebritatem gloria nec laetitiam uoluptatibus posse contingere.

An etiam causas cur id ita sit deprehendisti?

Tenui quidem ueluti rimula mihi uideor intueri, sed ex te apertius cognoscere malim.

Atqui promptissima ratio est. Quod enim simplex est indiuisumque natura, id error humanus separat et a uero atque perfecto ad falsum imperfectumque traducit. An tu arbitraris quod nihilo indigeat egere potentia?

Minime, inquam.

Recte tu quidem; nam si quid est quod in ulla re imbecillioris ualentiae sit, in hac praesidio necesse est egeat alieno.

Ita est, inquam.

Igitur sufficientiae potentiaeque una est eademque natura.

Sic uidetur.

Quod uero huius modi sit spernendumne esse censes an contra rerum omnium ueneratione dignissimum?

At hoc, inquam, ne dubitari quidem potest.

Addamus igitur sufficientiae potentiaeque reuerentiam, ut haec tria unum esse iudicemus.

Addamus, si quidem uera uolumus confiteri.

Quid uero, inquit, obscurum ne hoc atque ignobile censes esse an omni celebritate clarissimum? Considera uero, ne quod nihilo indigere, quod potentissimum, quod honore dignissimum esse concessum est, egere claritudine, quam sibi praestare non possit, atque ob id aliqua ex parte uideatur abiectius.

Non possum, inquam, quin hoc uti est ita etiam celeberrimum esse confitear.

Consequens igitur est ut claritudinem superioribus tribus nihil differre fateamur.

Consequitur, inquam.

'That, then, which needs nothing outside itself, which can accomplish all things in its own strength, which enjoys fame and compels reverence, must not this evidently be also fully crowned with joy?'

'In sooth, I cannot conceive,' said I, 'how any sadness can find entrance into such a state; wherefore I must needs acknowledge it full of joy—at least, if our former conclusions are to hold.'

'Then, for the same reasons, this also is necessary—that independence, power, renown, reverence, and sweetness of delight, are different only in name, but in substance differ no wise one from the other.'

'It is,' said I.

'This, then, which is one, and simple by nature, human perversity separates, and, in try-ing to win a part of that which has no parts, fails to attain not only that portion (since there are no portions), but also the whole, to which it does not dream of aspiring.'

'How so?' said I.

'He who, to escape want, seeks riches, gives himself no concern about power; he prefers a mean and low estate, and also denies himself many pleasures dear to nature to avoid losing the money which he has gained. But at this rate he does not even attain to independence—a weakling void of strength, vexed by distresses, mean and despised, and buried in obscurity. He, again, who thirsts alone for power squanders his wealth, despises pleasure, and thinks fame and rank alike worthless without power. But thou seest in how many ways his state also is defective. Sometimes it happens that he lacks necessaries, that he is gnawed by anxiet-ies, and, since he cannot rid himself of these inconveniences, even ceases to have that power which was his whole end and aim. In like manner may we cast up the reckoning in case of rank, of glory, or of pleasure. For since each one of these severally is identical with the rest, whosoever seeks any one of them without the others does not even lay hold of that one which he makes his aim.'

'Well,' said I, 'what then?'

'Suppose anyone desire to obtain them together, he does indeed wish for happiness as a whole; but will he find it in these things which, as we have proved, are unable to bestow what they promise?'

'Nay; by no means,' said I.

'Then, happiness must certainly not be sought in these things which severally are be-lieved to afford some one of the blessings most to be desired.'

'They must not, I admit. No conclusion could be more true.'

'So, then, the form and the causes of false happiness are set before thine eyes. Now turn thy gaze to the other side; there thou wilt straightway see the true happiness I promised.'

'Yea, indeed, 'tis plain to the blind.' said I. 'Thou didst point it out even now in seeking to unfold the causes of the false. For, unless I am mistaken, that is true and perfect happiness which crowns one with the union of independence, power, reverence, renown, and joy. And to prove to thee with how deep an insight I have listened—since all these are the same—that which can truly bestow one of them I know to be without doubt full and complete happiness.'

Quod igitur nullius egeat alieni, quod suis cuncta uiribus possit, quod sit clarum atque reuerendum, nonne hoc etiam constat esse laetissimum?

Sed unde huic, inquam, tali maeror ullus obrepat ne cogitare quidem possum; quare plenum esse laetitiae, si quidem superiora manebunt, necesse est confiteri.

Atqui illud quoque per eadem necessarium est, sufficientiae, potentiae, claritudinis, iucunditatis nomina quidem esse diuersa, nullo modo uero discrepare substantiam.

Necesse est, inquam.

Hoc igitur quod est unum simplexque natura prauitas humana dispertit et dum rei quae partibus caret partem conatur adipisci, nec portionem, quae nulla est, nec ipsam, quam minime affectat, assequitur.

Quonam, inquam, modo?

Qui diuitias, inquit, petit penuriae fuga, de potentia nihil laborat, uilis obscurusque esse mauult, multas etiam sibi naturales quoque subtrahit uoluptates, ne pecuniam quam parauit amittat. Sed hoc modo ne sufficientia quidem contingit ei quem ualentia deserit, quem molestia pungit, quem uilitas abicit, quem recondit obscuritas. Qui uero solum posse desiderat profligat opes, despicit uoluptates honoremque potentia carentem, gloriam quoque nihili pendit. Sed hunc quoque quam multa deficiant uides; fit enim ut aliquando necessariis egeat, ut anxietatibus mordeatur, cumque haec depellere nequeat etiam id quod maxime petebat, potens esse, desistat. Similiter ratiocinari de honoribus, gloria, uoluptatibus licet; nam cum unumquodque horum idem quod cetera sit, quisquis horum aliquid sine ceteris petit ne illud quidem quod desiderat apprehendit.

Quid igitur, inquam, si qui cuncta simul cupiat adipisci?

Summam quidem ille beatitudinis uelit; sed num in his eam repperiet quae demonstrauimus id quod pollicentur non posse conferre?

Minime, inquam.

In his igitur quae singula quaedam expetendorum praestare creduntur beatitudo nullo modo uestiganda est.

Fateor, inquam, et hoc nihil dici uerius potest.

Habes igitur, inquit, et formam falsae felicitatis et causas. Deflecte nunc in aduersum mentis intuitum; ibi enim ueram quam promisimus statim uidebis.

Atqui haec, inquam, uel caeco perspicua est eamque tu paulo ante monstrasti dum falsae causas aperire conaris. Nam nisi fallor, ea uera est et perfecta felicitas quae sufficientem, potentem, reuerendum, celebrem laetumque perficiat. Atque ut me interius animaduertisse cognoscas, quae unum horum, quoniam idem cuncta sunt, ueraciter praestare potest, hanc esse plenam beatitudinem sine ambiguitate cognosco.

'Happy art thou, my scholar, in this thy conviction; only one thing shouldst thou add.'

'What is that?' said I.

'Is there aught, thinkest thou, amid these mortal and perishable things which can produce a state such as this?'

'Nay, surely not; and this thou hast so amply demonstrated that no word more is needed.'

'Well, then, these things seem to give to mortals shadows of the true good, or some kind of imperfect good; but the true and perfect good they cannot bestow.'

'Even so,' said I.

'Since, then, thou hast learnt what that true happiness is, and what men falsely call happiness, it now remains that thou shouldst learn from what source to seek this.'

'Yes; to this I have long been eagerly looking forward.'

'Well, since, as Plato maintains in the "Timæus," we ought even in the most trivial matters to implore the Divine protection, what thinkest thou should we now do in order to deserve to find the seat of that highest good?'

'We must invoke the Father of all things,' said I; 'for without this no enterprise sets out from a right beginning.'

'Thou sayest well,' said she; and forthwith lifted up her voice and sang:

Song IX — Invocation[7]

Maker of earth and sky, from age to age
Who rul'st the world by reason; at whose word
Time issues from Eternity's abyss:
To all that moves the source of movement, fixed
Thyself and moveless. Thee no cause impelled
Extrinsic this proportioned frame to shape
From shapeless matter; but, deep-set within
Thy inmost being, the form of perfect good,
From envy free; and Thou didst mould the whole
To that supernal pattern. Beauteous
The world in Thee thus imaged, being Thyself
Most beautiful. So Thou the work didst fashion
In that fair likeness, bidding it put on
Perfection through the exquisite perfectness
Of every part's contrivance. Thou dost bind
The elements in balanced harmony,
So that the hot and cold, the moist and dry,
Contend not; nor the pure fire leaping up
Escape, or weight of waters whelm the earth.

---

7   The substance of this poem is taken from Plato's 'Timæus,' 29-42. See Jowett, vol. iii., pp. 448-462 (3rd ed.).

O te, alumne, hac opinione felicem, si quidem hoc, inquit, adieceris!

Quidnam? Inquam.

Essene aliquid in his mortalibus caducisque rebus putas quod huius modi statum possit afferre?

Minime, inquam, puto idque a te, nihil ut amplius desideretur, ostensum est.

Haec igitur uel imagines ueri boni uel imperfecta quaedam bona dare mortalibus uiden-tur, uerum autem atque perfectum bonum conferre non possunt.

Assentior, inquam.

Quoniam igitur agnouisti quae uera illa sit, quae autem beatitudinem mentiantur, nunc superest ut unde ueram hanc petere possis agnoscas.

Id quidem, inquam, iam dudum uehementer exspecto.

Sed cum, ut in Timaeo Platoni, inquit, nostro placet, in minimis quoque rebus diuinum praesidium debeat implorari, quid nunc faciendum censes ut illius summi boni sedem rep-perire mereamur?

Inuocandum, inquam, rerum omnium patrem, quo praetermisso nullum rite fundatur ex-ordium.

Recte, inquit; ac simul ita modulata est:

Metrum IX

O qui perpetua mundum ratione gubernas,
Terrarum caelique sator, qui tempus ab aeuo
Ire iubes stabilisque manens das cuncta moueri,
Quem non externae pepulerunt fingere causae
Materiae fluitantis opus uerum insita summi
Forma boni liuore carens, tu cuncta superno
Ducis ab exemplo, pulchrum pulcherrimus ipse
Mundum mente gerens similique in imagine formans
Perfectasque iubens perfectum absoluere partes.
Tu numeris elementa ligas, ut frigora flammis,
Arida conueniant liquidis, ne purior ignis
Euolet aut mersas deducant pondera terras.

Thou joinest and diffusest through the whole,
Linking accordantly its several parts,
A soul of threefold nature, moving all.
This, cleft in twain, and in two circles gathered,
Speeds in a path that on itself returns,
Encompassing mind's limits, and conforms
The heavens to her true semblance. Lesser souls
And lesser lives by a like ordinance
Thou sendest forth, each to its starry car
Affixing, and dost strew them far and wide
O'er earth and heaven. These by a law benign
Thou biddest turn again, and render back
To thee their fires. Oh, grant, almighty Father,
Grant us on reason's wing to soar aloft
To heaven's exalted height; grant us to see
The fount of good; grant us, the true light found,
To fix our steadfast eyes in vision clear
On Thee. Disperse the heavy mists of earth,
And shine in Thine own splendour. For Thou art
The true serenity and perfect rest
Of every pious soul—to see Thy face,
The end and the beginning—One the guide,
The traveller, the pathway, and the goal.

X.

'Since now thou hast seen what is the form of the imperfect good, and what the form of the perfect also, methinks I should next show in what manner this perfection of felicity is built up. And here I conceive it proper to inquire, first, whether any excellence, such as thou hast lately defined, can exist in the nature of things, lest we be deceived by an empty fiction of thought to which no true reality answers. But it cannot be denied that such does exist, and is, as it were, the source of all things good. For everything which is called imperfect is spoken of as imperfect by reason of the privation of some perfection; so it comes to pass that, whenever imperfection is found in any particular, there must necessarily be a perfection in respect of that particular also. For were there no such perfection, it is utterly inconceivable how that so-called imperfection should come into existence. Nature does not make a beginning with things mutilated and imperfect; she starts with what is whole and perfect, and falls away later to these feeble and inferior productions. So if there is, as we showed before, a happiness of a frail and imperfect kind, it cannot be doubted but there is also a happiness substantial and perfect.'

'Most true is thy conclusion, and most sure,' said I.

'Next to consider where the dwelling-place of this happiness may be. The common belief of all mankind agrees that God, the supreme of all things, is good. For since nothing can be imagined better than God, how can we doubt Him to be good than whom there is

Tu triplicis mediam naturae cuncta mouentem
Conectens animam per consona membra resoluis;
Quae cum secta duos motum glomerauit in orbes,
In semet reditura meat mentemque profundam
Circuit et simili conuertit imagine caelum.
Tu causis animas paribus uitasque minores
Prouehis et leuibus sublimes curribus aptans
In caelum terramque seris, quas lege benigna
Ad te conuersas reduci facis igne reuerti.
Da, pater, augustam menti conscendere sedem,
Da fontem lustrare boni, da luce reperta
In te conspicuos animi defigere uisus.
Dissice terrenae nebulas et pondera molis
Atque tuo splendore mica; tu namque serenum,
Tu requies tranquilla piis, te cernere finis,
Principium, uector, dux, semita, terminus idem.

Prosa X

Quoniam igitur quae sit imperfecti, quae etiam perfecti boni forma uidisti, nunc demonstrandum reor quonam haec felicitatis perfectio constituta sit. In quo illud primum arbitror inquirendum an aliquod huius modi bonum quale paulo ante definisti in rerum natura possit exsistere, ne nos praeter rei subiectae ueritatem cassa cogitationis imago decipiat. Sed quin exsistat sitque hoc ueluti quidam omnium fons bonorum, negari nequit; omne enim quod imperfectum esse dicitur id imminutione perfecti imperfectum esse perhibetur. Quo fit ut, si in quolibet genere imperfectum quid esse uideatur, in eo perfectum quoque aliquid esse necesse sit; etenim perfectione sublata unde illud quod imperfectum perhibetur exstiterit ne fingi quidem potest. Neque enim ab deminutis inconsummatisque natura rerum cepit exordium, sed ab integris absolutisque procedens in haec extrema atque effeta dilabitur. Quodsi, uti paulo ante monstrauimus, est quaedam boni fragilis imperfecta felicitas, esse aliquam solidam perfectamque non potest dubitari.

Firmissime, inquam, uerissimeque conclusum est.

Quo uero, inquit, habitet, ita considera. Deum, rerum omnium principem, bonum esse communis humanorum conceptio probat animorum; nam cum nihil deo melius excogitari

nothing better? Now, reason shows God to be good in such wise as to prove that in Him is perfect good. For were it not so, He would not be supreme of all things; for there would be something else more excellent, possessed of perfect good, which would seem to have the advantage in priority and dignity, since it has clearly appeared that all perfect things are prior to those less complete. Wherefore, lest we fall into an infinite regression, we must acknowledge the supreme God to be full of supreme and perfect good. But we have determined that true happiness is the perfect good; therefore true happiness must dwell in the supreme Deity.'

'I accept thy reasonings,' said I; 'they cannot in any wise be disputed.'

'But, come, see how strictly and incontrovertibly thou mayst prove this our assertion that the supreme Godhead hath fullest possession of the highest good.'

'In what way, pray?' said I.

'Do not rashly suppose that He who is the Father of all things hath received that highest good of which He is said to be possessed either from some external source, or hath it as a natural endowment in such sort that thou mightest consider the essence of the happiness possessed, and of the God who possesses it, distinct and different. For if thou deemest it received from without, thou mayst esteem that which gives more excellent than that which has received. But Him we most worthily acknowledge to be the most supremely excellent of all things. If, however, it is in Him by nature, yet is logically distinct, the thought is inconceivable, since we are speaking of God, who is supreme of all things. Who was there to join these distinct essences? Finally, when one thing is different from another, the things so conceived as distinct cannot be identical. Therefore that which of its own nature is distinct from the highest good is not itself the highest good—an impious thought of Him than whom, 'tis plain, nothing can be more excellent. For universally nothing can be better in nature than the source from which it has come; therefore on most true grounds of reason would I conclude that which is the source of all things to be in its own essence the highest good.'

'And most justly,' said I.

'But the highest good has been admitted to be happiness.'

'Yes.'

'Then,' said she, 'it is necessary to acknowledge that God is very happiness.'

'Yes,' said I; 'I cannot gainsay my former admissions, and I see clearly that this is a necessary inference therefrom.'

'Reflect, also,' said she, 'whether the same conclusion is not further confirmed by considering that there cannot be two supreme goods distinct one from the other. For the goods which are different clearly cannot be severally each what the other is: wherefore neither of the two can be perfect, since to either the other is wanting; but since it is not perfect, it cannot manifestly be the supreme good. By no means, then, can goods which are supreme be different one from the other. But we have concluded that both happiness and God are the supreme good; wherefore that which is highest Divinity must also itself necessarily be supreme happiness.'

'No conclusion,' said I, 'could be truer to fact, nor more soundly reasoned out, nor more worthy of God.'

queat, id quo melius nihil est bonum esse quis dubitet? Ita uero bonum esse deum ratio demonstrat ut perfectum quoque in eo bonum esse conuincat. Nam ni tale sit, rerum omnium princeps esse non poterit; erit enim eo praestantius aliquid perfectum possidens bonum, quod hoc prius atque antiquius esse uideatur; omnia namque perfecta minus integris priora esse claruerunt. Quare ne in infinitum ratio prodeat, confitendum est summum deum summi perfectique boni esse plenissimum; sed perfectum bonum ueram esse beatitudinem constitu⁻ imus: ueram igitur beatitudinem in summo deo sitam esse necesse est.

Accipio, inquam, nec est quod contra dici ullo modo queat.

Sed quaeso, inquit, te, uide quam id sancte atque inuiolabiliter probes quod boni summi summum deum diximus esse plenissimum.

Quonam, inquam, modo?

Ne hunc rerum omnium patrem illud summum bonum quo plenus esse perhibetur uel extrinsecus accepisse uel ita naturaliter habere praesumas quasi habentis dei habitaeque beatitudinis diuersam cogites esse substantiam. Nam si extrinsecus acceptum putes, praest⁻ antius id quod dederit ab eo quod acceperit existimare possis; sed hunc esse rerum omnium praecellentissimum dignissime confitemur. Quod si natura quidem inest sed est ratione di⁻ uersum, cum de rerum principe loquamur deo, fingat qui potest quis haec diuersa coniunxer⁻ it. Postremo, quod a qualibet re diuersum est id non est illud a quo intellegitur esse diuer⁻ sum; quare quod a summo bono diuersum est sui natura, id summum bonum non est; quod nefas est de eo cogitare, quo nihil constat esse praestantius. Omnino enim nullius rei natura suo principio melior poterit exsistere; quare quod omnium principium sit id etiam sui sub⁻ stantia summum esse bonum uerissima ratione concluserim.

Rectissime, inquam.

Sed summum bonum beatitudinem esse concessum est.

Ita est, inquam.

Igitur, inquit, deum esse ipsam beatitudinem necesse est confiteri.

Nec propositis, inquam, prioribus refragari queo et illis hoc inlatum consequens esse perspicio.

Respice, inquit, an hinc quoque idem firmius approbetur, quod duo summa bona quae a se diuersa sint esse non possunt. Etenim quae discrepant bona non esse alterum quod sit al⁻ terum liquet; quare neutrum poterit esse perfectum, cum alterutri alterum deest. Sed quod perfectum non sit id summum non esse manifestum est; nullo modo igitur quae summa sunt bona ea possunt esse diuersa. Atqui et beatitudinem et deum summum bonum esse col⁻ legimus: quare ipsam necesse est summam esse beatitudinem quae sit summa diuinitas.

Nihil, inquam, nec reapse uerius nec ratiocinatione firmius nec deo dignius concludi potest.

'Then, further,' said she, 'just as geometricians are wont to draw inferences from their demonstrations to which they give the name "deductions," so will I add here a sort of corollary. For since men become happy by the acquisition of happiness, while happiness is very Godship, it is manifest that they become happy by the acquisition of Godship. But as by the acquisition of justice men become just, and wise by the acquisition of wisdom, so by parity of reasoning by acquiring Godship they must of necessity become gods. So every man who is happy is a god; and though in nature God is One only, yet there is nothing to hinder that very many should be gods by participation in that nature.'

'A fair conclusion, and a precious,' said I, 'deduction or corollary, by whichever name thou wilt call it.'

'And yet,' said she, 'not one whit fairer than this which reason persuades us to add.'

'Why, what?' said I.

'Why, seeing happiness has many particulars included under it, should all these be regarded as forming one body of happiness, as it were, made up of various parts, or is there some one of them which forms the full essence of happiness, while all the rest are relative to this?'

'I would thou wouldst unfold the whole matter to me at large.'

'We judge happiness to be good, do we not?'

'Yea, the supreme good.'

'And this superlative applies to all; for this same happiness is adjudged to be the completest independence, the highest power, reverence, renown, and pleasure.'

'What then?'

'Are all these goods—independence, power, and the rest—to be deemed members of happiness, as it were, or are they all relative to good as to their summit and crown?'

'I understand the problem, but I desire to hear how thou wouldst solve it.'

'Well, then, listen to the determination of the matter. Were all these members composing happiness, they would differ severally one from the other. For this is the nature of parts—that by their difference they compose one body. All these, however, have been proved to be the same; therefore they cannot possibly be members, otherwise happiness will seem to be built up out of one member, which cannot be.'

'There can be no doubt as to that,' said I; 'but I am impatient to hear what remains.'

'Why, it is manifest that all the others are relative to the good. For the very reason why independence is sought is that it is judged good, and so power also, because it is believed to be good. The same, too, may be supposed of reverence, of renown, and of pleasant delight. Good, then, is the sum and source of all desirable things. That which has not in itself any good, either in reality or in semblance, can in no wise be desired. Contrariwise, even things which by nature are not good are desired as if they were truly good, if they seem to be so. Whereby it comes to pass that goodness is rightly believed to be the sum and hinge and cause of all things desirable. Now, that for the sake of which anything is desired itself seems to be most wished for. For instance, if anyone wishes to ride for the sake of health, he does not so much wish for the exercise of riding as the benefit of his health. Since, then, all things are sought for the sake of the good, it is not these so much as good itself that is sought by all.

Super haec, inquit, igitur ueluti geometrae solent demonstratis propositis aliquid inferre, quae porismata ipsi uocant, ita ego quoque tibi ueluti corollarium dabo. Nam quoniam beatitudinis adeptione fiunt homines beati, beatitudo uero est ipsa diuinitas, diuinitatis adeptione beatos fieri manifestum est. Sed uti iustitiae adeptione iusti, sapientiae sapientes fiunt, ita diuinitatem adeptos deos fieri simili ratione necesse est. Omnis igitur beatus deus. Sed natura quidem unus; participatione uero nihil prohibet esse quam plurimos.

Et pulchrum, inquam, hoc atque pretiosum siue porisma siue corollarium uocari mauis.

Atqui hoc quoque pulchrius nihil est quod his adnectendum esse ratio persuadet.

Quid? Inquam.

Cum multa, inquit, beatitudo continere uideatur, utrumne haec omnia unum ueluti corpus beatitudinis quadam partium uarietate coniungant an sit eorum aliquid quod beatitudinis substantiam compleat, ad hoc uero cetera referantur?

Vellem, inquam, id ipsarum rerum commemoratione patefaceres.

Nonne, inquit, beatitudinem bonum esse censemus?

Ac summum quidem, inquam.

Addas, inquit, hoc omnibus licet. Nam eadem sufficientia summa est, eadem summa potentia, reuerentia quoque, claritas ac uoluptas beatitudo esse iudicatur. Quid igitur, haecine omnia, bonum, sufficientia, potentia cetera que, ueluti quaedam beatitudinis membra sunt an ad bonum ueluti ad uerticem cuncta referuntur?

Intellego, inquam, quid inuestigandum proponas, sed quid constituas audire desidero.

Cuius discretionem rei sic accipe. Si haec omnia beatitudinis membra forent, a se quoque inuicem discreparent; haec est enim partium natura ut unum corpus diuersa componant. Atqui haec omnia idem esse monstrata sunt. Minime igitur membra sunt; alioquin ex uno membro beatitudo uidebitur esse coniuncta, quod fieri nequit.

Id quidem, inquam, dubium non est, sed id quod restat exspecto.

Ad bonum uero cetera referri palam est. Idcirco enim sufficientia petitur, quoniam bonum esse iudicatur; idcirco potentia, quoniam id quoque esse creditur bonum; idem de reuerentia, claritudine, iucunditate coniectare licet. Omnium igitur expetendorum summa atque causa bonum est; quod enim neque re neque similitudine ullum in se retinet bonum id expeti nullo modo potest. Contraque etiam quae natura bona non sunt tamen si esse uideantur quasi uere bona sint appetuntur. Quo fit uti summa, cardo atque causa expetendorum omnium bonitas esse iure credatur. Cuius uero causa quid expetitur id maxime uidetur optari, ueluti si salutis causa quispiam uelit equitare, non tam equitandi motum desiderat quam salutis effectum. Cum igitur omnia boni gratia petantur, non illa potius quam bonum ipsum

But that on account of which all other things are wished for was, we agreed, happiness; wherefore thus also it appears that it is happiness alone which is sought. From all which it is transparently clear that the essence of absolute good and of happiness is one and the same.'

'I cannot see how anyone can dissent from these conclusions.'

'But we have also proved that God and true happiness are one and the same.'

'Yes,' said I.

'Then we can safely conclude, also, that God's essence is seated in absolute good, and nowhere else.'

Song X – The True Light.

Hither come, all ye whose minds
Lust with rosy fetters binds—
Lust to bondage hard compelling
Th' earthy souls that are his dwelling—
Here shall be your labour's close;
Here your haven of repose.
Come, to your one refuge press;
Wide it stands to all distress!
Not the glint of yellow gold
Down bright Hermus' current rolled;
Not the Tagus' precious sands,
Nor in far-off scorching lands
All the radiant gems that hide
Under Indus' storied tide—
Emerald green and glistering white—
Can illume our feeble sight;
But they rather leave the mind
In its native darkness blind.
For the fairest beams they shed
In earth's lowest depths were fed;
But the splendour that supplies
Strength and vigour to the skies,
And the universe controls,
Shunneth dark and ruined souls.
He who once hath seen this light
Will not call the sunbeam bright.

desideratur ab omnibus. Sed propter quod cetera optantur beatitudinem esse concessimus; quare sic quoque sola quaeritur beatitudo. Ex quo liquido apparet ipsius boni et beatitudinis unam atque eandem esse substantiam.

Nihil uideo cur dissentire quispiam possit.

Sed deum ueramque beatitudinem unum atque idem esse monstrauimus.

Ita, inquam.

Securo igitur concludere licet dei quoque in ipso bono nec usquam alio sitam esse substantiam.

Metrum X

Huc omnes pariter uenite capti,
Quos fallax ligat improbis catenis
Terrenas habitans libido mentes:
Haec erit uobis requies laborum,
Hic portus placida manens quiete,
Hoc patens unum miseris asylum.
Non quicquid Tagus aureis harenis
Donat aut Hermus rutilante ripa
Aut Indus calido propinquus orbi
Candidis miscens uirides lapillos
Inlustrent aciem magisque caecos
In suas condunt animos tenebras.
Hoc, quicquid placet excitatque mentes,
Infimis tellus aluit cauernis;
Splendor quo regitur uigetque caelum
Vitat obscuras animae ruinas;
Hanc quisquis poterit notare lucem
Candidos Phoebi radios negabit.

XI.

'I quite agree,' said I, 'truly all thy reasonings hold admirably together.'

Then said she: 'What value wouldst thou put upon the boon shouldst thou come to the knowledge of the absolute good?'

'Oh, an infinite,' said I, 'if only I were so blest as to learn to know God also who is the good.'

'Yet this will I make clear to thee on truest grounds of reason, if only our recent conclusions stand fast.'

'They will.'

'Have we not shown that those things which most men desire are not true and perfect good precisely for this cause—that they differ severally one from another, and, seeing that one is wanting to another, they cannot bestow full and absolute good; but that they become the true good when they are gathered, as it were, into one form and agency, so that that which is independence is likewise power, reverence, renown, and pleasant delight, and unless they are all one and the same, they have no claim to be counted among things desirable?'

'Yes; this was clearly proved, and cannot in any wise be doubted.'

'Now, when things are far from being good while they are different, but become good as soon as they are one, is it not true that these become good by acquiring unity?'

'It seems so,' said I.

'But dost not thou allow that all which is good is good by participation in goodness?'

'It is.'

'Then, thou must on similar grounds admit that unity and goodness are the same; for when the effects of things in their natural working differ not, their essence is one and the same.'

'There is no denying it.'

'Now, dost thou know,' said she, 'that all which is abides and subsists so long as it continues one, but so soon as it ceases to be one it perishes and falls to pieces?'

'In what way?'

'Why, take animals, for example. When soul and body come together, and continue in one, this is, we say, a living creature; but when this unity is broken by the separation of these two, the creature dies, and is clearly no longer living. The body also, while it remains in one form by the joining together of its members, presents a human appearance; but if the separation and dispersal of the parts break up the body's unity, it ceases to be what it was. And if we extend our survey to all other things, without doubt it will manifestly appear that each several thing subsists while it is one, but when it ceases to be one perishes.'

'Yes; when I consider further, I see it to be even as thou sayest.'

'Well, is there aught,' said she, 'which, in so far as it acts conformably to nature, abandons the wish for life, and desires to come to death and corruption?'

'Looking to living creatures, which have some faults of choice, I find none that, without external compulsion, forego the will to live, and of their own accord hasten to destruction. For every creature diligently pursues the end of self-preservation, and shuns death and

Prosa XI

Assentior, inquam; cuncta enim firmissimis nexa rationibus constant.

Tum illa: quanti, inquit, aestimabis, si bonum ipsum quid sit agnoueris?

Infinito, inquam, si quidem mihi pariter deum quoque, qui bonum est, continget agnoscere.

Atqui hoc uerissima, inquit, ratione patefaciam, maneant modo quae paulo ante conclusa sunt.

Manebunt.

Nonne, inquit, monstrauimus ea quae appetuntur pluribus idcirco uera perfectaque bona non esse quoniam a se inuicem discreparent, cumque alteri abesset alterum plenum absolu‐ tumque bonum afferre non posse, tum autem uerum bonum fieri cum in unam ueluti formam atque efficientiam colliguntur, ut quae sufficientia est eadem sit potentia, reuerentia, claritas atque iucunditas, nisi uero unum atque idem omnia sint, nihil habere quo inter expetenda numerentur?

Demonstratum, inquam, nec dubitari ullo modo potest.

Quae igitur cum discrepant minime bona sunt, cum uero unum esse coeperint bona fiunt, nonne haec ut bona sint unitatis fieri adeptione contingit?

Ita, inquam, uidetur.

Sed omne quod bonum est boni participatione bonum esse concedis, an minime?

Ita est.

Oportet igitur idem esse unum atque bonum simili ratione concedas; eadem namque substantia est eorum quorum naturaliter non est diuersus effectus.

Negare, inquam, nequeo.

Nostine igitur, inquit, omne quod est tam diu manere atque subsistere quamdiu sit unum, sed interire atque dissolui pariter atque unum esse destiterit?

Quonam modo?

Vt in animalibus, inquit, cum in unum coeunt ac permanent anima corpusque id animal uocatur, cum uero haec unitas utriusque separatione dissoluitur interire nec iam esse animal liquet; ipsum quoque corpus cum in una forma membrorum coniunctione permanet humana uisitur species, at si distributae segregataeque partes corporis distraxerint unitatem desinit esse quod fuerat. Eoque modo percurrenti cetera procul dubio patebit subsistere unum‐ quodque dum unum est, cum uero unum esse desinit interire.

Consideranti, inquam, mihi plura minime aliud uidetur.

Estne igitur, inquit, quod, in quantum naturaliter agat, relicta subsistendi appetentia uenire ad interitum corruptionemque desideret?

Si animalia, inquam, considerem, quae habent aliquam uolendi nolendique naturam, ni‐ hil inuenio quod nullis extra cogentibus abiciant manendi intentionem et ad interitum sponte festinent. Omne namque animal tueri salutem laborat, mortem uero perniciemque deuitat.

destruction! As to herbs and trees, and inanimate things generally, I am altogether in doubt what to think.'

'And yet there is no possibility of question about this either, since thou seest how herbs and trees grow in places suitable for them, where, as far as their nature admits, they cannot quickly wither and die. Some spring up in the plains, others in the mountains; some grow in marshes, others cling to rocks; and others, again, find a fertile soil in the barren sands; and if you try to transplant these elsewhere, they wither away. Nature gives to each the soil that suits it, and uses her diligence to prevent any of them dying, so long as it is possible for them to continue alive. Why do they all draw their nourishment from roots as from a mouth dipped into the earth, and distribute the strong bark over the pith? Why are all the softer parts like the pith deeply encased within, while the external parts have the strong texture of wood, and outside of all is the bark to resist the weather's inclemency, like a champion stout in endurance? Again, how great is nature's diligence to secure universal propagation by multiplying seed! Who does not know all these to be contrivances, not only for the present maintenance of a species, but for its lasting continuance, generation after generation, for ever? And do not also the things believed inanimate on like grounds of reason seek each what is proper to itself? Why do the flames shoot lightly upward, while the earth presses downward with its weight, if it is not that these motions and situations are suitable to their respective natures? Moreover, each several thing is preserved by that which is agreeable to its nature, even as it is destroyed by things inimical. Things solid like stones resist disintegration by the close adhesion of their parts. Things fluid like air and water yield easily to what divides them, but swiftly flow back and mingle with those parts from which they have been severed, while fire, again, refuses to be cut at all. And we are not now treating of the voluntary motions of an intelligent soul, but of the drift of nature. Even so is it that we digest our food without thinking about it, and draw our breath unconsciously in sleep; nay, even in living creatures the love of life cometh not of conscious will, but from the principles of nature. For oftentimes in the stress of circumstances will chooses the death which nature shrinks from; and contrarily, in spite of natural appetite, will restrains that work of reproduction by which alone the persistence of perishable creatures is maintained. So entirely does this love of self come from drift of nature, not from animal impulse. Providence has furnished things with this most cogent reason for continuance: they must desire life, so long as it is naturally possible for them to continue living. Wherefore in no way mayst thou doubt but that things naturally aim at continuance of existence, and shun destruction.'

'I confess,' said I, 'that what I lately thought uncertain, I now perceive to be indubitably clear.'

'Now, that which seeks to subsist and continue desires to be one; for if its oneness be gone, its very existence cannot continue.'

'True,' said I.

'All things, then, desire to be one.'

'I agree.'

'But we have proved that one is the very same thing as good.'

'We have.'

Sed quid de herbis arboribus que, quid de inanimatis omnino consentiam rebus prorsus dubito.

Atqui non est quod de hoc quoque possis ambigere, cum herbas atque arbores intuearis primum sibi conuenientibus innasci locis, ubi, quantum earum natura queat, cito exarescere atque interire non possint. Nam aliae quidem campis, aliae montibus oriuntur, alias ferunt paludes, aliae saxis haerent, aliarum fecundae sunt steriles harenae, quas si in alia quispiam loca transferre conetur arescant. Sed dat cuique natura quod conuenit, et ne, dum manere possunt, intereant elaborat. Quid quod omnes uelut in terras ore demerso trahunt alimenta radicibus ac per medullas robur corticemque diffundunt? Quid quod mollissimum quidque, sicuti medulla est, interiore semper sede reconditur, extra uero quadam ligni firmitate, ultimus autem cortex aduersum caeli intemperiem quasi mali patiens defensor opponitur? Iam uero quanta est naturae diligentia ut cuncta semine multiplicato propagentur! Quae omnia non modo ad tempus manendi, uerum generatim quoque quasi in perpetuum permanendi ueluti quasdam machinas esse quis nesciat? Ea etiam quae inanimata esse creduntur nonne quod suum est quaeque simili ratione desiderant? Cur enim flammas quidem sursum leuitas uehit, terras uero deorsum pondus deprimit, nisi quod haec singulis loca motionesque conueniunt? Porro autem, quod cuique consentaneum est id unumquodque conseruat, sicuti ea quae sunt inimica corrumpunt. Iam uero quae dura sunt ut lapides adhaerent tenacissime partibus suis et ne facile dissoluantur resistunt. Quae uero liquentia ut aer atque aqua facile quidem diuidentibus cedunt, sed cito in ea rursus a quibus sunt abscisa relabuntur; ignis uero omnem refugit sectionem. Neque nunc nos de uoluntariis animae cognoscentis motibus, sed de naturali intentione tractamus, sicuti est quod acceptas escas sine cogitatione transigimus, quod in somno spiritum ducimus nescientes. Nam ne in animalibus quidem manendi amor ex animae uoluntatibus, uerum ex naturae principiis uenit. Nam saepe mortem cogentibus causis, quam natura reformidat, uoluntas amplectitur, contraque illud quo solo mortalium rerum durat diuturnitas, gignendi opus, quod natura semper appetit, interdum cohercet uoluntas. Adeo haec sui caritas non ex animali motione, sed ex naturali intentione procedit; dedit enim prouidentia creatis a se rebus hanc uel maximam manendi causam ut quoad possunt naturaliter manere desiderent. Quare nihil est quod ullo modo queas dubitare cuncta quae sunt appetere naturaliter constantiam permanendi, deuitare perniciem.

Confiteor, inquam, nunc me indubitato cernere quae dudum incerta uidebantur.

Quod autem, inquit, subsistere ac permanere petit id unum esse desiderat; hoc enim sublato ne esse quidem cuiquam permanebit.

Verum est, inquam.

Omnia igitur, inquit, unum desiderant.

Consensi.

Sed unum id ipsum monstrauimus esse quod bonum.

Ita quidem.

'All things, then, seek the good; indeed, you may express the fact by defining good as that which all desire.'

'Nothing could be more truly thought out. Either there is no single end to which all things are relative, or else the end to which all things universally hasten must be the highest good of all.'

Then she: 'Exceedingly do I rejoice, dear pupil; thine eye is now fixed on the very central mark of truth. Moreover, herein is revealed that of which thou didst erstwhile profess thyself ignorant.'

'What is that?' said I.

'The end and aim of the whole universe. Surely it is that which is desired of all; and, since we have concluded the good to be such, we ought to acknowledge the end and aim of the whole universe to be "the good."'

Song XI – Reminiscence[8]

Who truth pursues, who from false ways
His heedful steps would keep,
By inward light must search within
In meditation deep;
All outward bent he must repress
His soul's true treasure to possess.
Then all that error's mists obscured
Shall shine more clear than light,
This fleshly frame's oblivious weight
Hath quenched not reason quite;
The germs of truth still lie within,
Whence we by learning all may win.
Else how could ye the answer due
Untaught to questions give,
Were't not that deep within the soul
Truth's secret sparks do live?
If Plato's teaching erreth not,
We learn but that we have forgot.

---

8   The doctrine of Reminiscence—i.e., that all learning is really recollection—is set forth at length by Plato in the 'Meno,' 81–86, and the 'Phædo,' 72–76. See Jowett, vol. ii., pp. 40–47 and 213–218.

Cuncta igitur bonum petunt, quod quidem ita describas licet ipsum bonum esse quod desideretur ab omnibus.

Nihil, inquam, uerius excogitari potest; nam uel ad nihil unum cuncta referuntur et uno ueluti uertice destituta sine rectore fluitabunt aut si quid est ad quod uniuersa festinant id erit omnium summum bonorum.

Et illa: nimium, inquit, o alumne, laetor; ipsam enim mediae ueritatis notam mente fixisti. Sed in hoc patuit tibi quod ignorare te paulo ante dicebas.

Quid? Inquam.

Quis esset, inquit, rerum omnium finis. Is est enim profecto quod desideratur ab omnibus; quod quia bonum esse collegimus, oportet rerum omnium finem bonum esse fateamur.

Metrum XI

Quisquis profunda mente uestigat uerum
Cupitque nullis ille deuiis falli
In se reuoluat intimi lucem uisus
Longosque in orbem cogat inflectens motus
Animumque doceat quicquid extra molitur
Suis retrusum possidere thesauris;
Dudum quod atra texit erroris nubes
Lucebit ipso perspicacius Phoebo.
Non omne namque mente depulit lumen
Obliuiosam corpus inuehens molem;
Haeret profecto semen introrsum ueri
Quod excitatur uentilante doctrina
Nam cur rogati sponte recta censetis
Ni mersus alto uiueret fomes corde?
Quodsi Platonis Musa personat uerum,
Quod quisque discit immemor recordatur.

XII.

Then said I: 'With all my heart I agree with Plato; indeed, this is now the second time that these things have been brought back to my mind—first I lost them through the clogging contact of the body; then after through the stress of heavy grief.'

Then she continued: 'If thou wilt reflect upon thy former admissions, it will not be long before thou dost also recollect that of which erstwhile thou didst confess thyself ignorant.'

'What is that?' said I.

'The principles of the world's government,' said she.

'Yes; I remember my confession, and, although I now anticipate what thou intendest, I have a desire to hear the argument plainly set forth.'

'Awhile ago thou deemedst it beyond all doubt that God doth govern the world.'

'I do not think it doubtful now, nor shall I ever; and by what reasons I am brought to this assurance I will briefly set forth. This world could never have taken shape as a single system out of parts so diverse and opposite were it not that there is One who joins together these so diverse things. And when it had once come together, the very diversity of natures would have dissevered it and torn it asunder in universal discord were there not One who keeps together what He has joined. Nor would the order of nature proceed so regularly, nor could its course exhibit motions so fixed in respect of position, time, range, efficacy, and character, unless there were One who, Himself abiding, disposed these various vicissitudes of change. This power, whatsoever it be, whereby they remain as they were created, and are kept in motion, I call by the name which all recognise—God.'

Then said she: 'Seeing that such is thy belief, it will cost me little trouble, I think, to enable thee to win happiness, and return in safety to thy own country. But let us give our attention to the task that we have set before ourselves. Have we not counted independence in the category of happiness, and agreed that God is absolute happiness?'

'Truly, we have.'

'Then, He will need no external assistance for the ruling of the world. Otherwise, if He stands in need of aught, He will not possess complete independence.'

'That is necessarily so,' said I.

'Then, by His own power alone He disposes all things.'

'It cannot be denied.'

'Now, God was proved to be absolute good.'

'Yes; I remember.'

'Then, He disposes all things by the agency of good, if it be true that He rules all things by His own power whom we have agreed to be good; and He is, as it were, the rudder and helm by which the world's mechanism is kept steady and in order.'

'Heartily do I agree; and, indeed, I anticipated what thou wouldst say, though it may be in feeble surmise only.'

'I well believe it,' said she; 'for, as I think, thou now bringest to the search eyes quicker in discerning truth; but what I shall say next is no less plain and easy to see.'

'What is it?' said I.

Prosa XII

Tum ego: Platoni, inquam, uehementer assentior; nam me horum iam secundo commemoras, primum quod memoriam corporea contagione, dehinc cum maeroris mole pressus amisi.

Tum illa: si priora, inquit, concessa respicias, ne illud quidem longius aberit quin recorderis quod te dudum nescire confessus es.

Quid? Inquam.

Quibus, ait illa, gubernaculis mundus regatur.

Memini, inquam, me inscitiam meam fuisse confessum, sed quid afferas, licet iam prospiciam, planius tamen ex te audire desidero.

Mundum, inquit, hunc deo regi paulo ante minime dubitandum putabas.

Ne nunc quidem arbitror, inquam, nec umquam dubitandum putabo, quibusque in hoc rationibus accedam breuiter exponam. Mundus hic ex tam diuersis contrariisque partibus in unam formam minime conuenisset nisi unus esset qui tam diuersa coniungeret. Coniuncta uero naturarum ipsa diuersitas inuicem discors dissociaret atque diuelleret nisi unus esset qui quod nexuit contineret. Non tam uero certus naturae ordo procederet nec tam dispositos motus locis, temporibus, efficientia, spatiis, qualitatibus explicarent nisi unus esset qui has mutationum uarietates manens ipse disponeret. Hoc, quicquid est, quo condita manent atque agitantur usitato cunctis uocabulo deum nomino.

Tum illa: cum haec, inquit, ita sentias, paruam mihi restare operam puto ut felicitatis compos patriam sospes reuisas. Sed quae proposuimus intueamur. Nonne in beatitudine sufficientiam numerauimus deumque beatitudinem ipsam esse consensimus?

Ita quidem.

Et ad mundum igitur, inquit, regendum nullis extrinsecus amminiculis indigebit; alioquin si quo egeat, plenam sufficientiam non habebit.

Id, inquam, ita est necessarium.

Per se igitur solum cuncta disponit?

Negari, inquam, nequit.

Atqui deus ipsum bonum esse monstratus est.

Memini, inquam.

Per bonum igitur cuncta disponit, si quidem per se regit omnia quem bonum esse consensimus, et hic est ueluti quidam clauus atque gubernaculum quo mundana machina stabilis atque incorrupta seruatur.

Vehementer assentior, inquam, et id te paulo ante dicturam tenui licet suspicione prospexi.

Credo, inquit; iam enim, ut arbitror, uigilantius ad cernenda uera oculos deducis. Sed quod dicam non minus ad contuendum patet.

Quid? Inquam.

'Why,' said she, 'since God is rightly believed to govern all things with the rudder of goodness, and since all things do likewise, as I have taught, haste towards good by the very aim of nature, can it be doubted that His governance is willingly accepted, and that all submit themselves to the sway of the Disposer as conformed and attempered to His rule?'

'Necessarily so,' said I; 'no rule would seem happy if it were a yoke imposed on reluctant wills, and not the safe-keeping of obedient subjects.'

'There is nothing, then, which, while it follows nature, endeavours to resist good.'

'No; nothing.'

'But if anything should, will it have the least success against Him whom we rightly agreed to be supreme Lord of happiness?'

'It would be utterly impotent.'

'There is nothing, then, which has either the will or the power to oppose this supreme good.'

'No; I think not.'

'So, then,' said she, 'it is the supreme good which rules in strength, and graciously disposes all things.'

Then said I: 'How delighted am I at thy reasonings, and the conclusion to which thou hast brought them, but most of all at these very words which thou usest! I am now at last ashamed of the folly that so sorely vexed me.'

'Thou hast heard the story of the giants assailing heaven; but a beneficent strength disposed of them also, as they deserved. But shall we submit our arguments to the shock of mutual collision?—it may be from the impact some fair spark of truth may be struck out.'

'If it be thy good pleasure,' said I.

'No one can doubt that God is all-powerful.'

'No one at all can question it who thinks consistently.'

'Now, there is nothing which One who is all-powerful cannot do.'

'Nothing.'

'But can God do evil, then?'

'Nay; by no means.'

'Then, evil is nothing,' said she, 'since He to whom nothing is impossible is unable to do evil.'

'Art thou mocking me,' said I, 'weaving a labyrinth of tangled arguments, now seeming to begin where thou didst end, and now to end where thou didst begin, or dost thou build up some wondrous circle of Divine simplicity? For, truly, a little before thou didst begin with happiness, and say it was the supreme good, and didst declare it to be seated in the supreme Godhead. God Himself, too, thou didst affirm to be supreme good and all-complete happiness; and from this thou didst go on to add, as by the way, the proof that no one would be happy unless he were likewise God. Again, thou didst say that the very form of good was the essence both of God and of happiness, and didst teach that the absolute One was the absolute good which was sought by universal nature. Thou didst maintain, also, that God rules the universe by the governance of goodness, that all things obey Him willingly, and that evil

Cum Deus, inquit, omnia bonitatis clauo gubernare iure credatur eademque omnia, sicuti docui, ad bonum naturali intentione festinent, num dubitari potest quin uoluntaria regantur seque ad disponentis nutum ueluti conuenientia contemperataque rectori sponte conuertant?

Ita, inquam, necesse est; nec beatum regimen esse uideretur, si quidem detrectantium iugum foret, non obtemperantium salus.

Nihil est igitur, quod naturam seruans deo contra ire conetur?

Nihil, inquam.

Quodsi conetur, ait, num tandem proficiet quicquam aduersus eum quem iure beatitudinis potentissimum esse concessimus?

Prorsus, inquam, nihil ualeret.

Non est igitur aliquid quod summo huic bono uel uelit uel possit obsistere?

Non, inquam, arbitror.

Est igitur summum, inquit, bonum quod regit cuncta fortiter suauiterque disponit.

Tum ego: quam, inquam, me non modo ea quae conclusa est summa rationum, uerum multo magis haec ipsa quibus uteris uerba delectant, ut tandem aliquando stultitiam magna lacerantem sui pudeat!

Accepisti, inquit, in fabulis lacessentes caelum Gigantas; sed illos quoque, uti condignum fuit, benigna fortitudo disposuit. Sed uisne rationes ipsas inuicem collidamus? Forsitan ex huius modi conflictatione pulchra quaedam ueritatis scintilla dissiliat. — Tuo, inquam, arbitratu.

Deum, inquit, esse omnium potentem nemo dubitauerit.

Qui quidem, inquam, mente consistat nullus prorsus ambigat.

Qui uero est, inquit, omnium potens, nihil est quod ille non possit.

Nihil, inquam.

Num igitur deus facere malum potest?

Minime, inquam.

Malum igitur, inquit, nihil est, cum id facere ille possit qui nihil non potest.

Ludisne, inquam, me inextricabilem labyrinthum rationibus texens, quae nunc quidem qua egrediaris introeas, nunc uero quo introieris egrediare, an mirabilem quendam diuinae simplicitatis orbem complicas? Etenim paulo ante beatitudine incipiens eam summum bonum esse dicebas, quam in summo deo sitam loquebare. Ipsum quoque deum summum esse bonum plenamque beatitudinem disserebas, ex quo neminem beatum fore nisi qui pariter deus esset quasi munusculum dabas. Rursus ipsam boni formam dei ac beatitudinis loquebaris esse substantiam ipsumque unum id ipsum esse bonum docebas quod ab omni rerum natura peteretur. Deum quoque bonitatis gubernaculis uniuersitatem regere disputabas uolentiaque cuncta

has no existence in nature. And all this thou didst unfold without the help of assumptions from without, but by inherent and proper proofs, drawing credence one from the other.'

Then answered she: 'Far is it from me to mock thee; nay, by the blessing of God, whom we lately addressed in prayer, we have achieved the most important of all objects. For such is the form of the Divine essence, that neither can it pass into things external, nor take up any-thing external into itself; but, as Parmenides says of it,

"'In body like to a sphere on all sides perfectly rounded,"

it rolls the restless orb of the universe, keeping itself motionless the while. And if I have also employed reasonings not drawn from without, but lying within the compass of our sub-ject, there is no cause for thee to marvel, since thou hast learnt on Plato's authority that words ought to be akin to the matter of which they treat.'

Song XII – Orpheus and Eurydice.

Blest he whose feet have stood
Beside the fount of good;
Blest he whose will could break
Earth's chains for wisdom's sake!
The Thracian bard, 'tis said,
Mourned his dear consort dead;
To hear the plaintive strain
The woods moved in his train,
And the stream ceased to flow,
Held by so soft a woe;
The deer without dismay
Beside the lion lay;
The hound, by song subdued,
No more the hare pursued,
But the pang unassuaged
In his own bosom raged.
The music that could calm
All else brought him no balm.
Chiding the powers immortal,
He came unto Hell's portal;
There breathed all tender things
Upon his sounding strings,
Each rhapsody high-wrought
His goddess-mother taught—
All he from grief could borrow
And love redoubling sorrow,
Till, as the echoes waken,
All Tænarus is shaken;
Whilst he to ruth persuades
The monarch of the shades

parere nec ullam mali esse naturam. Atque haec nullis extrinsecus sumptis, sed ex altero [altero] fidem trahente insitis domesticisque probationibus explicabas.

Tum illa: minime, inquit, ludimus remque omnium maximam dei munere, quem dudum deprecabamur, exegimus. Ea est enim diuinae forma substantiae ut neque in externa dilabatur nec in se externum aliquid ipsa suscipiat, sed, sicut de ea Parmenides ait,

"Πάντοθεν εὐκύκλου σφαίρας ἐναλίγκιον ὄγκῳ,"[6]

rerum orbem mobilem rotat dum se immobilem ipsa conseruat. Quodsi rationes quoque non extra petitas sed intra rei quam tractabamus ambitum collocatas agitauimus, nihil est quod ammirere, cum Platone sanciente didiceris cognatos de quibus loquuntur rebus oportere esse sermones.

Metrum XII

Felix, qui potuit boni
Fontem uisere lucidum,
Felix, qui potuit grauis
Terrae soluere uincula.
Quondam funera coniugis
Vates Threicius gemens
Postquam flebilibus modis
Siluas currere mobiles,
Amnes stare coegerat
Iunxitque intrepidum latus
Saeuis cerua leonibus
Nec uisum timuit lepus
Iam cantu placidum canem,
Cum flagrantior intima
Feruor pectoris ureret
Nec qui cuncta subegerant
Mulcerent dominum modi,
Immites superos querens
Infernas adiit domos.
Illic blanda sonantibus
Chordis carmina temperans
Quicquid praecipuis deae
Matris fontibus hauserat,
Quod luctus dabat impotens,
Quod luctum geminans amor
Deflet Taenara commouens

---

6   Velut pilam omnino circularem.

With dulcet prayer. Spell-bound,
The triple-headed hound
At sounds so strangely sweet
Falls crouching at his feet.
The dread Avengers, too,
That guilty minds pursue
With ever-haunting fears,
Are all dissolved in tears.
Ixion, on his wheel,
A respite brief doth feel;
For, lo! the wheel stands still.
And, while those sad notes thrill,
Thirst-maddened Tantalus
Listens, oblivious
Of the stream's mockery
And his long agony.
The vulture, too, doth spare
Some little while to tear
At Tityus' rent side,
Sated and pacified.
At length the shadowy king,
His sorrows pitying,
'He hath prevailèd!' cried;
'We give him back his bride!
To him she shall belong,
As guerdon of his song.
One sole condition yet
Upon the boon is set:
Let him not turn his eyes
To view his hard-won prize,
Till they securely pass
The gates of Hell.' Alas!
What law can lovers move?
A higher law is love!
For Orpheus—woe is me!—
On his Eurydice—
Day's threshold all but won—
Looked, lost, and was undone!
Ye who the light pursue,
This story is for you,
Who seek to find a way
Unto the clearer day.
If on the darkness past
One backward look ye cast,
Your weak and wandering eyes
Have lost the matchless prize.

Et dulci ueniam prece
Vmbrarum dominos rogat.
Stupet tergeminus nouo
Captus carmine ianitor;
Quae sontes agitant metu
Vltrices scelerum deae
Iam maestae lacrimis madent;
Non Ixionium caput
Velox praecipitat rota
Et longa site perditus
Spernit flumina Tantalus;
Vultur dum satur est modis
Non traxit Tityi iecur.
Tandem 'uincimur' arbiter
Vmbrarum miserans ait.
'Donamus comitem uiro
Emptam carmine coniugem;
Sed lex dona coherceat,
Ne dum Tartara liquerit
Fas sit lumina flectere.'
Quis legem det amantibus?
Maior lex amor est sibi.
Heu, noctis prope terminos
Orpheus Eurydicen suam
Vidit, perdidit, occidit.
Vos haec fabula respicit
Quicumque in superum diem
Mentem ducere quaeritis;
Nam qui Tartareum in specus
Victus lumina flexerit,
Quicquid praecipuum trahit
Perdit dum uidet inferos.

Book IV – Good and Ill Fortune

I.

Softly and sweetly Philosophy sang these verses to the end without losing aught of the dignity of her expression or the seriousness of her tones; then, forasmuch as I was as yet unable to forget my deeply-seated sorrow, just as she was about to say something further, I broke in and cried: 'O thou guide into the way of true light, all that thy voice hath uttered from the beginning even unto now has manifestly seemed to me at once divine contemplated in itself, and by the force of thy arguments placed beyond the possibility of overthrow. Moreover, these truths have not been altogether unfamiliar to me heretofore, though because of indignation at my wrongs they have for a time been forgotten. But, lo! herein is the very chiefest cause of my grief—that, while there exists a good ruler of the universe, it is possible that evil should be at all, still more that it should go unpunished. Surely thou must see how deservedly this of itself provokes astonishment. But a yet greater marvel follows: While wickedness reigns and flourishes, virtue not only lacks its reward, but is even thrust down and trampled under the feet of the wicked, and suffers punishment in the place of crime. That this should happen under the rule of a God who knows all things and can do all things, but wills only the good, cannot be sufficiently wondered at nor sufficiently lamented.'

Then said she: 'It would indeed be infinitely astounding, and of all monstrous things most horrible, if, as thou esteemest, in the well-ordered home of so great a householder, the base vessels should be held in honour, the precious left to neglect. But it is not so. For if we hold unshaken those conclusions which we lately reached, thou shall learn that, by the will of Him of whose realm we are speaking, the good are always strong, the bad always weak and impotent; that vices never go unpunished, nor virtues unrewarded; that good fortune ever befalls the good, and ill fortune the bad, and much more of the sort, which shall hush thy murmurings, and stablish thee in the strong assurance of conviction. And since by my late instructions thou hast seen the form of happiness, hast learnt, too, the seat where it is to be found, all due preliminaries being discharged, I will now show thee the road which will lead thee home. Wings, also, will I fasten to thy mind wherewith thou mayst soar aloft, that so, all disturbing doubts removed, thou mayst return safe to thy country, under my guidance, in the path I will show thee, and by the means which I furnish.'

Song I – The Soul's Flight.

Wings are mine; above the pole
Far aloft I soar.

Liber Quartus

Prosa I

Haec cum philosophia dignitate uultus et oris grauitate seruata leniter suauiterque cecinisset, tum ego nondum penitus insiti maeroris oblitus intentionem dicere adhuc aliquid parantis abrupi et: o, inquam, ueri praeuia luminis, quae usque adhuc tua fudit oratio cum sui speculatione diuina tum tuis rationibus inuicta patuerunt, eaque mihi etsi ob iniuriae dolor‑ em nuper oblita non tamen antehac prorsus ignorata dixisti. Sed ea ipsa est uel maxima nostri causa maeroris quod, cum rerum bonus rector exsistat, uel esse omnino mala possint uel im‑ punita praetereant; quod solum quanta dignum sit ammiratione profecto consideras. At huic aliud maius adiungitur; nam imperante florenteque nequitia uirtus non solum praemiis caret, uerum etiam sceleratorum pedibus subiecta calcatur et in locum facinorum supplicia luit. Quae fieri in regno scientis omnia, potentis omnia, sed bona tantummodo uolentis dei nemo satis potest nec ammirari nec conqueri.

Tum illa: et esset, inquit, infiniti stuporis omnibusque horribilius monstris si, uti tu aes‑ timas, in tanti uelut patris familias dispositissima domo uilia uasa colerentur, pretiosa sordes‑ cerent. Sed non ita est; nam si ea quae paulo ante conclusa sunt inconuulsa seruantur, ipso de cuius nunc regno loquimur auctore cognosces semper quidem potentes esse bonos, malos uero abiectos semper atque imbecilles, nec sine poena umquam esse uitia nec sine praemio uirtutes, bonis felicia malis semper infortunata contingere multaque id genus, quae sopitis querelis firma te soliditate corroborent. Et quoniam uerae formam beatitudinis me dudum monstrante uidisti, quo etiam sita sit agnouisti, decursis omnibus quae praemittere necessari‑ um puto uiam tibi quae te domum reuehat ostendam. Pennas etiam tuae menti quibus se in altum tollere possit adfigam, ut perturbatione depulsa sospes in patriam meo ductu, mea semita, meis etiam uehiculis reuertaris.

Metrum I

Sunt etenim pennae uolucres mihi
Quae celsa conscendant poli;

Clothed with these, my nimble soul
Scorns earth's hated shore,
Cleaves the skies upon the wind,
Sees the clouds left far behind.

Soon the glowing point she nears,
Where the heavens rotate,
Follows through the starry spheres
Phœbus' course, or straight
Takes for comrade 'mid the stars
Saturn cold or glittering Mars;
Thus each circling orb explores
Through Night's stole that peers;
Then, when all are numbered, soars
Far beyond the spheres,
Mounting heaven's supremest height
To the very Fount of light.

There the Sovereign of the world
His calm sway maintains;
As the globe is onward whirled
Guides the chariot reins,
And in splendour glittering
Reigns the universal King.

Hither if thy wandering feet
Find at last a way,
Here thy long-lost home thou'lt greet:'
Dear lost land,' thou'lt say,'
Though from thee I've wandered wide,
Hence I came, here will abide.'

Yet if ever thou art fain
Visitant to be
Of earth's gloomy night again,
Surely thou wilt see
Tyrants whom the nations fear
Dwell in hapless exile here.

II.

Then said I: 'Verily, wondrous great are thy promises; yet I do not doubt but thou canst make them good: only keep me not in suspense after raising such hopes.'

'Learn, then, first,' said she, 'how that power ever waits upon the good, while the bad are left wholly destitute of strength.[1] Of these truths the one proves the other; for since good

---

1   The paradoxes in this chapter and chapter iv. are taken from Plato's 'Gorgias.' See Jowett, vol. ii., pp. 348—366, and also pp. 400, 401 ('Gorgias,' 466—479, and 508, 509).

Quas sibi cum uelox mens induit

Terras perosa despicit,

Aeris immensi superat globum

Nubesque postergum uidet

Quique agili motu calet aetheris

Transcendit ignis uerticem,

Donec in astriferas surgat domos

Phoeboque coniungat uias

Aut comitetur iter gelidi senis

Miles corusci sideris

Vel quocumque micans nox pingitur

Recurrat astri circulum

Atque ubi iam exhausti fuerit satis

Polum relinquat extimum

Dorsaque uelocis premat aetheris

Compos uerendi luminis.

Hic regum sceptrum dominus tenet

Orbisque habenas temperat

Et uolucrem currum stabilis regit

Rerum coruscus arbiter.

Huc te si reducem referat uia

Quam nunc requiris immemor,

Haec, dices, memini, patria est mihi,

Hinc ortus, hic sistam gradum.

Quodsi terrarum placeat tibi

Noctem relictam uisere,

Quos miseri toruos populi timent

Cernes tyrannos exsules.

Prosa II

Tum ego: papae, inquam, ut magna promittis! Nec dubito quin possis efficere, tu modo quem excitaueris ne moreris.

Primum igitur, inquit, bonis semper adesse potentiam, malos cunctis uiribus esse desertos agnoscas licebit, quorum quidem alterum demonstratur ex altero. Nam cum bonum

and evil are contraries, if it is made plain that good is power, the feebleness of evil is clearly seen, and, conversely, if the frail nature of evil is made manifest, the strength of good is thereby known. However, to win ampler credence for my conclusion, I will pursue both paths, and draw confirmation for my statements first in one way and then in the other.

'The carrying out of any human action depends upon two things—to wit, will and power; if either be wanting, nothing can be accomplished. For if the will be lacking, no attempt at all is made to do what is not willed; whereas if there be no power, the will is all in vain. And so, if thou seest any man wishing to attain some end, yet utterly failing to attain it, thou canst not doubt that he lacked the power of getting what he wished for.'

'Why, certainly not; there is no denying it.'

'Canst thou, then, doubt that he whom thou seest to have accomplished what he willed had also the power to accomplish it?'

'Of course not.'

'Then, in respect of what he can accomplish a man is to be reckoned strong, in respect of what he cannot accomplish weak?'

'Granted,' said I.

'Then, dost thou remember that, by our former reasonings, it was concluded that the whole aim of man's will, though the means of pursuit vary, is set intently upon happiness?'

'I do remember that this, too, was proved.'

'Dost thou also call to mind how happiness is absolute good, and therefore that, when happiness is sought, it is good which is in all cases the object of desire?'

'Nay, I do not so much call to mind as keep it fixed in my memory.'

'Then, all men, good and bad alike, with one indistinguishable purpose strive to reach good?'

'Yes, that follows.'

'But it is certain that by the attainment of good men become good?'

'It is.'

'Then, do the good attain their object?'

'It seems so.'

'But if the bad were to attain the good which is their object, they could not be bad?'

'No.'

'Then, since both seek good, but while the one sort attain it, the other attain it not, is there any doubt that the good are endued with power, while they who are bad are weak?'

'If any doubt it, he is incapable of reflecting on the nature of things, or the consequences involved in reasoning.'

'Again, supposing there are two things to which the same function is prescribed in the course of nature, and one of these successfully accomplishes the function by natural action, the other is altogether incapable of that natural action, instead of which, in a way other than is agreeable to its nature, it—I will not say fulfils its function, but feigns to fulfil it: which of these two would in thy view be the stronger?'

'I guess thy meaning, but I pray thee let me hear thee more at large.'

malumque contraria sint, si bonum potens esse constiterit liquet imbecillitas mali, at si fragil-
itas clarescat mali boni firmitas nota est. Sed uti nostrae sententiae fides abundantior sit, alterutro calle procedam nunc hinc nunc inde proposita confirmans. Duo sunt, quibus omnis
humanorum actuum constat effectus, uoluntas scilicet ac potestas, quorum si alterutrum desit,
nihil est quod explicari queat. Deficiente etenim uoluntate ne aggreditur quidem quisque
quod non uult, at si potestas absit uoluntas frustra sit. Quo fit ut, si quem uideas adipisci
uelle quod minime adipiscatur, huic obtinendi quod uoluerit defuisse ualentiam dubitare non
possis.

Perspicuum est, inquam, nec ullo modo negari potest.

Quem uero effecisse quod uoluerit uideas, num etiam potuisse dubitatis?

Minime.

Quod uero quisque potest in eo ualidus, quod uero non potest in hoc imbecillis esse
censendus est.

Fateor, inquam.

Meministine igitur, inquit, superioribus rationibus esse collectum intentionem omnem
uoluntatis humanae, quae diuersis studiis agitur, ad beatitudinem festinare?

Memini, inquam, illud quoque esse demonstratum.

Num recordaris beatitudinem ipsum esse bonum eoque modo, cum beatitudo petitur, ab
omnibus desiderari bonum?

Minime, inquam, recordor, quoniam id memoriae fixum teneo.

Omnes igitur homines boni pariter ac mali indiscreta intentione ad bonum peruenire
nituntur?

Ita, inquam, consequens est.

Sed certum adeptione boni bonos fieri?

Certum.

Adipiscuntur igitur boni, quod appetunt?

Sic uidetur.

Mali uero si adipiscerentur quod appetunt, bonum, mali esse non possent.

Ita est.

Cum igitur utrique bonum petant, sed hi quidem adipiscantur, illi uero minime, num
dubium est bonos quidem potentes esse, qui uero mali sint imbecilles?

Quisquis, inquam, dubitat nec rerum naturam nec consequentiam potest considerare
rationum.

Rursus, inquit, si duo sint quibus idem secundum naturam propositum sit, eorumque
unus naturali officio id ipsum agat atque perficiat, alter uero naturale illud officium minime
amministrare queat, alio uero modo quam naturae conuenit non quidem impleat propositum
suum sed imitetur implentem, quemnam horum ualentiorem esse decernis?

Etsi coniecto, inquam, quid uelis, planius tamen audire desidero.

'Walking is man's natural motion, is it not?'

'Certainly.'

'Thou dost not doubt, I suppose, that it is natural for the feet to discharge this function?'

'No; surely I do not.'

'Now, if one man who is able to use his feet walks, and another to whom the natural use of his feet is wanting tries to walk on his hands, which of the two wouldst thou rightly es-teem the stronger?'

'Go on,' said I; 'no one can question but that he who has the natural capacity has more strength than he who has it not.'

'Now, the supreme good is set up as the end alike for the bad and for the good; but the good seek it through the natural action of the virtues, whereas the bad try to attain this same good through all manner of concupiscence, which is not the natural way of attaining good. Or dost thou think otherwise?'

'Nay; rather, one further consequence is clear to me: for from my admissions it must needs follow that the good have power, and the bad are impotent.'

'Thou anticipatest rightly, and that as physicians reckon is a sign that nature is set work-ing, and is throwing off the disease. But, since I see thee so ready at understanding, I will heap proof on proof. Look how manifest is the extremity of vicious men's weakness; they cannot even reach that goal to which the aim of nature leads and almost constrains them. What if they were left without this mighty, this well-nigh irresistible help of nature's guid-ance! Consider also how momentous is the powerlessness which incapacitates the wicked. Not light or trivial[10] are the prizes which they contend for, but which they cannot win or hold; nay, their failure concerns the very sum and crown of things. Poor wretches! they fail to compass even that for which they toil day and night. Herein also the strength of the good conspicuously appears. For just as thou wouldst judge him to be the strongest walker whose legs could carry him to a point beyond which no further advance was possible, so must thou needs account him strong in power who so attains the end of his desires that nothing further to be desired lies beyond. Whence follows the obvious conclusion that they who are wicked are seen likewise to be wholly destitute of strength. For why do they forsake virtue and fol-low vice? Is it from ignorance of what is good? Well, what is more weak and feeble than the blindness of ignorance? Do they know what they ought to follow, but lust drives them aside out of the way? If it be so, they are still frail by reason of their incontinence, for they cannot fight against vice. Or do they knowingly and wilfully forsake the good and turn aside to vice? Why, at this rate, they not only cease to have power, but cease to be at all. For they who forsake the common end of all things that are, they likewise also cease to be at all. ⟨Now, to some it may seem strange that we should assert that the bad, who form the greater part of mankind, do not exist. But the fact is so. I do not, indeed, deny that they who are bad are bad, but that they are in an unqualified and absolute sense I deny. Just as we call a corpse a dead man, but cannot call it simply "man," so I would allow the vicious to be bad, but that they are in an absolute sense I cannot allow. That only is which maintains its place and keeps its nature; whatever falls away from this forsakes the existence which is essential to its

---

10   'No trivial game is here; the strife Is waged for Turnus' own dear life.' —Conington. See Virgil, 'Æneid,' xii. 764, 745: cf. 'Iliad,' xxii. 159–162.

Ambulandi, inquit, motum secundum naturam esse hominibus num negabis?

Minime, inquam.

Eiusque rei pedum officium esse naturale num dubitas?

Ne hoc quidem, inquam.

Si quis igitur pedibus incedere ualens ambulet alius que, cui hoc naturale pedum desit officium, manibus nitens ambulare conetur, quis horum iure ualentior existimari potest?

Contexe, inquam, cetera; nam quin naturalis officii potens eo qui idem nequeat ualentior sit nullus ambigat.

Sed summum bonum, quod aeque malis bonisque propositum boni quidem naturali officio uirtutum petunt, mali uero uariam per cupiditatem, quod adipiscendi boni naturale officium non est, idem ipsum conantur adipisci; an tu aliter existimas?

Minime, inquam; nam etiam quod est consequens patet. Ex his enim quae concesserim bonos quidem potentes, malos uero esse necesse est imbecilles.

Recte, inquit, praecurris id que, uti medici sperare solent, indicium est erectae iam resistentisque naturae. Sed quoniam te ad intellegendum promptissimum esse conspicio, crebras coaceruabo rationes; uide enim quanta uitiosorum hominum pateat infirmitas, qui ne ad hoc quidem peruenire queunt ad quod eos naturalis ducit ac paene compellit intentio. Et quid, si hoc tam magno ac paene inuicto praeeuntis naturae desererentur auxilio? Considera uero quanta sceleratos homines habeat impotentia. Neque enim leuia aut ludicra praemia petunt quae consequi atque obtinere non possunt, sed circa ipsam rerum summam uerticemque deficiunt nec in eo miseris contingit effectus quod solum dies noctesque moliuntur; in qua re bonorum uires eminent. Sicut enim eum qui pedibus incedens ad eum locum usque peruenire potuisset quod nihil ulterius peruium iaceret incessui ambulandi potentissimum esse censeres, ita eum qui expetendorum finem quo nihil ultra est apprehendit potentissimum necesse est iudices. Ex quo fit, quod huic obiacet, ut idem scelesti idem uiribus omnibus uideantur esse deserti. Cur enim relicta uirtute uitia sectantur? Inscitiane bonorum — Sed quid eneruatius ignorantiae caecitate? — An sectanda nouerunt, sed transuersos eos libido praecipitat? Sic quoque intemperantia fragiles, qui obluctari uitio nequeunt. An scientes uolentesque bonum deserunt, ad uitia deflectunt? Sed hoc modo non solum potentes esse, sed omnino esse desinunt; nam qui communem omnium quae sunt finem relinquunt pariter quoque esse desistunt.

Quod quidem cuipiam mirum forte uideatur, ut malos, qui plures hominum sunt, eosdem non esse dicamus; sed ita sese res habet. Nam qui mali sunt eos malos esse non abnuo; sed eosdem esse pure atque simpliciter nego. Nam uti cadauer hominem mortuum dixeris, simpliciter uero hominem appellare non possis, ita uitiosos malos quidem esse concesserim, sed esse absolute nequeam confiteri. Est enim quod ordinem retinet seruatque naturam;

nature. "But" thou wilt say, "the bad have an ability." Nor do I wish to deny it; only this ability of theirs comes not from strength, but from impotence. For their ability is to do evil, which would have had no efficacy at all if they could have continued in the performance of good. So this ability of theirs proves them still more plainly to have no power. For if, as we concluded just now, evil is nothing, 'tis clear that the wicked can effect nothing, since they are only able to do evil.'

'Tis evident.'

'And that thou mayst understand what is the precise force of this power, we determined, did we not, awhile back, that nothing has more power than supreme good?'

'We did,' said I.

'But that same highest good cannot do evil?'

'Certainly not.'

'Is there anyone, then, who thinks that men are able to do all things?'

'None but a madman.'

'Yet they are able to do evil?'

'Ay; would they could not!'

'Since, then, he who can do only good is omnipotent, while they who can do evil also are not omnipotent, it is manifest that they who can do evil have less power. There is this also: we have shown that all power is to be reckoned among things desirable, and that all desirable things are referred to good as to a kind of consummation of their nature. But the ability to commit crime cannot be referred to the good; therefore it is not a thing to be desired. And yet all power is desirable; it is clear, then, that ability to do evil is not power. From all which considerations appeareth the power of the good, and the indubitable weakness of the bad, and it is clear that Plato's judgment was true; the wise alone are able to do what they would, while the wicked follow their own hearts' lust, but can notaccomplish what they would. For they go on in their wilfulness fancying they will attain what they wish for in the paths of delight; but they are very far from its attainment, since shameful deeds lead not to happiness.'

Song II — The Bondage of Passion.

When high-enthroned the monarch sits, resplendent in the pride
Of purple robes, while flashing steel guards him on every side;
When baleful terrors on his brow with frowning menace lower,
And Passion shakes his labouring breast—how dreadful seems his power!
But if the vesture of his state from such a one thou tear,
Thou'lt see what load of secret bonds this lord of earth doth wear.
Lust's poison rankles; o'er his mind rage sweeps in tempest rude;
Sorrow his spirit vexes sore, and empty hopes delude.
Then thou'lt confess: one hapless wretch, whom many lords oppress,
Does never what he would, but lives in thraldom's helplessness.

quod uero ab hac deficit esse etiam, quod in sua natura situm est, derelinquit. Sed possunt, inquies, mali; ne ego quidem negauerim, sed haec eorum potentia non a uiribus sed ab imbe-cillitate descendit. Possunt enim mala, quae minime ualerent si in bonorum efficientia manere potuissent. Quae possibilitas eos euidentius nihil posse demonstrat; nam si, uti paulo ante collegimus, malum nihil est, cum mala tantummodo possint, nihil posse improbos liquet.

Perspicuum est.

Atque ut intellegas quaenam sit huius potentiae uis: summo bono nihil potentius esse paulo ante definiuimus.

Ita est, inquam.

Sed idem, inquit, facere malum nequit.

Minime.

Est igitur, inquit, aliquis qui omnia posse homines putet?

Nisi quis insaniat, nemo.

Atqui idem possunt mala.

Vtinam quidem, inquam, non possent!

Cum igitur bonorum tantummodo potens possit omnia, non uero queant omnia potentes etiam malorum, eosdem qui mala possunt, minus posse manifestum est. Huc accedit quod omnem potentiam inter expetenda numerandam omniaque expetenda referri ad bonum uelut ad quoddam naturae suae cacumen ostendimus. Sed patrandi sceleris possibilitas referri ad bonum non potest, expetenda igitur non est. Atqui omnis potentia expetenda est; liquet igit-ur malorum possibilitatem non esse potentiam. Ex quibus omnibus bonorum quidem poten-tia, malorum uero minime dubitabilis apparet infirmitas ueramque illam Platonis esse senten-tiam liquet solos quod desiderent facere posse sapientes, improbos uero exercere quidem quod libeat, quod uero desiderent explere non posse. Faciunt enim quaelibet, dum per ea quibus delectantur id bonum quod desiderant se adepturos putant; sed minime adipiscuntur, quoniam ad beatitudinem probra non ueniunt.

Metrum II

Quos uides sedere celsos solii culmine reges,
Purpura claros nitente, saeptos tristibus armis,
Ore toruo comminantes, rabie cordis anhelos,
Detrahat si quis superbis uani tegmina cultus,
Iam uidebit intus artas dominos ferre catenas;
Hinc enim libido uersat auidis corda uenenis,
Hinc flagellat ira mentem fluctus turbida tollens,
Maeror aut captus fatigat aut spes lubrica torquet.
Ergo cum caput tot unum cernas ferre tyrannos,
Non facit quod optat ipse, dominis pressus iniquis.

III.

'Thou seest, then, in what foulness unrighteous deeds are sunk, with what splendour righteousness shines. Whereby it is manifest that goodness never lacks its reward, nor crime its punishment. For, verily, in all manner of transactions that for the sake of which the particular action is done may justly be accounted the reward of that action, even as the wreath for the sake of which the race is run is the reward offered for running. Now, we have shown happiness to be that very good for the sake of which all things are done. Absolute good, then, is offered as the common prize, as it were, of all human actions. But, truly, this is a reward from which it is impossible to separate the good man, for one who is without good cannot properly be called good at all; wherefore righteous dealing never misses its reward. Rage the wicked, then, never so violently, the crown shall not fall from the head of the wise, nor wither. Verily, other men's unrighteousness cannot pluck from righteous souls their proper glory. Were the reward in which the soul of the righteous delighteth received from without, then might it be taken away by him who gave it, or some other; but since it is conferred by his own righteousness, then only will he lose his prize when he has ceased to be righteous. Lastly, since every prize is desired because it is believed to be good, who can account him who possesses good to be without reward? And what a prize, the fairest and grandest of all! For remember the corollary which I chiefly insisted on a little while back, and reason thus: Since absolute good is happiness, 'tis clear that all the good must be happy for the very reason that they are good. But it was agreed that those who are happy are gods. So, then, the prize of the good is one which no time may impair, no man's power lessen, no man's unrighteousness tarnish; 'tis very Godship. And this being so, the wise man cannot doubt that punishment is inseparable from the bad. For since good and bad, and likewise reward and punishment, are contraries, it necessarily follows that, corresponding to all that we see accrue as reward of the good, there is some penalty attached as punishment of evil. As, then, righteousness itself is the reward of the righteous, so wickedness itself is the punishment of the unrighteous. Now, no one who is visited with punishment doubts that he is visited with evil. Accordingly, if they were but willing to weigh their own case, could they think themselves free from punishment whom wickedness, worst of all evils, has not only touched, but deeply tainted?

'See, also, from the opposite standpoint—the standpoint of the good—what a penalty attends upon the wicked. Thou didst learn a little since that whatever is is one, and that unity itself is good. Accordingly, by this way of reckoning, whatever falls away from goodness ceases to be; whence it comes to pass that the bad cease to be what they were, while only the outward aspect is still left to show they have been men. Wherefore, by their perversion to badness, they have lost their true human nature. Further, since righteousness alone can raise men above the level of humanity, it must needs be that unrighteousness degrades below man's level those whom it has cast out of man's estate. It results, then, that thou canst not consider him human whom thou seest transformed by vice. The violent despoiler of other men's goods, enflamed with covetousness, surely resembles a wolf. A bold and restless spirit, ever wrangling in law-courts, is like some yelping cur. The secret schemer, taking pleasure in fraud and stealth, is own brother to the fox. The passionate man, phrenzied with rage, we might believe to be animated with the soul of a lion. The coward and runaway, afraid where

Prosa III

Videsne igitur quanto in caeno probra uoluantur, qua probitas luce resplendeat? In quo perspicuum est numquam bonis praemia, numquam sua sceleribus deesse supplicia. Rerum etenim quae gerentur illud propter quod unaquaeque res geritur eiusdem rei praemium esse non iniuria uideri potest, uti currendi in stadio propter quam curritur iacet praemium corona. Sed beatitudinem esse id ipsum bonum propter quod omnia geruntur ostendimus; est igitur humanis actibus ipsum bonum ueluti praemium commune propositum. Atqui hoc a bonis non potest separari — Neque enim bonus ultra iure uocabitur, qui careat bono — Quare probos mores sua praemia non relinquunt. Quantumlibet igitur saeuiant mali, sapienti tamen corona non decidet, non arescet; neque enim probis animis proprium decus aliena decerpit improbitas. Quodsi extrinsecus accepto laetaretur, poterat hoc uel alius quispiam uel ipse etiam qui contulisset auferre; sed quoniam id sua cuique probitas confert, tum suo praemio carebit cum probus esse desierit. Postremo, cum omne praemium idcirco appetatur bonum esse creditur, quis boni compotem praemii iudicet expertem? At cuius praemii? Omnium pulcherrimi maximi que; memento etenim corollarii illius quod paulo ante praecipuum dedi ac sic collige. Cum ipsum bonum beatitudo sit, bonos omnes eo ipso quod boni sint fieri beatos liquet. Sed qui beati sint deos esse conuenit. Est igitur praemium bonorum, quod nullus deterat dies, nullius minuat potestas, nullius fuscet improbitas, deos fieri. Quae cum ita sint, de malorum quoque inseparabili poena dubitare sapiens nequeat; nam cum bonum malum que, item poenae atque praemium aduersa fronte dissideant, quae in boni praemio uidemus accedere eadem necesse est in mali poena contraria parte respondeant. Sicut igitur probis probitas ipsa fit praemium ita improbis nequitia ipsa supplicium est. Iam uero quisquis afficitur poena malo se affectum esse non dubitat. Si igitur sese ipsi aestimare uelint, possuntne sibi supplicii expertes uideri, quos — Omnium malorum extremo — Nequitia non affecit modo, uerum etiam uehementer infecit?

Vide autem ex aduersa parte bonorum quae improbos poena comitetur; omne namque quod sit unum esse ipsumque unum bonum esse paulo ante didicisti; cui consequens est ut omne quod sit id etiam bonum esse uideatur. Hoc igitur modo quicquid a bono deficit esse desistit. Quo fit ut mali desinant esse quod fuerant. — Sed fuisse homines adhuc ipsa humani corporis reliqua species ostentat — Quare uersi in malitiam humanam quoque amisere naturam. Sed cum ultra homines quemque prouehere sola probitas possit, necesse est ut quod ab humana condicione deiecit infra homines merito detrudat improbitas; euenit igitur ut quem transformatum uitiis uideas hominem aestimare non possis. Auaritia feruet alienarum opum uiolentus ereptor: lupis similem dixeris. Ferox atque inquies linguam litigiis exercet: cani comparabis. Insidiator occultus subripuisse fraudibus gaudet: uulpeculis exaequetur. Irae intemperans fremit: leonis animum gestare credatur. Pauidus ac fugax non metuenda formidat:

no fear is, may be likened to the timid deer. He who is sunk in ignorance and stupidity lives like a dull ass. He who is light and inconstant, never holding long to one thing, is for all the world like a bird. He who wallows in foul and unclean lusts is sunk in the pleasures of a filthy hog. So it comes to pass that he who by forsaking righteousness ceases to be a man cannot pass into a Godlike condition, but actually turns into a brute beast.'

Song III — Circe's Cup.

Th' Ithacan discreet,
And all his storm-tossed fleet,
Far o'er the ocean wave
The winds of heaven drave—
Drave to the mystic isle,
Where dwelleth in her guile
That fair and faithless one,
The daughter of the Sun.
There for the stranger crew
With cunning spells she knew
To mix th' enchanted cup.
For whoso drinks it up,
Must suffer hideous change
To monstrous shapes and strange.
One like a boar appears;
This his huge form uprears,
Mighty in bulk and limb—
An Afric lion—grim
With claw and fang. Confessed
A wolf, this, sore distressed
When he would weep, doth howl;
And, strangely tame, these prowl
The Indian tiger's mates.

And though in such sore straits,
The pity of the god
Who bears the mystic rod
Had power the chieftain brave
From her fell arts to save;
His comrades, unrestrained,
The fatal goblet drained.
All now with low-bent head,
Like swine, on acorns fed;
Man's speech and form were reft,
No human feature left;
But steadfast still, the mind,
Unaltered, unresigned,

ceruis similis habeatur. Segnis ac stupidus torpet: asinum uiuit. Leuis atque inconstans studia permutat: nihil auibus differt. Foedis immundisque libidinibus immergitur: sordidae suis uoluptate detinetur. Ita fit ut qui probitate deserta homo esse desierit, cum in diuinam condicionem transire non possit, uertatur in beluam.

Metrum III

Vela Neritii ducis
Et uagas pelago rates
Eurus appulit insulae,
Pulchra qua residens dea
Solis edita semine
Miscet hospitibus nouis
Tacta carmine pocula.
Quos ut in uarios modos
Vertit herbipotens manus,
Hunc apri facies tegit,
Ille Marmaricus Leo
Dente crescit et unguibus;
Hic lupis nuper additus
Flere dum parat ululat,
Ille tigris ut Indica
Tecta mitis obambulat.
Sed licet uariis malis
Numen Arcadis alitis
Obsitum miserans ducem
Peste soluerit hospitis,
Iam tamen mala remiges
Ore pocula traxerant,
Iam sues Cerealia
Glande pabula uerterant
Et nihil manet integrum
Voce, corpore perditis.
Sola mens stabilis super

The monstrous change bewailed.
How little, then, availed
The potencies of ill!
These herbs, this baneful skill,
May change each outward part,
But cannot touch the heart.
In its true home, deep-set,
Man's spirit liveth yet.
Those poisons are more fell,
More potent to expel
Man from his high estate,
Which subtly penetrate,
And leave the body whole,
But deep infect the soul.

IV.

Then said I: 'This is very true. I see that the vicious, though they keep the outward form of man, are rightly said to be changed into beasts in respect of their spiritual nature; but, inasmuch as their cruel and polluted minds vent their rage in the destruction of the good, I would this license were not permitted to them.'

'Nor is it,' said she, 'as shall be shown in the fitting place. Yet if that license which thou believest to be permitted to them were taken away, the punishment of the wicked would be in great part remitted. For verily, incredible as it may seem to some, it needs must be that the bad are more unfortunate when they have accomplished their desires than if they are unable to get them fulfilled. If it is wretched to will evil, to have been able to accomplish evil is more wretched; for without the power the wretched will would fail of effect. Accordingly, those whom thou seest to will, to be able to accomplish, and to accomplish crime, must needs be the victims of a threefold wretchedness, since each one of these states has its own measure of wretchedness.'

'Yes,' said I; 'yet I earnestly wish they might speedily be quit of this misfortune by losing the ability to accomplish crime.'

'They will lose it,' said she, 'sooner than perchance thou wishest, or they themselves think likely; since, verily, within the narrow bounds of our brief life there is nothing so late in coming that anyone, least of all an immortal spirit, should deem it long to wait for. Their great expectations, the lofty fabric of their crimes, is oft overthrown by a sudden and unlooked-for ending, and this but sets a limit to their misery. For if wickedness makes men wretched, he is necessarily more wretched who is wicked for a longer time; and were it not that death, at all events, puts an end to the evil doings of the wicked, I should account them wretched to the last degree. Indeed, if we have formed true conclusions aboutthe ill fortune of wickedness, that wretchedness is plainly infinite which is doomed to be eternal.'

Then said I: 'A wonderful inference, and difficult to grant; but I see that it agrees entirely with our previous conclusions.'

Monstra quae patitur gemit.

O leuem nimium manum

Nec potentia gramina,

Membra quae ualeant licet,

Corda uertere non ualent!

Intus est hominum uigor

Arce conditus abdita.

Haec uenena potentius

Detrahunt hominem sibi

Dira quae penitus meant

Nec nocentia corpori

Mentis uulnere saeuiunt.

Prosa IV

Tum ego: fateor, inquam, nec iniuria dici uideo uitiosos, tametsi humani corporis spe‑ ciem seruent, in beluas tamen animorum qualitate mutari; sed quorum atrox scelerataque mens bonorum pernicie saeuit, id ipsum eis licere noluissem.

Nec licet, inquit, uti conuenienti monstrabitur loco, sed tamen, si id ipsum quod eis licere creditur auferatur, magna ex parte sceleratorum hominum poena releuetur. Etenim, quod incredibile cuiquam forte uideatur, infeliciores esse necesse est malos cum cupita perfe‑ cerint quam si ea quae cupiunt implere non possint. Nam si miserum est uoluisse praua, potuisse miserius est, sine quo uoluntatis miserae langueret effectus. Itaque cum sua singulis miseria sit, triplici infortunio necesse est urgueantur quos uideas scelus uelle, posse, per‑ ficere.

Accedo, inquam, sed uti hoc infortunio cito careant patrandi sceleris possibilitate deserti uehementer exopto.

Carebunt, inquit, ocius quam uel tu forsitan uelis uel illi sese aestiment esse carituros; neque enim est aliquid in tam breuibus uitae metis ita serum quod exspectare longum immor‑ talis praesertim animus putet. Quorum magna spes et excelsa facinorum machina repentino atque insperato saepe fine destruitur. Quod quidem illis miseriae modum statuit; nam si nequitia miseros facit, miserior sit necesse est diuturnior nequam. Quos infelicissimos esse iudicarem si non eorum malitiam saltem mors extrema finiret; etenim si de prauitatis infortu‑ nio uera conclusimus, infinitam liquet esse miseriam quam esse constat aeternam.

Tum ego: mira quidem, inquam, et concessu difficilis inlatio, sed his eam quae prius con‑ cessa sunt nimium conuenire cognosco.

'Thou art right,' said she; 'but if anyone finds it hard to admit the conclusion, he ought in fairness either to prove some falsity in the premises, or to show that the combination of pro-positions does not adequately enforce the necessity of the conclusion; otherwise, if the premises be granted, nothing whatever can be said against the inference of the conclusion. And here is another statement which seems not less wonderful, but on the premises assumed is equally necessary.'

'What is that?'

'The wicked are happier in undergoing punishment than if no penalty of justice chasten them. And I am not now meaning what might occur to anyone—that bad character is amended by retribution, and is brought into the right path by the terror of punishment, or that it serves as an example to warn others to avoid transgression; but I believe that in anoth-er way the wicked are more unfortunate when they go unpunished, even though no account be taken of amendment, and no regard be paid to example.'

'Why, what other way is there beside these?' said I.

Then said she: 'Have we not agreed that the good are happy, and the evil wretched?'

'Yes,' said I.

'Now, if,' said she, 'to one in affliction there be given along with his misery some good thing, is he not happier than one whose misery is misery pure and simple without admixture of any good?'

'It would seem so.'

'But if to one thus wretched, one destitute of all good, some further evil be added be-sides those which make him wretched, is he not to be judged far more unhappy than he whose ill fortune is alleviated by some share of good?'

'It could scarcely be otherwise.'

'Surely, then, the wicked, when they are punished, have a good thing added to them—to wit, the punishment which by the law of justice is good; and likewise, when they escape punishment, a new evil attaches to them in that very freedom from punishment which thou hast rightly acknowledged to be an evil in the case of the unrighteous.'

'I cannot deny it.'

'Then, the wicked are far more unhappy when indulged with an unjust freedom from punishment than when punished by a just retribution. Now, it is manifest that it is just for the wicked to be punished, and for them to escape unpunished is unjust.'

'Why, who would venture to deny it?'

'This, too, no one can possibly deny—that all which is just is good, and, conversely, all which is unjust is bad.'

Then I answered: 'These inferences do indeed follow from what we lately concluded; but tell me,' said I, 'dost thou take no account of the punishment of the soul after the death of the body?'

'Nay, truly,' said she, 'great are these penalties, some of them inflicted, I imagine, in the severity of retribution, others in the mercy of purification. But it is not my present purpose to speak of these. ❰So far, my aim hath been to make thee recognise that the power of the bad which shocked thee so exceedingly is no power; to make thee see that those of whose

Recte, inquit, aestimas, sed qui conclusioni accedere durum putat aequum est uel falsum aliquid praecessisse demonstret uel collocationem propositionum non esse efficacem necessariae conclusionis ostendat; alioquin concessis praecedentibus nihil prorsus est quod de inlatione causetur. Nam hoc quoque quod dicam non minus mirum uideatur, sed ex his quae sumpta sunt aeque est necessarium.

Quidnam? Inquam.

Feliciores, inquit, esse improbos supplicia luentes quam si eos nulla iustitiae poena coherceat. Neque id nunc molior quod cuiuis ueniat in mentem, corrigi ultione prauos mores et ad rectum supplicii terrore deduci, ceteris quoque exemplum esse culpanda fugiendi; sed alio quodam modo infeliciores esse improbos arbitror impunitos, tametsi nulla ratio correctionis, nullus respectus habeatur exempli.

Et quis erit, inquam, praeter hos alius modus?

Et illa: bonos, inquit, esse felices, malos uero miseros nonne concessimus?

Ita est, inquam.

Si igitur, inquit, miseriae cuiuspiam bonum aliquid addatur, nonne felicior est eo cuius pura ac solitaria sine cuiusquam boni ammixtione miseria est?

Sic, inquam, uidetur.

Quid si eidem misero, qui cunctis careat bonis, praeter ea quibus miser est malum aliud fuerit adnexum, nonne multo infelicior eo censendus est cuius infortunium boni participatione releuatur?

Quidni? Inquam.

Habent igitur improbi cum puniuntur quidem boni aliquid adnexum, poenam ipsam scilicet, quae ratione iustitiae bona est, idemque cum supplicio carent inest eis aliquid ulterius mali, ipsa impunitas, quam iniquitatis merito malum esse confessus es.

Negare non possum.

Multo igitur infeliciores improbi sunt iniusta impunitate donati quam iusta ultione puniti. Sed puniri improbos iustum, impunitos uero elabi iniquum esse manifestum est.

Quis id neget?

Sed ne illud quidem, ait, quisquam negabit bonum esse quod iustum est contraque quod iniustum est malum.

Liquere respondi. Tum ego: ista quidem consequentia sunt eis quae paulo ante conclusa sunt; sed quaeso, inquam, te, nullane animarum supplicia post defunctum morte corpus relinquis?

Et magna quidem, inquit, quorum alia poenali, alia uero purgatoria clementia exerceri puto; sed nunc de his disserere consilium non est.

Id uero hactenus egimus ut quae indignissima tibi uidebatur malorum potestas eam nullam esse cognosceres, quosque impunitos querebare uideres numquam improbitatis suae

freedom from punishment thou didst complain are never without the proper penalties of their unrighteousness; to teach thee that the license which thou prayedst might soon come to an end is not long-enduring; that it would be more unhappy if it lasted longer, most unhappy of all if it lasted for ever; thereafter that the unrighteous are more wretched if unjustly let go without punishment than if punished by a just retribution—from which point of view it follows that the wicked are afflicted with more severe penalties just when they are supposed to escape punishment.'

Then said I: 'While I follow thy reasonings, I am deeply impressed with their truth; but if I turn to the common convictions of men, I find few who will even listen to such arguments, let alone admit them to be credible.'

'True,' said she; 'they cannot lift eyes accustomed to darkness to the light of clear truth, and are like those birds whose vision night illumines and day blinds; for while they regard, not the order of the universe, but their own dispositions of mind, they think the license to commit crime, and the escape from punishment, to be fortunate. But mark the ordinance of eternal law. Hast thou fashioned thy soul to the likeness of the better, thou hast no need of a judge to award the prize—by thine own act hast thou raised thyself in the scale of excellence; hast thou perverted thy affections to baser things, look not for punishment from one without thee—thine own act hath degraded thee, and thrust thee down. Even so, if alternately thou turn thy gaze upon the vile earth and upon the heavens, though all without thee stand still, by the mere laws of sight thou seemest now sunk in the mire, now soaring among the stars. But the common herd regards not these things. What, then? Shall we go over to those whom we have shown to be like brute beasts? Why, suppose, now, one who had quite lost his sight should likewise forget that he had ever possessed the faculty of vision, and should imagine that nothing was wanting in him to human perfection, should we deem those who saw as well as ever blind? Why, they will not even assent to this, either—that they who do wrong are more wretched than those who suffer wrong, though the proof of this rests on grounds of reason no less strong.'

'Let me hear these same reasons,' said I.

'Wouldst thou deny that every wicked man deserves punishment?'

'I would not, certainly.'

'And that those who are wicked are unhappy is clear in manifold ways?'

'Yes,' I replied.

'Thou dost not doubt, then, that those who deserve punishment are wretched?'

'Agreed,' said I.

'So, then, if thou wert sitting in judgment, on whom wouldst thou decree the infliction of punishment—on him who had done the wrong, or on him who had suffered it?'

'Without doubt, I would compensate the sufferer at the cost of the doer of the wrong.'

'Then, the injurer would seem more wretched than the injured?'

'Yes; it follows. And so for this and other reasons resting on the same ground, inasmuch as baseness of its own nature makes men wretched, it is plain that a wrong involves the misery of the doer, not of the sufferer.'

carere suppliciis, licentiam quam cito finiri precabaris nec longam esse disceres infeliciorem-que fore si diuturnior, infelicissimam uero si esset aeterna; post haec miseriores esse impro-bos iniusta impunitate dimissos quam iusta ultione punitos. Cui sententiae consequens est ut tum demum grauioribus suppliciis urgueantur cum impuniti esse creduntur.

Tum ego: cum tuas, inquam, rationes considero, nihil dici uerius puto; at si ad hominum iudicia reuertar, quis ille est cui haec non credenda modo sed saltem audienda uideantur?

Ita est, inquit illa. Nequeunt enim oculos tenebris assuetos ad lucem perspicuae ueritatis attollere similesque auibus sunt quarum intuitum nox inluminat, dies caecat; dum enim non rerum ordinem sed suos intuentur affectus, uel licentiam uel impunitatem scelerum putant esse felicem.

Vide autem quid aeterna lex sanciat. Melioribus animum conformaueris: nihil opus est iudice praemium deferente, tu te ipse excellentioribus addidisti;studium ad peiora deflexer-is: extra ne quaesieris ultorem, tu te ipse in deteriora trusisti ueluti, si uicibus sordidam hu-mum caelumque respicias, cunctis extra cessantibus ipsa cernendi ratione nunc caeno nunc sideribus interesse uidearis. At uulgus ista non respicit. Quid igitur, hisne accedamus quos beluis similes esse monstrauimus? Quid, si quis amisso penitus uisu ipsum etiam se habuisse obliuisceretur intuitum nihilque sibi ad humanam perfectionem deesse arbitraretur, num uidentes eadem caeco putaremus? Nam ne illud quidem adquiescent quod aeque ualidis ra-tionum nititur firmamentis, infeliciores eos esse qui faciant quam qui patiantur iniuriam.

Vellem, inquam, has ipsas audire rationes.

Omnem, inquit, improbum num supplicio dignum negas?

Minime.

Infelices uero esse qui sint improbi multipliciter liquet.

Ita, inquam.

Qui igitur supplicio digni sunt miseros esse non dubitas.

Conuenit, inquam.

Si igitur cognitor, ait, resideres, cui supplicium inferendum putares, eine qui fecisset an qui pertulisset iniuriam?

Nec ambigo, inquam, quin perpesso satisfacerem dolore facientis.

Miserior igitur tibi iniuriae inlator quam acceptor esse uiderentur.

Consequitur, inquam. Hac igitur aliisque causis ea radice nitentibus quod turpitudo suapte natura miseros faciat apparet inlatam cuilibet iniuriam non accipientis sed inferentis esse miseriam.

'And yet,' says she, 'the practice of the law-courts is just the opposite: advocates try to arouse the commiseration of the judges for those who have endured some grievous and cruel wrong; whereas pity is rather due to the criminal, who ought to be brought to the judgment-seat by his accusers in a spirit not of anger, but of compassion and kindness, as a sick man to the physician, to have the ulcer of his fault cut away by punishment. Whereby the business of the advocate would either wholly come to a standstill, or, did men prefer to make it service-able to mankind, would be restricted to the practice of accusation. The wicked themselves also, if through some chink or cranny they were permitted to behold the virtue they have for-saken, and were to see that by the pains of punishment they would rid themselves of the un-cleanness of their vices, and win in exchange the recompense of righteousness, they would no longer think these sufferings pains; they would refuse the help of advocates, and would commit themselves wholly into the hands of their accusers and judges. Whence it comes to pass that for the wise no place is left for hatred; ⟨only the most foolish would hate the good, ⟨and to hate the bad is unreasonable. For if vicious propensity is, as it were, a disease of the soul like bodily sickness, even as we account the sick in body by no means deserving of hate, but rather of pity, so, and much more, should they be pitied whose minds are assailed by wickedness, which is more frightful than any sickness.'

Song IV — *The Unreasonableness of Hatred.*

Why all this furious strife? Oh, why
With rash and wilful hand provoke death's destined day?
If death ye seek—lo! Death is nigh,
Not of their master's will those coursers swift delay!
The wild beasts vent on man their rage,
Yet 'gainst their brothers' lives men point the murderous steel;
Unjust and cruel wars they wage,
And haste with flying darts the death to meet or deal.
No right nor reason can they show;
'Tis but because their lands and laws are not the same.
Wouldst thou give each his due; then know
Thy love the good must have, the bad thy pity claim.

V.

On this I said: 'I see how there is a happiness and misery founded on the actual deserts of the righteous and the wicked. Nevertheless, I wonder in myself whether there is not some good and evil in fortune as the vulgar understand it. Surely, no sensible man would rather be exiled, poor and disgraced, than dwell prosperously in his own country, powerful, wealthy, and high in honour. Indeed, the work of wisdom is more clear and manifest in its operation when the happiness of rulers is somehow passed on to the people around them, especially considering that the prison, the law, and the other pains of legal punishment are properly due only to mischievous citizens on whose account they were originally instituted. Accordingly, I do exceedingly marvel why all this is completely reversed—why the good are harassed

Atqui nunc, ait, contra faciunt oratores; pro his enim qui graue quid acerbumque perpessi sunt miserationem iudicum excitare conantur, cum magis admittentibus iustior miseratio debeatur; quos ab iratis sed a propitiis potius miserantibusque accusatoribus ad iudicium ueluti aegros ad medicum duci oportebat ut culpae morbos supplicio resecarent. Quo pacto defensorum opera uel tota frigeret uel si prodesse hominibus mallet in accusationis habitum uerteretur. Ipsi quoque improbi, si eis aliqua rimula uirtutem relictam fas esset aspicere uitiorumque sordes poenarum cruciatibus se deposituros uiderent, compensatione adipiscendae probitatis nec hos cruciatus esse ducerent defensorumque operam repudiarent ac se totos accusatoribus iudicibusque permitterent. Quo fit ut apud sapientes nullus prorsus odio locus relinquatur,

Nam bonos quis nisi stultissimus oderit?

Malos uero odisse ratione caret. Nam si uti corporum languor ita uitiositas quidam est quasi morbus animorum, cum aegros corpore minime dignos odio sed potius miseratione iudicemus, multo magis non insequendi sed miserandi sunt quorum mentes omni languore atrocior urguet improbitas.

Metrum IV

Quid tantos iuuat excitare motus
Et propria fatum sollicitare manu?
Si mortem petitis, propinquat ipsa
Sponte sua uolucres nec remoratur equos.
Quos serpens, leo, tigris, ursus, aper
Dente petunt idem se tamen ense petunt.
An distant quia dissidentque mores,
Iniustas acies et fera bella mouent
Alternisque uolunt perire telis?
Non est iusta satis saeuitiae ratio.
Vis aptam meritis uicem referre:
Dilige iure bonos et miseresce malis.

Prosa V

Hic ego: uideo, inquam, quae sit uel felicitas uel miseria in ipsis proborum atque improborum meritis constituta. Sed in hac ipsa fortuna populari non nihil boni maliue inesse perpendo; neque enim sapientum quisquam exsul inops ignominiosusque esse malit potius quam pollens opibus, honore reuerendus, potentia ualidus in sua permanens urbe florere. Sic enim clarius testatiusque sapientiae tractatur officium, cum in contingentes populos regentium quodam modo beatitudo transfunditur, cum praesertim carcer, nex ceteraque legalium tormenta poenarum perniciosis potius ciuibus, propter quos etiam constitutae sunt, debeantur. Cur haec igitur uersa uice mutentur scelerumque supplicia bonos premant, praemia uirtutum

with the penalties due to crime, and the bad carry off the rewards of virtue; and I long to hear from thee what reason may be found for so unjust a state of disorder. For assuredly I should wonder less if I could believe that all things are the confused result of chance. But now my belief in God's governance doth add amazement to amazement. For, seeing that He sometimes assigns fair fortune to the good and harsh fortune to the bad, and then again deals harshly with the good, and grants to the bad their hearts' desire, how does this differ from chance, unless some reason is discovered for it all?'

'Nay; it is not wonderful,' said she, 'if all should be thought random and confused when the principle of order is not known. And though thou knowest not the causes on which this great system depends, yet forasmuch as a good ruler governs the world, doubt not for thy part that all is rightly done.'

Song V — Wonder and Ignorance.

Who knoweth not how near the pole
Bootes' course doth go,
Must marvel by what heavenly law
He moves his Wain so slow;
Why late he plunges 'neath the main,
And swiftly lights his beams again.
When the full-orbèd moon grows pale
In the mid course of night,
And suddenly the stars shine forth
That languished in her light,
Th' astonied nations stand at gaze,
And beat the air in wild amaze.[3]
None marvels why upon the shore
The storm-lashed breakers beat,
Nor why the frost-bound glaciers melt
At summer's fervent heat;
For here the cause seems plain and clear,
Only what's dark and hid we fear.
Weak-minded folly magnifies
All that is rare and strange,
And the dull herd's o'erwhelmed with awe
At unexpected change.
But wonder leaves enlightened minds,
When ignorance no longer blinds.

---

3   To frighten away the monster swallowing the moon. The superstition was once common. See Tylor's 'Primitive Culture,' pp. 296—302.

mali rapiant, uehementer ammiror, quaeque tam iniustae confusionis ratio uideatur ex te scire desidero. Minus etenim mirarer si misceri omnia fortuitis casibus crederem. Nunc stuporem meum deus rector exaggerat. Qui cum saepe bonis iucunda, malis aspera contraque bonis dura tribuat, malis optata concedat, nisi causa deprehenditur, quid est quod a fortuitis casibus differre uideatur?

Nec mirum, si quid ordinis ignorata ratione temerarium confusumque credatur; sed tu quamuis causam tantae dispositionis ignores, tamen, quoniam bonus mundum rector temperat, recte fieri cuncta ne dubites.

Metrum V

Si quis Arcturi sidera nescit
Propinqua summo cardine labi,
Cur regat tardus plaustra Bootes
Mergatque seras aequore flammas,
Cum nimis celeres explicet ortus,
Legem stupebit aetheris alti.
Palleant plenae cornua lunae
Infecta metis noctis opacae,
Quaeque fulgenti texerat ore,
Confusa Phoebe detegat astra:
Commouet gentes publicus error
Lassantque crebris pulsibus aera.
Nemo miratur flamina Cori
Litus frementi tundere fluctu
Nec niuis duram frigore molem
Feruente Phoebi soluier aestu.
Hic enim causas cernere promptum est,
Illic latentes pectora turbant.
Cuncta quae rara prouehit aetas
Stupetque subitis mobile uulgus;
Cedat inscitiae nubilus error,
Cessent profecto mira uideri!

VI.

'True,' said I; 'but, since it is thy office to unfold the hidden cause of things, and explain principles veiled in darkness, inform me, I pray thee, of thine own conclusions in this matter, since the marvel of it is what more than aught else disturbs my mind.'

A smile played one moment upon her lips as she replied: 'Thou callest me to the greatest of all subjects of inquiry, a task for which the most exhaustive treatment barely suffices. Such is its nature that, as fast as one doubt is cut away, innumerable others spring up like Hydra's heads, nor could we set any limit to their renewal did we not apply the mind's living fire to suppress them. For there come within its scope the questions of the essential simplicity of providence, of the order of fate, of unforeseen chance, of the Divine knowledge and predestination, and of the freedom of the will. How heavy is the weight of all this thou canst judge for thyself. But, inasmuch as to know these things also is part of the treatment of thy malady, we will try to give them some consideration, despite the restrictions of the narrow limits of our time. Moreover, thou must for a time dispense with the pleasures of music and song, if so be that thou findest any delight therein, whilst I weave together the connected train of reasons in proper order.'

'As thou wilt,' said I.

Then, as if making a new beginning, she thus discoursed: 'The coming into being of all things, the whole course of development in things that change, every sort of thing that moves in any wise, receives its due cause, order, and form from the steadfastness of the Divine mind. This mind, calm in the citadel of its own essential simplicity, has decreed that the method of its rule shall be manifold. Viewed in the very purity of the Divine intelligence, this method is called providence; but viewed in regard to those things which it moves and disposes, it is what the ancients called fate. That these two are different will easily be clear to anyone who passes in review their respective efficacies. Providence is the Divine reason itself, seated in the Supreme Being, which disposes all things; fate is the disposition inherent in all things which move, through which providence joins all things in their proper order. Providence embraces all things, however different, however infinite; fate sets in motion separately individual things, and assigns to them severally their position, form, and time.

'So the unfolding of this temporal order unified into the foreview of the Divine mind is providence, while the same unity broken up and unfolded in time is fate. And although these are different, yet is there a dependence between them; for the order of destiny issues from the essential simplicity of providence. For as the artificer, forming in his mind beforehand the idea of the thing to be made, carries out his design, and develops from moment to moment what he had before seen in a single instant as a whole, so God in His providence ordains all things as parts of a single unchanging whole, but carries out these very ordinances by fate in a time of manifold unity. So whether fate is accomplished by Divine spirits as the ministers of providence, or by a soul, or by the service of all nature—whether by the celestial motion of the stars, by the efficacy of angels, or by the many-sided cunning of demons—whether by all or by some of these the destined series is woven, this, at least, is manifest: that providence is the fixed and simple form of destined events, fate their shifting series in order of time, as by the disposal of the Divine simplicity they are to take place. ⸿ Whereby it is that all things which are under fate are subjected also to providence, on which fate itself is dependent;

Prosa VI

Ita est, inquam; sed cum tui muneris sit latentium rerum causas euoluere uelatasque cali-gine explicare rationes, quaeso uti quae hinc decernas, quoniam hoc me miraculum maxime perturbat, edisseras.

Tum illa paulisper arridens: ad rem me, inquit, omnium quaesitu maximam uocas, cui uix exhausti quicquam satis sit. Talis namque materia est ut una dubitatione succisa innumer-abiles aliae uelut hydrae capita succrescant; nec ullus fuerit modus nisi quis eas uiuacissimo mentis igne coherceat. In hac enim de prouidentiae simplicitate, de fati serie, de repentinis casibus, de cognitione ac praedestinatione diuina, de arbitrii libertate quaeri solet, quae quanti oneris sint ipse perpendis. Sed quoniam haec quoque te nosse quaedam medicinae tuae portio est, quamquam angusto limite temporis saepti tamen aliquid deliberare con-abimur. Quodsi te musici carminis oblectamenta delectant, hanc oportet paulisper differas uoluptatem dum nexas sibi ordine contexo rationes.

Vt libet, inquam.

Tunc uelut ab alio orsa principio ita disseruit: omnium generatio rerum cunctusque mut-abilium naturarum progressus et quicquid aliquo mouetur modo causas, ordinem, formas ex diuinae mentis stabilitate sortitur. Haec in suae simplicitatis arce composita multiplicem re-bus gerendis modum statuit. Qui modus cum in ipsa diuinae intellegentiae puritate conspi-citur, prouidentia nominatur; cum uero ad ea quae mouet atque disponit refertur, fatum a ueteribus appellatum est. Quae diuersa esse facile liquebit si quis utriusque uim mente con-spexerit; nam prouidentia est ipsa illa diuina ratio in summo omnium principe constituta quae cuncta disponit, fatum uero inhaerens rebus mobilibus dispositio per quam prouidentia suis quaeque nectit ordinibus. Prouidentia namque cuncta pariter quamuis diuersa quamuis infinita complectitur, fatum uero singula digerit in motum locis, formis ac temporibus distributa.

Vt haec temporalis ordinis explicatio in diuinae mentis adunata prospectum prouidentia sit, eadem uero adunatio digesta atque explicata temporibus fatum uocetur. Quae licet di-uersa sint, alterum tamen pendet ex altero; ordo namque fatalis ex prouidentiae simplicitate procedit. Sicut enim artifex faciendae rei formam mente praecipiens mouet operis effectum et quod simpliciter praesentarieque prospexerat per temporales ordines ducit, ita deus prouidentia quidem singulariter stabiliterque facienda disponit, fato uero haec ipsa quae dis-posuit multipliciter ac temporaliter amministrat. Siue igitur famulantibus quibusdam prouidentiae diuinis spiritibus fatum exercetur seu anima seu tota inseruiente natura seu cae-lestibus siderum motibus seu angelica uirtute seu daemonum uaria sollertia seu aliquibus hor-um seu omnibus fatalis series texitur, illud certe manifestum est immobilem simplicemque gerendarum formam rerum esse prouidentiam, fatum uero eorum quae diuina simplicitas ger-enda disposuit mobilem nexum atque ordinem temporalem.

Quo fit ut omnia quae fato subsunt prouidentiae quoque subiecta sint, cui ipsum etiam subiacet fatum, quaedam uero quae sub prouidentia locata sunt fati seriem superent; ea uero

whereas certain things which are set under providence are above the chain of fate—viz., those things which by their nearness to the primal Divinity are steadfastly fixed, and lie outside the order of fate's movements. For as the innermost of several circles revolving round the same centre approaches the simplicity of the midmost point, and is, as it were, a pivot round which the exterior circles turn, while the outermost, whirled in ampler orbit, takes in a wider and wider sweep of space in proportion to its departure from the indivisible unity of the centre—while, further, whatever joins and allies itself to the centre is narrowed to a like simplicity, and no longer expands vaguely into space—even so whatsoever departs widely from primal mind is involved more deeply in the meshes of fate, and things are free from fate in proportion as they seek to come nearer to that central pivot; while if aught cleaves close to supreme mind in its absolute fixity, this, too, being free from movement, rises above fate's necessity. Therefore, as is reasoning to pure intelligence, as that which is generated to that which is, time to eternity, a circle to its centre, so is the shifting series of fate to the steadfastness and simplicity of providence.

'It is this causal series which moves heaven and the stars, attempers the elements to mutual accord, and again in turn transforms them into new combinations; this which renews the series of all things that are born and die through like successions of germ and birth; it is its operation which binds the destinies of men by an indissoluble nexus of causality, and, since it issues in the beginning from unalterable providence, these destinies also must of necessity be immutable. Accordingly, the world is ruled for the best if this unity abiding in the Divine mind puts forth an inflexible order of causes. And this order, by its intrinsic immutability, restricts things mutable which otherwise would ebb and flow at random. ℂAnd so it happens that, although to you, who are not altogether capable of understanding this order, all things seem confused and disordered, nevertheless there is everywhere an appointed limit which guides all things to good. Verily, nothing can be done for the sake of evil even by the wicked themselves; for, as we abundantly proved, they seek good, but are drawn out of the way by perverse error; far less can this order which sets out from the supreme centre of good turn aside anywhither from the way in which it began.

'"Yet what confusion," thou wilt say, "can be more unrighteous than that prosperity and adversity should indifferently befall the good, what they like and what they loathe come alternately to the bad!" Yes; but have men in real life such soundness of mind that their judgments of righteousness and wickedness must necessarily correspond with facts? Why, on this very point their verdicts conflict, and those whom some deem worthy of reward, others deem worthy of punishment. ℂYet granted there were one who could rightly distinguish the good and bad, yet would he be able to look into the soul's inmost constitution, as it were, if we may borrow an expression used of the body? The marvel here is not unlike that which astonishes one who does not know why in health sweet things suit some constitutions, and bitter others, or why some sick men are best alleviated by mild remedies, others by severe. But the physician who distinguishes the precise conditions and characteristics of health and sickness does not marvel. Now, the health of the soul is nothing but righteousness, and vice is its sickness. God, the guide and physician of the mind, it is who preserves the good and banishes the bad. And He looks forth from the lofty watch-tower of His providence, perceives what is suited to each, and assigns what He knows to be suitable.

sunt quae primae propinqua diuinitati stabiliter fixa fatalis ordinem mobilitatis excedunt. Nam ut orbium circa eundem cardinem sese uertentium qui est intimus ad simplicitatem medietatis accedit ceterorumque extra locatorum ueluti cardo quidam circa quem uersentur exsistit, extimus uero maiore ambitu rotatus quanto a puncti media indiuiduitate discedit tanto amplioribus spatiis explicatur, si quid uero illi se medio conectat et societ in simplicitatem cogitur diffundique ac diffluere cessat: simili ratione quod longius a prima mente discedit maioribus fati nexibus implicatur ac tanto aliquid fato liberum est quanto illum rerum cardinem uicinius petit. Quodsi supernae mentis haeserit firmitati, motu carens fati quoque supergreditur necessitatem. Igitur uti est ad intellectum ratiocinatio, ad id quod est id quod gignitur, ad aeternitatem tempus, ad punctum medium circulus, ita est fati series mobilis ad prouidentiae stabilem simplicitatem.

Ea series caelum ac sidera mouet, elementa in se inuicem temperat et alterna commutatione transformat, eadem nascentia occidentiaque omnia per similes fetuum seminumque renouat progressus. Haec actus etiam fortunasque hominum indissolubili causarum conexione constringit; quae cum ab immobilis prouidentiae proficiscatur exordiis, ipsas quoque immutabiles esse necesse est. Ita enim res optime reguntur si manens in diuina mente simplicitas indeclinabilem causarum ordinem promat, hic uero ordo res mutabiles et alioquin temere fluituras propria incommutabilitate coërceat.

Quo fit ut, tametsi uobis hunc ordinem minime considerare ualentibus confusa omnia perturbataque uideantur, nihilo minus tamen suus modus ad bonum dirigens cuncta disponat. Nihil est enim quod mali causa ne ab ipsis quidem improbis fiat; quos, ut uberrime demonstratum est, bonum quaerentes prauus error auertit, nedum ordo de summi boni cardine proficiens a suo quoquam deflectat exordio.

Quae uero, inquies, potest ulla iniquior esse confusio quam ut bonis tum aduersa tum prospera, malis etiam tum optata tum odiosa contingant? Num igitur ea mentis integritate homines degunt ut quos probos improbosue censuerunt eos quoque uti existimant esse necesse sit? Atqui in hoc hominum iudicia depugnant et quos alii praemio alii supplicio dignos arbitrantur.

Sed concedamus ut aliquis possit bonos malosque discernere; num igitur poterit intueri illam intimam temperiem, uelut in corporibus dici solet, animorum? Non enim dissimile est miraculum nescienti cur sanis corporibus his quidem dulcia illis uero amara conueniant, cur aegri etiam quidam lenibus quidam uero acribus adiuuantur. At hoc medicus, qui sanitatis ipsius atque aegritudinis modum temperamentumque dinoscit, minime miratur. Quid uero aliud animorum salus uidetur esse quam probitas, quid aegritudo quam uitia? Quis autem alius uel seruator bonorum uel malorum depulsor quam rector ac medicator mentium Deus? Qui cum ex alta prouidentiae specula respexit, quid unicuique conueniat agnoscit et quod conuenire nouit accommodat.

'This, then, is what that extraordinary mystery of the order of destiny comes to—that something is done by one who knows, whereat the ignorant are astonished. ⟨But let us consider a few instances whereby appears what is the competency of human reason to fathom the Divine unsearchableness. Here is one whom thou deemest the perfection of justice and scrupulous integrity; to all-knowing Providence it seems far otherwise. We all know our Lucan's admonition that it was the winning cause that found favour with the gods, the beaten cause with Cato. So, shouldst thou see anything in this world happening differently from thy expectation, doubt not but events are rightly ordered; it is in thy judgment that there is perverse confusion.

'Grant, however, there be somewhere found one of so happy a character that God and man alike agree in their judgments about him; yet is he somewhat infirm in strength of mind. It may be, if he fall into adversity, he will cease to practise that innocency which has failed to secure his fortune. Therefore, God's wise dispensation spares him whom adversity might make worse, will not let him suffer who is ill fitted for endurance. Another there is perfect in all virtue, so holy and nigh to God that providence judges it unlawful that aught untoward should befall him; nay, doth not even permit him to be afflicted with bodily disease. As one more excellent than I[4] hath said:

'"The very body of the holy saint Is built of purest ether."

Often it happens that the governance is given to the good that a restraint may be put upon superfluity of wickedness. To others providence assigns some mixed lot suited to their spiritual nature; some it will plague lest they grow rank through long prosperity; others it will suffer to be vexed with sore afflictions to confirm their virtues by the exercise and practice of patience. Some fear overmuch what they have strength to bear; others despise overmuch that to which their strength is unequal. All these it brings to the test of their true self through misfortune. Some also have bought a name revered to future ages at the price of a glorious death; some by invincible constancy under their sufferings have afforded an example to others that virtue cannot be overcome by calamity—all which things, without doubt, come to pass rightly and in due order, and to the benefit of those to whom they are seen to happen.

'As to the other side of the marvel, that the bad now meet with affliction, now get their hearts' desire, this, too, springs from the same causes. As to the afflictions, of course no one marvels, because all hold the wicked to be ill deserving. The truth is, their punishments both frighten others from crime, and amend those on whom they are inflicted; while their prosperity is a powerful sermon to the good, what judgments they ought to pass on good fortune of this kind, which often attends the wicked so assiduously.

'There is another object which may, I believe, be attained in such cases: there is one, perhaps, whose nature is so reckless and violent that poverty would drive him more desperately into crime. His disorder providence relieves by allowing him to amass money. Such a one, in the uneasiness of a conscience stained with guilt, while he contrasts his character with his fortune, perchance grows alarmed lest he should come to mourn the loss of that whose possession is so pleasant to him. He will, then, reform his ways, and through the fear of losing his fortune he forsakes his iniquity. Some, through a prosperity unworthily borne,

---

4   Parmenides. Boethius seems to forget for the moment that Philosophy is speaking.

Hic iam fit illud fatalis ordinis insigne miraculum, cum ab sciente geritur quod stupeant ignorantes.

Nam ut pauca, quae ratio ualet humana, de diuina profunditate perstringam, de hoc quem tu iustissimum et aequi seruantissimum putas omnia scienti prouidentiae diuersum uidetur. Et uictricem quidem causam dis, uictam uero Catoni placuisse familiaris noster Lucanus ammonuit. Hic igitur quicquid citra spem uideas geri rebus quidem rectus ordo est, opinioni uero tuae peruersa confusio. ⟨Sed sit aliquis ita bene moratus ut de eo diuinum iudicium pariter humanumque consentiat, sed est animi uiribus infirmus, cui si quid eueniat aduersi desinet colere forsitan innocentiam per quam non potuit retinere fortunam. Parcit itaque sapiens dispensatio ei quem deteriorem facere possit aduersitas, ne cui non conuenit laborare patiatur. Est alius cunctis uirtutibus absolutus sanctusque ac deo proximus: hunc contingi quibuslibet aduersis nefas prouidentia iudicat adeo ut ne corporeis quidem morbis agitari sinat. Nam ut quidam me quoque excellentior:

Ἀνδρὸς ἱεροῦ σῶμα δεμάς οἰκοδομοῦσι.[7]

Fit autem saepe uti bonis summa rerum regenda deferatur ut exuberans retundatur improbitas. Aliis mixta quaedam pro animorum qualitate distribuit: quosdam ... Remordet ne longa felicitate luxurient, alios duris [sinit] agitari ut uirtutes animi patientiae usu atque exercitatione confirment. Alii plus aequo metuunt quod ferre possunt, alii plus aequo despiciunt quod ferre non possunt; hos in experimentum sui tristibus ducit. Nonnulli uenerandum saeculis nomen gloriosae pretio mortis emerunt, quidem suppliciis inexpugnabiles exemplum ceteris praetulerunt inuictam malis esse uirtutem; quae quam recte atque disposite et ex eorum bono quibus accedere uidentur fiant nulla dubitatio est.

Nam illud quoque, quod improbis nunc tristia nunc optata proueniunt, ex eisdem ducitur causis. Ac de tristibus quidem nemo miratur, quod eos male meritos omnes existimant; quorum quidem supplicia tum ceteros ab sceleribus deterrent tum ipsos quibus inuehuntur emendant. Laeta uero magnum bonis argumentum loquuntur, quid de huius modi felicitate debeant iudicare quam famulari saepe improbis cernant.

In qua re illud etiam dispensari credo quod est forsitan alicuius tam praeceps atque importuna natura ut eum in scelera potius exacerbare possit rei familiaris inopia; huius morbo prouidentia collatae pecuniae remedio medetur. Hic foedatam probris conscientiam spectans et se cum fortuna sua comparans forsitan pertimescit ne cuius ei iucundus usus est sit tristis amissio; mutabit igitur mores ac dum fortunam metuit amittere nequitiam derelinquit. Alios in cladem meritam praecipitauit indigne acta felicitas; quibusdam permissum puniendi ius ut

---

7   Hominis sacri corpus faciunt ut vivat.

have been hurled headlong to ruin; to some the power of the sword has been committed, to the end that the good may be tried by discipline, and the bad punished. For while there can be no peace between the righteous and the wicked, neither can the wicked agree among themselves. How should they, when each is at variance with himself, because his vices rend his conscience, and ofttimes they do things which, when they are done, they judge ought not to have been done. Hence it is that this supreme providence brings to pass this notable marvel—that the bad make the bad good. For some, when they see the injustice which they themselves suffer at the hands of evil-doers, are inflamed with detestation of the offenders, and, in the endeavour to be unlike those whom they hate, return to the ways of virtue. It is the Divine power alone to which things evil are also good, in that, by putting them to suitable use, it bringeth them in the end to some good issue. For order in some way or other embraceth all things, so that even that which has departed from the appointed laws of the order, nevertheless falleth within an order, though another order, that nothing in the realm of providence may be left to haphazard. But

'"Hard were the task, as a god, to recount all, nothing omitting."'

Nor, truly, is it lawful for man to compass in thought all the mechanism of the Divine work, or set it forth in speech. Let us be content to have apprehended this only—that God, the creator of universal nature, likewise disposeth all things, and guides them to good; and while He studies to preserve in likeness to Himself all that He has created, He banishes all evil from the borders of His commonweal through the links of fatal necessity. Whereby it comes to pass that, if thou look to disposing providence, thou wilt nowhere find the evils which are believed so to abound on earth.

'But I see thou hast long been burdened with the weight of the subject, and fatigued with the prolixity of the argument, and now lookest for some refreshment of sweet poesy. Listen, then, and may the draught so restore thee that thou wilt bend thy mind more resolutely to what remains.'

Song VI – The Universal Aim.

Wouldst thou with unclouded mind
View the laws by God designed,
Lift thy steadfast gaze on high
To the starry canopy;
See in rightful league of love
All the constellations move.
Fiery Sol, in full career,
Ne'er obstructs cold Phoebe's sphere;
When the Bear, at heaven's height,
Wheels his coursers' rapid flight,
Though he sees the starry train
Sinking in the western main,
He repines not, nor desires
In the flood to quench his fires.

exercitii bonis et malis esset causa supplicii. Nam ut probis atque improbis nullum foedus est ita ipsi inter se improbi nequeunt conuenire. Quidni, cum a semet ipsis discerpentibus conscientiam uitiis quisque dissentiat faciantque saepe quae cum gesserint non fuisse gerenda decernant? Ex quo saepe summa illa prouidentia protulit insigne miraculum, ut malos mali bonos facerent. Nam dum iniqua sibi a pessimis quidam perpeti uidentur, noxiorum odio flagrantes ad uirtutis frugem rediere, dum se eis dissimiles student esse quos oderant. Sola est enim diuina uis cui mala quoque bona sint, cum eis competenter utendo alicuius boni elicit effectum. Ordo enim quidam cuncta complectitur, ut quod adsignata ordinis ratione decesserit hoc licet in alium, tamen ordinem relabatur, ne quid in regno prouidentiae liceat temeritati.

Ἀργαλέον δ' ἐμὲ ταῦτα θεὸν ὡς πάντ' ἀγορεύειν.[8]

Neque enim fas est homini cunctas diuinae operae machinas uel ingenio comprehendere uel explicare sermone. Hoc tantum perspexisse sufficiat quod naturarum omnium proditor Deus idem ad bonum dirigens cuncta disponat, dumque ea quae protulit in sui similitudinem retinere festinat, malum omne de rei publicae suae terminis per fatalis seriem necessitatis eliminet. Quo fit ut quae in terris abundare creduntur, si disponentem prouidentiam spectes, nihil usquam mali esse perpendas.

Sed uideo te iam dudum et pondere quaestionis oneratum et rationis prolixitate fatigatum aliquam carminis exspectare dulcedinem; accipe igitur haustum quo refectus firmior in ulteriora contendas.

Metrum VI

Si uis celsi iura Tonantis
Pura sollers cernere mente,
Aspice summi culmina caeli;
Illic iusto foedere rerum
Veterem seruant sidera pacem.
Non sol rutilo concitus igne
Gelidum Phoebes impedit axem
Nec quae summo uertice mundi
Flectit rapidos Vrsa meatus
Numquam occiduo lota profundo
Cetera cernens sidera mergi
Cupit Oceano tinguere flammas;

---

8 Difficile autem mihi tamquam deo omnia narrare.

In true sequence, as decreed,
Daily morn and eve succeed;
Vesper brings the shades of night,
Lucifer the morning light.
Love, in alternation due,
Still the cycle doth renew,
And discordant strife is driven
From the starry realm of heaven.
Thus, in wondrous amity,
Warring elements agree;
Hot and cold, and moist and dry,
Lay their ancient quarrel by;
High the flickering flame ascends,
Downward earth for ever tends.
So the year in spring's mild hours
Loads the air with scent of flowers;
Summer paints the golden grain;
Then, when autumn comes again,
Bright with fruit the orchards glow;
Winter brings the rain and snow.
Thus the seasons' fixed progression,
Tempered in a due succession,
Nourishes and brings to birth
All that lives and breathes on earth.
Then, soon run life's little day,
All it brought it takes away.
But One sits and guides the reins,
He who made and all sustains;
King and Lord and Fountain-head,
Judge most holy, Law most dread;
Now impels and now keeps back,
Holds each waverer in the track.
Else, were once the power withheld
That the circling spheres compelle
dIn their orbits to revolve,
This world's order would dissolve,
And th' harmonious whole would all
In one hideous ruin fall.
But through this connected frame
Runs one universal aim;
Towards the Good do all things tend,
Many paths, but one the end.
For naught lasts, unless it turns
Backward in its course, and yearns

Semper uicibus temporis aequis
Vesper seras nuntiat umbras
Reuehitque diem Lucifer almum.
Sic aeternos reficit cursus
Alternus amor, sic astrigeris
Bellum discors exsulat oris.
Haec concordia temperat aequis
Elementa modis, ut pugnantia
Vicibus cedant humida siccis
Iungantque fidem frigora flammis,
Pendulus ignis surgat in altum
Terraeque graues pondere sidant.
His de causis uere tepenti
Spirat florifer annus odores,
Aestas cererem feruida siccat,
Remeat pomis grauis autumnus,
Hiemem defluus inrigat imber.
Haec temperies alit ac profert
Quicquid uitam spirat in orbe;
Eadem rapiens condit et aufert
Obitu mergens orta supremo.
Sedet interea conditor altus
Rerumque regens flectit habenas,
Rex et dominus, fons et origo,
Lex et sapiens arbiter aequi,
Et quae motu concitat ire
Sistit retrahens ac uaga firmat;
Nam nisi rectos reuocans itus
Flexos iterum cogat in orbes,
Quae nunc stabilis continet ordo
Dissaepta suo fonte fatiscant.
Hic est cunctis communis amor
Repetuntque boni fine teneri,
Quia non aliter durare queant

To that Source to flow again
Whence its being first was ta'en.

VII.

'Dost thou, then, see the consequence of all that we have said?'

'Nay; what consequence?'

'That absolutely every fortune is good fortune.'

'And how can that be?' said I.

'Attend,' said she. 'Since every fortune, welcome and unwelcome alike, has for its object the reward or trial of the good, and the punishing or amending of the bad, every fortune must be good, since it is either just or useful.'

'The reasoning is exceeding true,' said I, 'the conclusion, so long as I reflect upon the providence and fate of which thou hast taught me, based on a strong foundation. Yet, with thy leave, we will count it among those which just now thou didst set down as paradoxical.'

'And why so?' said she.

'Because ordinary speech is apt to assert, and that frequently, that some men's fortune is bad.'

'Shall we, then, for awhile approach more nearly to the language of the vulgar, that we may not seem to have departed too far from the usages of men?'

'At thy good pleasure,' said I.

'That which advantageth thou callest good, dost thou not?'

'Certainly.'

'And that which either tries or amends advantageth?'

'Granted.'

'Is good, then?'

'Of course.'

'Well, this is their case who have attained virtue and wage war with adversity, or turn from vice and lay hold on the path of virtue.'

'I cannot deny it.'

'What of the good fortune which is given as reward of the good—do the vulgar adjudge it bad?'

'Anything but that; they deem it to be the best, as indeed it is.'

'What, then, of that which remains, which, though it is harsh, puts the restraint of just punishment on the bad—does popular opinion deem it good?'

'Nay; of all that can be imagined, it is accounted the most miserable.'

'Observe, then, if, in following popular opinion, we have not ended in a conclusion quite paradoxical.'

'How so?' said I.

Nisi conuerso rursus amore
Refluant causae quae dedit esse.

Prosa VII

Iamne igitur uides quid haec omnia quae diximus consequatur?

Quidnam? Inquam.

Omnem, inquit, bonam prorsus esse fortunam.

Et qui id, inquam, fieri potest?

Attende, inquit. Cum omnis fortuna uel iucunda uel aspera tum remunerandi exercendiue bonos tum puniendi corrigendiue improbos causa deferatur, omnis bona quam uel iustam constat esse uel utilem.

Nimis quidem, inquam, uera ratio et, si quam paulo ante docuisti prouidentiam fatumue considerem, firmis uiribus nixa sententia. Sed eam, si placet, inter eas quas inopinabiles paulo ante posuisti numeremus.

Qui? Inquit.

Quia id hominum sermo communis usurpat, et quidem crebro, quorundam malam esse fortunam.

Visne igitur, inquit, paulisper uulgi sermonibus accedamus ne nimium uelut ab humanitatis usu recessisse uideamur?

Vt placet, inquam.

Nonne igitur bonum censes esse quod prodest?

Ita est, inquam.

Quae uero aut exercet aut corrigit, prodest?

Fateor, inquam.

Bona igitur?

Quidni?

Sed haec eorum est qui uel in uirtute positi contra aspera bellum gerunt uel a uitiis declinantes uirtutis iter arripiunt.

Negare, inquam, nequeo.

Quid uero iucunda, quae in praemium tribuitur bonis, num uulgus malam esse decernit?

Nequaquam, uerum uti est ita quoque esse optimam censet.

Quid reliqua, quae cum sit aspera iusto supplicio malos cohercet, num bonam populus putat?

Immo omnium, inquam, quae excogitari possunt iudicat esse miserrimam.

Vide igitur ne opinionem populi sequentes quiddam ualde inopinabile confecerimus.

Quid? Inquam.

'Why, it results from our admissions that of all who have attained, or are advancing in, or are aiming at virtue, the fortune is in every case good, while for those who remain in their wickedness fortune is always utterly bad.'

'It is true,' said I; 'yet no one dare acknowledge it.'

'Wherefore,' said she, 'the wise man ought not to take it ill, if ever he is involved in one of fortune's conflicts, any more than it becomes a brave soldier to be offended when at any time the trumpet sounds for battle. The time of trial is the express opportunity for the one to win glory, for the other to perfect his wisdom. Hence, indeed, virtue gets its name, because, relying on its own efficacy, it yieldeth not to adversity. And ye who have taken your stand on virtue's steep ascent, it is not for you to be dissolved in delights or enfeebled by pleasure; ye close in conflict—yea, in conflict most sharp—with all fortune's vicissitudes, lest ye suffer foul fortune to overwhelm or fair fortune to corrupt you. Hold the mean with all your strength. Whatever falls short of this, or goes beyond, is fraught with scorn of happiness, and misses the reward of toil. It rests with you to make your fortune what you will. Verily, every harsh-seeming fortune, unless it either disciplines or amends, is punishment.'

Song VII – The Hero's Path.

Ten years a tedious warfare raged,
Ere Ilium's smoking ruins paid
For wedlock stained and faith betrayed,
And great Atrides' wrath assuaged.

But when heaven's anger asked a life,
And baffling winds his course withstood,
The king put off his fatherhood,
And slew his child with priestly knife.

When by the cavern's glimmering light
His comrades dear Odysseus saw
In the huge Cyclops' hideous maw
Engulfed, he wept the piteous sight.

But blinded soon, and wild with pain—
In bitter tears and sore annoy—
For that foul feast's unholy joy
Grim Polyphemus paid again.

His labours for Alcides win
A name of glory far and wide;
He tamed the Centaur's haughty pride,
And from the lion reft his skin.

The foul birds with sure darts he slew;
The golden fruit he stole—in vain
The dragon's watch; with triple chain
From hell's depths Cerberus he drew.

Ex his enim, ait, quae concessa sunt euenit eorum quidem qui uel sunt uel in possessione uel in prouectu uel in adeptione uirtutis omnem quaecumque sit bonam, in improbitate uero manentibus omnem pessimam esse fortunam.

Hoc, inquam, uerum est, tametsi nemo audeat confiteri.

Quare, inquit, ita uir sapiens moleste ferre non debet quotiens in fortunae certamen adducitur, ut uirum fortem non decet indignari quotiens increpuit bellicus tumultus. Vtriqueque enim huic quidem gloriae propagandae illi uero conformandae sapientiae difficultas ipsa materia est. Ex quo etiam uirtus uocatur, quod suis uiribus nitens non superetur aduersis; neque enim uos in prouectu positi uirtutis diffluere deliciis et emarcescere uoluptate uenistis. Proelium cum omni fortuna animis acre conseritis ne uos aut tristis opprimat aut iucunda corrumpat. Firmis medium uiribus occupate; quicquid aut infra subsistit aut ultra progreditur habet contemptum felicitatis, non habet praemium laboris. In uestra enim situm manu qualem uobis fortunam formare malitis; omnis enim quae uidetur aspera, nisi aut exercet aut corrigit, punit.

Metrum VII

Bella bis quinis operatus annis
Vltor Atrides Phrygiae ruinis
Fratris amissos thalamos piauit;
Ille dum Graiae dare uela classi
Optat et uentos redimit cruore,
Exuit patrem miserumque tristis
Foederat natae iugulum sacerdos.
Fleuit amissos Ithacus sodales,
Quos ferus uasto recubans in antro
Mersit immani Polyphemus aluo;
Sed tamen caeco furibundus ore
Gaudium maestis lacrimis rependit.
Herculem duri celebrant labores:
Ille Centauros domuit superbos,
Abstulit saeuo spolium leoni,
Fixit et certis uolucres sagittis,
Poma cernenti rapuit draconi
Aureo laeuam grauior metallo,
Cerberum traxit triplici catena,
Victor immitem posuisse fertur

With their fierce lord's own flesh he fed
The wild steeds; Hydra overcame
With fire. 'Neath his own waves in shame
Maimed Achelous hid his head.

Huge Cacus for his crimes was slain;
On Libya's sands Antæus hurled;
The shoulders that upheld the world
The great boar's dribbled spume did stain.

Last toil of all—his might sustained
The ball of heaven, nor did he bend
Beneath; this toil, his labour's end,
The prize of heaven's high glory gained.

Brave hearts, press on! Lo, heavenward lead
These bright examples! From the fight
Turn not your backs in coward flight;
Earth's conflict won, the stars your meed!

Pabulum saeuis dominum quadrigis,
Hydra combusto periit ueneno,
Fronte turpatus Achelous amnis
Ora demersit pudibunda ripis,
Strauit Antaeum Libycis harenis,
Cacus Euandri satiauit iras,
Quosque pressurus foret altus orbis
Saetiger spumis umeros notauit;
Vltimus caelum labor inreflexo
Sustulit collo pretiumque rursus
Vltimi caelum meruit laboris.
Ite nunc, fortes, ubi celsa magni
Ducit exempli uia. Cur inertes
Terga nudatis? Superata tellus
Sidera donat.

Book V – Free Will and God's Foreknowledge

I.

She ceased, and was about to pass on in her discourse to the exposition of other matters, when I break in and say: 'Excellent is thine exhortation, and such as well beseemeth thy high authority; but I am even now experiencing one of the many difficulties which, as thou saidst but now, beset the question of providence. I want to know whether thou deemest that there is any such thing as chance at all, and, if so, what it is.'

Then she made answer: 'I am anxious to fulfil my promise completely, and open to thee a way of return to thy native land. As for these matters, though very useful to know, they are yet a little removed from the path of our design, and I fear lest digressions should fatigue thee, and thou shouldst find thyself unequal to completing the direct journey to our goal.'

'Have no fear for that,' said I. 'It is rest to me to learn, where learning brings delight so exquisite, especially when thy argument has been built up on all sides with undoubted conviction, and no place is left for uncertainty in what follows.'

She made answer: 'I will accede to thy request;' and forthwith she thus began: 'If chance be defined as a result produced by random movement without any link of causal connection, I roundly affirm that there is no such thing as chance at all, and consider the word to be altogether without meaning, except as a symbol of the thing designated. What place can be left for random action, when God constraineth all things to order? For "ex nihilo nihil" is sound doctrine which none of the ancients gainsaid, although they used it of material substance, not of the efficient principle; this they laid down as a kind of basis for all their reasonings concerning nature. Now, if a thing arise without causes, it will appear to have arisen from nothing. But if this cannot be, neither is it possible for there to be chance in accordance with the definition just given.'

'Well,' said I, 'is there, then, nothing which can properly be called chance or accident, or is there something to which these names are appropriate, though its nature is dark to the vulgar?'

'Our good Aristotle,' says she, 'has defined it concisely in his "Physics," and closely in accordance with the truth.'

'How, pray?' said I.

'Thus,' says she: 'Whenever something is done for the sake of a particular end, and for certain reasons some other result than that designed ensues, this is called chance; for instance, if a man is digging the earth for tillage, and finds a mass of buried gold. Now, such a find is regarded as accidental; yet it is not "ex nihilo," for it has its proper causes, the

Liber Quintus

Prosa I

Dixerat orationisque cursum ad alia quaedam tractanda atque expedienda uertebat. Tum ego: recta quidem, inquam, exhortatio tuaque prorsus auctoritate dignissima, sed quod tu dudum de prouidentia quaestionem pluribus aliis implicitam esse dixisti re experior. Quaero enim an esse aliquid omnino et quidnam esse casum arbitrere.

Tum illa: festino, inquit, debitum promissionis absoluere uiamque tibi qua patriam reueharis aperire. Haec autem etsi perutilia cognitu tamen a propositi nostri tramite paulisper auersa sunt, uerendumque est ne deuiis fatigatus ad emetiendum rectum iter sufficere non possis.

Ne id, inquam, prorsus uereare; nam quietis mihi loco fuerit ea quibus maxime delector agnoscere. Simul, cum omne disputationis tuae latus indubitata fide constiterit, nihil de sequentibus ambigatur.

Tum illa: morem, inquit, geram tibi, simulque sic orsa est: si quidem, inquit, aliquis euentum temerario motu nullaque causarum conexione productum casum esse definiat, nihil omnino casum esse confirmo et praeter subiectae rei significationem inanem prorsus uocem esse decerno. Quis enim cohercente in ordinem cuncta deo locus esse ullus temeritati reliquus potest? Nam nihil ex nihilo exsistere uera sententia est, cui nemo umquam ueterum refragatus est, quamquam id illi non de operante principio sed de materiali subiecto hoc omnium de natura rationum quasi quoddam iecerint fundamentum. At si nullis ex causis aliquid oriatur, id de nihilo ortum esse uidebitur; quodsi hoc fieri nequit, ne casum quidem huius modi esse possibile est qualem paulo ante definiuimus.

Quid igitur, inquam, nihilne est quod uel casus uel fortuitum iure appellari queat? An est aliquid, tametsi uulgus lateat, cui uocabula ista conueniant?

Aristoteles meus id, inquit, in Physicis et breui et ueri propinqua ratione definiuit.

Quonam, inquam, modo?

Quotiens, ait, aliquid cuiuspiam rei gratia geritur aliudque quibusdam de causis quam quod intendebatur obtingit casus uocatur, ut si quis colendi agri causa fodiens humum defossi auri pondus inueniat. Hoc igitur fortuitu quidem creditur accidisse, uerum non de nihilo est;

unforeseen and unexpected concurrence of which has brought the chance about. For had not the cultivator been digging, had not the man who hid the money buried it in that precise spot, the gold would not have been found. These, then, are the reasons why the find is a chance one, in that it results from causes which met together and concurred, not from any intention on the part of the discoverer. Since neither he who buried the gold nor he who worked in the field intended that the money should be found, but, as I said, it happened by coincidence that one dug where the other buried the treasure. We may, then, define chance as being an unexpected result flowing from a concurrence of causes where the several factors had some definite end. But the meeting and concurrence of these causes arises from that inevitable chain of order which, flowing from the fountain-head of Providence, disposes all things in their due time and place.'

Song I – Chance.

In the rugged Persian highlands,
Where the masters of the bow
Skill to feign a flight, and, fleeing,
Hurl their darts and pierce the foe;
There the Tigris and Euphrates
At one source[5] their waters blend,
Soon to draw apart, and plainward
Each its separate way to wend.
When once more their waters mingle
In a channel deep and wide,
All the flotsam comes together
That is borne upon the tide:
Ships, and trunks of trees, uprooted
In the torrent's wild career,
Meet, as 'mid the swirling waters
Chance their random way may steer.
Yet the shelving of the channel
And the flowing water's force
Guides each movement, and determines
Every floating fragment's course.
Thus, where'er the drift of hazard
Seems most unrestrained to flow,
Chance herself is reined and bitted,
And the curb of law doth know.

---

5   This is not, of course, literally true, though the Tigris and Euphrates rise in the same mountain district.

nam proprias causas habet, quarum inprouisus inopinatusque concursus casum uidetur operatus. Nam nisi cultor agri humum foderet, nisi eo loci pecuniam suam depositor obruisset,
aurum non esset inuentum. Hae sunt igitur fortuiti causae compendii, quod ex obuiis sibi et
confluentibus causis, non ex gerentis intentione prouenit. Neque enim uel qui aurum obruit
uel qui agrum exercuit ut ea pecunia repperiretur intendit, sed, uti dixi, quo ille obruit hunc
fodisse conuenit atque concurrit. Licet igitur definire casum esse inopinatum ex confluentibus causis in his quae ob aliquid geruntur euentum. Concurrere uero atque confluere causas
facit ordo ille ineuitabili conexione procedens qui de prouidentiae fonte descendens cuncta
suis locis temporibusque disponit.

Metrum I

Rupis Achaemeniae scopulis, ubi uersa sequentum
Pectoribus figit spicula pugna fugax,
Tigris et Euphrates uno se fonte resoluunt
Et mox abiunctis dissociantur aquis.
Si coeant cursumque iterum reuocentur in unum,
Confluat alterni quod trahit unda uadi,
Conuenient puppes et uulsi flumine trunci
Mixtaque fortuitos implicet unda modos;
Quos tamen ipsa uagos terrae decliuia casus
Gurgitis et lapsi defluus ordo regit.
Sic quae permissis fluitare uidetur habenis
Fors patitur frenos ipsaque lege meat.

II.

'I am following needfully,' said I, 'and I agree that it is as thou sayest. But in this series of linked causes is there any freedom left to our will, or does the chain of fate bind also the very motions of our souls?'

'There is freedom,' said she; 'nor, indeed, can any creature be rational, unless he be endowed with free will. For that which hath the natural use of reason has the faculty of discriminative judgment, and of itself distinguishes what is to be shunned or desired. Now, everyone seeks what he judges desirable, and avoids what he thinks should be shunned. Wherefore, beings endowed with reason possess also the faculty of free choice and refusal. But I suppose this faculty not equal alike in all. The higher Divine essences possess a clear-sighted judgment, an uncorrupt will, and an effective power of accomplishing their wishes. Human souls must needs be comparatively free while they abide in the contemplation of the Divine mind, less free when they pass into bodily form, and still less, again, when they are enwrapped in earthly members. But when they are given over to vices, and fall from the possession of their proper reason, then indeed their condition is utter slavery. For when they let their gaze fall from the light of highest truth to the lower world where darkness reigns, soon ignorance blinds their vision; they are disturbed by baneful affections, by yielding and assenting to which they help to promote the slavery in which they are involved, and are in a manner led captive by reason of their very liberty. Yet He who seeth all things from eternity beholdeth these things with the eyes of His providence, and assigneth to each what is predestined for it by its merits:

'"All things surveying, all things overhearing."'

Song II – The True Sun.

Homer with mellifluous tongue
Phœbus' glorious light hath sung,
Hymning high his praise;
Yet his feeble rays
Ocean's hollows may not brighten,
Nor earth's central gloom enlighten.
But the might of Him, who skilled
This great universe to build,
Is not thus confined;
Not earth's solid rind,
Nor night's blackest canopy,
Baffle His all-seeing eye.
All that is, hath been, shall be,
In one glance's compass, He
Limitless descries;
And, save His, no eyes
All the world survey—no, none!
Him, then, truly name the Sun.

Prosa II

Animaduerto, inquam, idque uti tu dicis ita esse consentio. Sed in hac haerentium sibi serie causarum estne ulla nostri arbitrii libertas an ipsos quoque humanorum motus animorum fatalis catena constringit?

Est, inquit; neque enim fuerit ulla rationalis natura quin eidem libertas adsit arbitrii. Nam quod ratione uti naturaliter potest id habet iudicium quo quidque discernat; per se igitur fugienda optandaue dinoscit. Quod uero quis optandum esse iudicat petit, refugit uero quod aestimat esse fugiendum. Quare quibus in ipsis inest ratio etiam uolendi nolendique libertas, sed hanc non in omnibus aequam esse constituo. Nam supernis diuinisque substantiis et perspicax iudicium et incorrupta uoluntas et efficax optatorum praesto est potestas. Humanas uero animas liberiores quidem esse necesse est cum se in mentis diuinae speculatione conseruant, minus uero cum dilabuntur ad corpora, minusque etiam cum terrenis artubus colligantur. Extrema uero est seruitus cum uitiis deditae rationis propriae possessione ceciderunt. Nam ubi oculos a summae luce ueritatis ad inferiora et tenebrosa deiecerint, mox inscitiae nube caligant, perniciosis turbantur affectibus, quibus accedendo consentiendoque quam inuexere sibi adiuuant seruitutem et sunt quodam modo propria libertate captiuae. Quae tamen ille ab aeterno cuncta prospiciens prouidentiae cernit intuitus et suis quaeque meritis praedestinata disponit.

πάντ᾽ ἐφορᾷ καὶ πάντ᾽ ἐπακούειν.[9]

Metrum II

Puro clarum lumine Phoebum
Melliflui canit oris Homerus;
Qui tamen intima uiscera terrae
Non ualet aut pelagi radiorum
Infirma perrumpere luce.
Haud sic magni conditor orbis:
Huic ex alto cuncta tuenti
Nulla terrae mole resistunt,
Non nox astris nubibus obstat;
Quae sint, quae fuerint ueniantque
Vno mentis cernit in ictu;
Quem quia respicit omnia solus
Verum possis dicere solem.

---

9   Omnia videre et omnia audire.

III.

Then said I: 'But now I am once more perplexed by a problem yet more difficult.'

'And what is that?' said she; 'yet, in truth, I can guess what it is that troubles you.'

'It seems,' said I, 'too much of a paradox and a contradiction that God should know all things, and yet there should be free will. For if God foresees everything, and can in no wise be deceived, that which providence foresees to be about to happen must necessarily come to pass. Wherefore, if from eternity He foreknows not only what men will do, but also their designs and purposes, there can be no freedom of the will, seeing that nothing can be done, nor can any sort of purpose be entertained, save such as a Divine providence, incapable of being deceived, has perceived beforehand. For if the issues can be turned aside to some other end than that foreseen by providence, there will not then be any sure foreknowledge of the future, but uncertain conjecture instead, and to think this of God I deem impiety.

'Moreover, I do not approve the reasoning by which some think to solve this puzzle. For they say that it is not because God has foreseen the coming of an event that therefore it is sure to come to pass, but, conversely, because something is about to come to pass, it cannot be hidden from Divine providence; and accordingly the necessity passes to the opposite side, and it is not that what is foreseen must necessarily come to pass, but that what is about to come to pass must necessarily be foreseen. But this is just as if the matter in debate were, which is cause and which effect—whether foreknowledge of the future cause of the necessity, or the necessity of the future of the foreknowledge. But we need not be at the pains of demonstrating that, whatsoever be the order of the causal sequence, the occurrence of things foreseen is necessary, even though the foreknowledge of future events does not in itself impose upon them the necessity of their occurrence. ❲For example, if a man be seated, the supposition of his being seated is necessarily true; and, conversely, if the supposition of his being seated is true, because he is really seated, he must necessarily be sitting. So, in either case, there is some necessity involved—in this latter case, the necessity of the fact; in the former, of the truth of the statement. But in both cases the sitter is not therefore seated because the opinion is true, but rather the opinion is true because antecedently he was sitting as a matter of fact. Thus, though the cause of the truth of the opinion comes from the other side,[6] yet there is a necessity on both sides alike. ❲We can obviously reason similarly in the case of providence and the future. Even if future events are foreseen because they are about to happen, and do not come to pass because they are foreseen, still, all the same, there is a necessity, both that they should be foreseen by God as about to come to pass, and that when they are foreseen they should happen, and this is sufficient for the destruction of free will. However, it is preposterous to speak of the occurrence of events in time as the cause of eternal foreknowledge. And yet if we believe that God foresees future events because they are about to come to pass, what is it but to think that the occurrence of events is the cause of His supreme providence? Further, just as when I know that anything is, that thing necessarily is, so when I know that anything will be, it will necessarily be. It follows, then, that things foreknown come to pass inevitably.

---

6   I.e., the necessity of the truth of the statement from the fact.

Prosa III

Tum ego: en, inquam, difficiliore rursus ambiguitate confundor.

Quaenam, inquit, ista est? Iam enim quibus pertubere, coniecto.

Nimium, inquam, aduersari ac repugnare uidetur praenoscere uniuersa deum et esse ullum libertatis arbitrium. Nam si cuncta prospicit deus neque falli ullo modo potest, euenire necesse est quod prouidentia futurum esse praeuiderit. Quare si ab aeterno non facta hominum modo sed etiam consilia uoluntatesque praenoscit, nulla erit arbitrii libertas; neque enim uel factum aliud ullum uel quaelibet exsistere poterit uoluntas nisi quam nescia falli prouidentia diuina praesenserit. Nam si aliorsum quam prouisa sunt detorqueri ualent, non iam erit futuri firma praescientia, sed opinio potius incerta; quod de deo credere nefas iudico.

Neque enim illam probo rationem qua se quidam credunt hunc quaestionis nodum posse dissoluere. Aiunt enim non ideo quid esse euenturum quoniam id prouidentia futurum esse prospexerit, sed e contrario potius quoniam quid futurum est id diuinam prouidentiam latere non posse eoque modo necessarium hoc in contrariam relabi partem. Neque enim necesse esse contingere quae prouidentur, sed necesse esse quae futura sunt prouideri quasi uero quae cuius rei causa sit, praescientiane futurorum necessitatis an futurorum necessitas prouidentiae, laboretur ac non illud demonstrare nitamur, quoquo modo sese habeat ordo causarum necessarium esse euentum praescitarum rerum etiam si praescientia futuris rebus eueniendi necessitatem non uideatur inferre.

Etenim si quispiam sedeat, opinionem quae eum sedere coniectat ueram esse necesse est; atque e conuerso rursus, si de quopiam uera sit opinio quoniam sedet, eum sedere necesse est. In utroque igitur necessitas inest, in hoc quidem sedendi, at uero in altero ueritatis. Sed non idcirco quisque sedet quoniam uera est opinio, sed haec potius uera est quoniam quempiam sedere praecessit. Ita cum causa ueritatis ex altera parte procedat, inest tamen communis in utraque necessitas.

Similia de prouidentia futurisque rebus ratiocinari patet. Nam etiam si idcirco quoniam futura sunt prouidentur, non uero ideo quoniam prouidentur eueniunt, nihilo minus tamen a deo uel uentura prouideri uel prouisa necesse est euenire prouisa, quod ad perimendam arbitrii libertatem solum satis est. Iam uero quam praeposterum est ut aeternae praescientiae temporalium rerum euentus causa esse dicatur! Quid est autem aliud arbitrari ideo deum futura quoniam sunt euentura prouidere quam putare quae olim acciderunt causam summae illius esse prouidentiae? Ad haec, sicuti cum quid esse scio id ipsum esse necesse est ita cum quid futurum noui id ipsum futurum esse necesse est; sic fit igitur ut euentus praescitae rei nequeat euitari.

'Lastly, to think of a thing as being in any way other than what it is, is not only not knowledge, but it is false opinion widely different from the truth of knowledge. Consequently, if anything is about to be, and yet its occurrence is not certain and necessary, how can anyone foreknow that it will occur? For just as knowledge itself is free from all admixture of falsity, so any conception drawn from knowledge cannot be other than as it is conceived. For this, indeed, is the cause why knowledge is free from falsehood, because of necessity each thing must correspond exactly with the knowledge which grasps its nature. ⦅In what way, then, are we to suppose that God foreknows these uncertainties as about to come to pass? For if He thinks of events which possibly may not happen at all as inevitably destined to come to pass, He is deceived; and this it is not only impious to believe, but even so much as to express in words. If, on the other hand, He sees them in the future as they are in such a sense as to know that they may equally come to pass or not, what sort of foreknowledge is this which comprehends nothing certain nor fixed? What better is this than the absurd vaticination of Teiresias?

'"Whate'er I say Shall either come to pass—or not."

In that case, too, in what would Divine providence surpass human opinion if it holds for uncertain things the occurrence of which is uncertain, even as men do? But if at that perfectly sure Fountain-head of all things no shadow of uncertainty can possibly be found, then the occurrence of those things which He has surely foreknown as coming is certain. ⦅Wherefore there can be no freedom in human actions and designs; but the Divine mind, which foresees all things without possibility of mistake, ties and binds them down to one only issue. But this admission once made, what an upset of human affairs manifestly ensues! Vainly are rewards and punishments proposed for the good and bad, since no free and voluntary motion of the will has deserved either one or the other; nay, the punishment of the wicked and the reward of the righteous, which is now esteemed the perfection of justice, will seem the most flagrant injustice, since men are determined either way not by their own proper volition, but by the necessity of what must surely be. And therefore neither virtue nor vice is anything, but rather good and ill desert are confounded together without distinction. Moreover, seeing that the whole course of events is deduced from providence, and nothing is left free to human design, it comes to pass that our vices also are referred to the Author of all good—a thought than which none more abominable can possibly be conceived. Again, no ground is left for hope or prayer, since how can we hope for blessings, or pray for mercy, when every object of desire depends upon the links of an unalterable chain of causation? ⦅Gone, then, is the one means of intercourse between God and man—the communion of hope and prayer—if it be true that we ever earn the inestimable recompense of the Divine favour at the price of a due humility; for this is the one way whereby men seem able to hold communion with God, and are joined to that unapproachable light by the very act of supplication, even before they obtain their petitions. Then, since these things can scarcely be believed to have any efficacy, if the necessity of future events be admitted, what means will there be whereby we may be brought near and cleave to Him who is the supreme Head of all? Wherefore it needs must be that the human race, even as thou didst erstwhile declare in song, parted and dissevered from its Source, should fall to ruin.'

Postremo si quid aliquis aliorsum atque sese res habet, existimet, id non modo scientia non est, sed est opinio fallax ab scientiae ueritate longe diuersa. Quare si quid ita futurum est ut eius certus ac necessarius non sit euentus, id euenturum esse praesciri qui poterit? Sicut enim scientia ipsa impermixta est falsitati ita id quod ab ea concipitur esse aliter atque con‐ cipitur nequit. Ea namque causa est cur mendacio scientia careat, quod se ita rem quamque habere necesse est uti eam sese habere scientia comprehendit.

Quid igitur, quonam modo deus haec incerta futura praenoscit? Nam si ineuitabiliter euentura censet quae etiam non euenire possibile est, fallitur, quod non sentire modo nefas est sed etiam uoce proferre. At si ita uti sunt ita ea futura esse decernit, ut aeque uel fieri ea uel non fieri posse cognoscat, quae est haec praescientia, quae nihil certum, nihil stabile com‐ prehendit? Aut quid hoc refert uaticinio illo ridiculo Tiresiae:

'Quicquid dicam aut erit aut non?'

Quid etiam diuina prouidentia opinione praestiterit si uti homines incerta iudicat quor‐ um est incertus euentus? Quodsi apud illum rerum omnium certissimum fontem nihil incerti esse potest, certus eorum est euentus quae futura firmiter ille praescierit.

Quare nulla est humanis consiliis actionibusque libertas, quas diuina mens sine falsitatis errore cuncta prospiciens ad unum alligat et constringit euentum. Quo semel recepto quantus occasus humanarum rerum consequatur liquet. Frustra enim bonis malisque praemia poen‐ aeue proponuntur, quae nullus meruit liber ac uoluntarius motus animorum. Idque omnium uidebitur iniquissimum quod nunc aequissimum iudicatur, uel puniri improbos uel remuner‐ ari probos, quos ad alterutrum non propria mittit uoluntas sed futuri cogit certa necessitas. Nec uitia igitur nec uirtutes quicquam fuerint, sed omnium meritorum potius mixta atque in‐ discreta confusio; quoque nihil sceleratius excogitari potest, cum ex prouidentia rerum omnis ordo ducatur nihilque consiliis liceat humanis, fit ut uitia quoque nostra ad bonorum omnium referantur auctorem. Igitur nec sperandi aliquid nec deprecandi ulla ratio est; quid enim uel speret quisque uel etiam deprecetur quando optanda omnia series indeflexa conectit?

Auferetur igitur unicum illud inter homines deumque commercium, sperandi scilicet ac deprecandi, si quidem iustae humilitatis pretio inaestimabilem uicem diuinae gratiae promeremur; qui solus modus est quo cum deo colloqui homines posse uideantur illique inac‐ cessae luci prius quoque quam impetrent ipsa supplicandi ratione coniungi. Quae si recepta futurorum necessitate nihil uirium habere credantur, quid erit quo summo illi rerum principi conecti atque adhaerere possimus? Quare necesse erit humanum genus, uti paulo ante canta‐ bas, dissaeptum atque disiunctum suo fonte fatiscere.

Song III — Truth's Paradoxes.

Why does a strange discordance break
The ordered scheme's fair harmony?
Hath God decreed 'twixt truth and truth
There may such lasting warfare be,
That truths, each severally plain,
We strive to reconcile in vain?

Or is the discord not in truth,
Since truth is self consistent ever?
But, close in fleshly wrappings held,
The blinded mind of man can never
Discern—so faint her taper shines—
The subtle chain that all combines?

Ah! then why burns man's restless mind
Truth's hidden portals to unclose?
Knows he already what he seeks?
Why toil to seek it, if he knows?
Yet, haply if he knoweth not,
Why blindly seek he knows not what?[7]

Who for a good he knows not sighs?
Who can an unknown end pursue?
How find? How e'en when haply found
Hail that strange form he never knew?
Or is it that man's inmost soul
Once knew each part and knew the whole?

Now, though by fleshly vapours dimmed,
Not all forgot her visions past;
For while the several parts are lost,
To the one whole she cleaveth fast;
Whence he who yearns the truth to find
Is neither sound of sight nor blind.

For neither does he know in full,
Nor is he reft of knowledge quite;
But, holding still to what is left,
He gropes in the uncertain light,
And by the part that still survives
To win back all he bravely strives.

IV.

Then said she: 'This debate about providence is an old one, and is vigorously discussed by Cicero in his "Divination"; thou also hast long and earnestly pondered the problem, yet no

---

7   Compare Plato, 'Meno', 80; Jowett, vol. ii., pp. 39, 40.

Metrum III

Quaenam discors foedera rerum
Causa resoluit? Quis tanta deus
Veris statuit bella duobus
Vt quae carptim singula constent
Eadem nolint mixta iugari?
An nulla est discordia ueris
Semperque sibi certa cohaerent,
Sed mens caecis obruta membris
Nequit oppressi luminis igne
Rerum tenues noscere nexus?
Sed cur tanto flagrat amore
Veri tectas reperire notas?
Scitne quod appetit anxia nosse?
Sed quis nota scire laborat?
At si nescit, quid caeca petit?
Quis enim quicquam optet?
Aut quis ualeat nescita sequi
Quoue inueniat? Quis reppertam
Queat ignarus noscere formam?
An cum mentem cerneret altam
Pariter summam et singula norat,
Nunc membrorum condita nube
Non in totum est oblita sui
Summamque tenet singula perdens?
Igitur quisquis uera requirit
Neutro est habitu; nam neque nouit
Nec penitus tamen omnia nescit,
Sed quam retinens meminit summam
Consulit alte uisa retractans,
Vt seruatis queat oblitas
Addere partes.

Prosa IV

Tum illa: uetus, inquit, haec est de prouidentia querela M.que Tullio, cum diuinationem distribuit, uehementer agitata tibique ipsi res diu prorsus multumque quaesita, sed

one has had diligence and perseverance enough to find a solution. And the reason of this ob-scurity is that the movement of human reasoning cannot cope with the simplicity of the Divine foreknowledge; for if a conception of its nature could in any wise be framed, no shadow of uncertainty would remain. With a view of making this at last clear and plain, I will begin by considering the arguments by which thou art swayed. First, I inquire into the reasons why thou art dissatisfied with the solution proposed, which is to the effect that, seeing the fact of foreknowledge is not thought the cause of the necessity of future events, foreknow-ledge is not to be deemed any hindrance to the freedom of the will. Now, surely the sole ground on which thou arguest the necessity of the future is that things which are foreknown cannot fail to come to pass. But if, as thou wert ready to acknowledge just now, the fact of foreknowledge imposes no necessity on things future, what reason is there for supposing the results of voluntary action constrained to a fixed issue? ⟨Suppose, for the sake of argument, and to see what follows, we assume that there is no foreknowledge. Are willed actions, then, tied down to any necessity in this case?'

'Certainly not.'

'Let us assume foreknowledge again, but without its involving any actual necessity; the freedom of the will, I imagine, will remain in complete integrity. But thou wilt say that, even although the foreknowledge is not the necessity of the future event's occurrence, yet it is a sign that it will necessarily happen. Granted; but in this case it is plain that, even if there had been no foreknowledge, the issues would have been inevitably certain. For a sign only indic-ates something which is, does not bring to pass that of which it is the sign. We require to show beforehand that all things, without exception, happen of necessity in order that a pre-conception may be a sign of this necessity. Otherwise, if there is no such universal necessity, neither can any preconception be a sign of a necessity which exists not. Manifestly, too, a proof established on firm grounds of reason must be drawn not from signs and loose general arguments, but from suitable and necessary causes. ⟨But how can it be that things foreseen should ever fail to come to pass? Why, this is to suppose us to believe that the events which providence foresees to be coming were not about to happen, instead of our supposing that, although they should come to pass, yet there was no necessity involved in their own nature compelling their occurrence. Take an illustration that will help to convey my meaning. There are many things which we see taking place before our eyes—the movements of charioteers, for instance, in guiding and turning their cars, and so on. Now, is any one of these movements compelled by any necessity?'

'No; certainly not. There would be no efficacy in skill if all motions took place perforce.'

'Then, things which in taking place are free from any necessity as to their being in the present must also, before they take place, be about to happen without necessity. Wherefore there are things which will come to pass, the occurrence of which is perfectly free from ne-cessity. At all events, I imagine that no one will deny that things now taking place were about to come to pass before they were actually happening. Such things, however much fore-known, are in their occurrence free. For even as knowledge of things present imports no ne-cessity into things that are taking place, so foreknowledge of the future imports none into things that are about to come. But this, thou wilt say, is the very point in dispute—whether any foreknowing is possible of things whose occurrence is not necessary. For here there

haudquaquam ab ullo uestrum hactenus satis diligenter ac firmiter expedita. Cuius caliginis causa est quod humanae ratiocinationis motus ad diuinae praescientiae simplicitatem non potest ammoueri; quae si ullo modo cogitari queat, nihil prorsus relinquetur ambigui. Quod ita demum patefacere atque expedire temptabo, si prius ea quibus moueris expendero. Quaero enim cur illam soluentium rationem minus efficacem putes quae quia praescientiam non esse futuris rebus causam necessitatis existimat nihil impediri praescientia arbitrii libertatem putat. Num enim tu aliunde argumentum futurorum necessitatis trahis nisi quod ea quae praesciuntur non euenire non possunt? Si igitur praenotio nullam futuris rebus adicit necessitatem, quod tu etiam paulo ante fatebare, quid est quod uoluntarii exitus rerum ad certum cogantur euentum?

Etenim positionis gratia, ut quid consequatur aduertas, statuamus nullam esse praescientiam. Num igitur, quantum ad hoc attinet, quae ex arbitrio ueniunt ad necessitatem cogantur?

Minime.

Statuamus iterum esse, sed nihil rebus necessitatis iniungere; manebit, ut opinor, eadem uoluntatis integra atque absoluta libertas. Sed praescienta, inquies, tametsi futuris eueniendi necessitas non est, signum tamen est necessario ea esse uentura. Hoc igitur modo, etiam si praecognitio non fuisset, necessarios futurorum exitus esse constaret; omne etenim signum tantum quid sit ostendit, non uero efficit quod designat. Quare demonstrandum prius est nihil non ex necessitate contingere, ut praenotionem signum esse huius necessitatis appareat; alioquin si haec nulla est, ne illa quidem eius rei signum poterit esse quae non est. Iam uero probationem firma ratione subnixam constat non ex signis neque petitis extrinsecus argumentis sed ex conuenientibus necessariisque causis esse ducendam.

Sed qui fieri potest ut ea non proueniant quae futura esse prouidentur? Quasi uero nos ea quae prouidentia futura esse praenoscit non esse euentura credamus ac non illud potius arbitremur, licet eueniant, nihil tamen ut euenirent sui natura necessitatis habuisse. Quod hinc facile perpendas licebit: plura etenim dum fiunt subiecta oculis intuemur, ut ea quae in quadrigis moderandis atque flectendis facere spectantur aurigae, atque ad hunc modum cetera. Num igitur quicquam illorum ita fieri necessitas ulla compellit?

Minime; frustra enim esset artis effectus si omnia coacta mouerentur.

Quae igitur cum fiunt carent exsistendi necessitate eadem prius quam fiant sine necessitate futura sunt. Quare sunt quaedam euentura quorum exitus ab omni necessitate sit absolutus. Nam illud quidem nullum arbitror esse dicturum, quod quae nunc fiunt prius quam fierint euentura non fuerint. Haec igitur etiam praecognita liberos habent euentus. Nam sicut scientia praesentium rerum nihil his quae fiunt ita praescientia futurorum nihil his quae uentura sunt necessitatis importat. Sed hoc, inquis, ipsum dubitatur an earum rerum quae necessarios exitus non habent ulla possit esse praenotio. Dissonare etenim uidentur, putasque si

seems to thee a contradiction, and, if they are foreseen, their necessity follows; whereas if there is no necessity, they can by no means be foreknown; and thou thinkest that nothing can be grasped as known unless it is certain, but if things whose occurrence is uncertain are fore-known as certain, this is the very mist of opinion, not the truth of knowledge. For to think of things otherwise than as they are, thou believest to be incompatible with the soundness of knowledge.

'Now, the cause of the mistake is this—that men think that all knowledge is cognized purely by the nature and efficacy of the thing known. Whereas the case is the very reverse: all that is known is grasped not conformably to its own efficacy, but rather conformably to the faculty of the knower. An example will make this clear: the roundness of a body is recog-nised in one way by sight, in another by touch. Sight looks upon it from a distance as a whole by a simultaneous reflection of rays; touch grasps the roundness piecemeal, by contact and at-tachment to the surface, and by actual movement round the periphery itself. ⟨Man himself, likewise, is viewed in one way by Sense, in another by Imagination, in another way, again, by Thought, in another by pure Intelligence. Sense judges figure clothed in material sub-stance, Imagination figure alone without matter. Thought transcends this again, and by its contemplation of universals considers the type itself which is contained in the individual. The eye of Intelligence is yet more exalted; for overpassing the sphere of the universal, it will behold absolute form itself by the pure force of the mind's vision. Wherein the main point to be considered is this: the higher faculty of comprehension embraces the lower, while the lower cannot rise to the higher. For Sense has no efficacy beyond matter, nor can Imagination behold universal ideas, nor Thought embrace pure form; but Intelligence, look-ing down, as it were, from its higher standpoint in its intuition of form, discriminates also the several elements which underlie it; but it comprehends them in the same way as it compre-hends that form itself, which could be cognized by no other than itself. For it cognizes the universal of Thought, the figure of Imagination, and the matter of Sense, without employing Thought, Imagination, or Sense, but surveying all things, so to speak, under the aspect of pure form by a single flash of intuition. Thought also, in considering the universal, embraces images and sense-impressions without resorting to Imagination or Sense. For it is Thought which has thus defined the universal from its conceptual point of view: "Man is a two-legged animal endowed with reason." This is indeed a universal notion, yet no one is ignorant that the thing is imaginable and presentable to Sense, because Thought considers it not by Ima-gination or Sense, but by means of rational conception. Imagination, too, though its faculty of viewing and forming representations is founded upon the senses, nevertheless surveys sense-impressions without calling in Sense, not in the way of Sense-perception, but of Imagina-tion. See'st thou, then, how all things in cognizing use rather their own faculty than the fac-ulty of the things which they cognize? Nor is this strange; for since every judgment is the act of the judge, it is necessary that each should accomplish its task by its own, not by another's power.'

praeuideantur consequi necessitatem, si necessitas desit minime praesciri, nihilque scientia comprehendi posse nisi certum. Quodsi quae incerti sunt exitus ea quasi certa prouidentur, opinionis id esse caliginem non scientiae ueritatem; aliter enim ac sese res habeat arbitrari ab integritate scientiae credis esse diuersum.

Cuius erroris causa quod omnia quae quisque nouit ex ipsorum tantum ui atque natura cognosci aestimat quae sciuntur. Quod totum contra est; omne enim quod cognoscitur non secundum sui uim sed secundum cognoscentium potius comprehenditur facultatem. Nam ut hoc breui liqueat exemplo, eandem corporis rotunditatem aliter uisus aliter tactus agnoscit; ille eminus manens totum simul iactis radiis intuetur, hic uero cohaerens orbi atque coniunctus circa ipsum motus ambitum rotunditatem partibus comprehendit.

Ipsum quoque hominem aliter sensus, aliter imaginatio, aliter ratio, aliter intellegentia contuetur. Sensus enim figuram in subiecta materia constitutam, imaginatio uero solam sine materia iudicat figuram. Ratio uero hanc quoque transcendit speciemque ipsam quae singularibus inest uniuersali consideratione perpendit. Intellegentiae uero celsior oculus exsistit; supergressa namque uniuersitatis ambitum ipsam illam simplicem formam pura mentis acie contuetur. In quo illud maxime considerandum est: nam superior comprehendendi uis amplectitur inferiorem, inferior uero ad superiorem nullo modo consurgit. Neque enim sensus aliquid extra materiam ualet uel uniuersales species imaginatio contuetur uel ratio capit simplicem formam; sed intellegentia quasi desuper spectans concepta forma quae subsunt etiam cuncta diiudicat, sed eo modo quo formam ipsam, quae nulli alii nota esse poterat, comprehendit. Nam et rationis uniuersum et imaginationis figuram et materiale sensibile cognoscit nec ratione utens nec imaginatione nec sensibus, sed illo uno ictu mentis formaliter, ut ita dicam, cuncta prospiciens. Ratio quoque cum quid uniuersale respicit nec imaginatione nec sensibus utens imaginabilia uel sensibilia comprehendit. Haec est enim quae conceptionis suae uniuersale ita definit: homo est animal bipes rationale. Quae cum uniuersalis notio sit, tum imaginabilem sensibilemque esse rem nullus ignorat quod illa non imaginatione uel sensu sed in rationali conceptione considerat. Imaginatio quoque, tametsi ex sensibus uisendi formandique figuras sumpsit exordium, sensu tamen absente sensibilia quaeque collustrat non sensibili sed imaginaria ratione iudicandi. Videsne igitur ut in cognoscendo cuncta sua potius facultate quam eorum quae cognoscuntur utantur? Neque id iniuria; nam cum omne iudicium iudicantis actus exsistat, necesse est ut suam quisque operam non ex aliena sed ex propria potestate perficiat.

Song IV – A Psychological Fallacy[8]

From the Porch's murky depths
Comes a doctrine sage,
That doth liken living mind
To a written page;
Since all knowledge comes through
Sense, Graven by Experience.
'As,' say they, 'the pen its marks
Curiously doth trace
On the smooth unsullied white
Of the paper's face,
So do outer things impress
Images on consciousness.'
But if verily the mind
Thus all passive lies;
If no living power within
Its own force supplies;
If it but reflect again,
Like a glass, things false and vain—
Whence the wondrous faculty
That perceives and knows,
That in one fair ordered scheme
Doth the world dispose;
Grasps each whole that Sense presents,
Or breaks into elements?
So divides and recombines,
And in changeful wise
Now to low descends, and now
To the height doth rise;
Last in inward swift review
Strictly sifts the false and true?
Of these ample potencies
Fitter cause, I ween,
Were Mind's self than marks impressed
By the outer scene.
Yet the body through the sense
Stirs the soul's intelligence.
When light flashes on the eye,
Or sound strikes the ear,
Mind aroused to due response

---

8   A criticism of the doctrine of the mind as a blank sheet of paper on which experience writes, as held by the
     Stoics in anticipation of Locke. See Zeller, 'Stoics, Epicureans, and Sceptics,' Reichel's translation, p. 76.

Metrum IV

Quondam Porticus attulit
Obscuros nimium senes,
Qui sensus et imagines
E corporibus extimis
Credant mentibus imprimi,
Vt quondam celeri stilo
Mos est aequore paginae
Quae nullas habeat notas
Pressas figere litteras.
Sed mens si propriis uigens
Nihil motibus explicat,
Sed tantum patiens iacet
Notis subdita corporum
Cassasque in speculi uicem
Rerum reddit imagines,
Vnde haec sic animis uiget
Cernens omnia notio?
Quae uis singula perspicit
Aut quae cognita diuidit?
Quae diuisa recolligit
Alternumque legens iter
Nunc summis caput inserit,
Nunc decedit in infima,
Tum sese referens sibi
Veris falsa redarguit?
Haec est efficiens magis
Longe causa potentior
Quam quae materiae modo
Impressas patitur notas.
Praecedit tamen excitans
Ac uires animi mouens
Viuo in corpore passio
Cum uel lux oculos ferit
Vel uox auribus instrepit.
Tum mentis uigor excitus
Quas intus species tenet
Ad motus similes uocans

Makes the message clear;
And the dumb external signs
With the hidden forms combines.

V.

'Now, although in the case of bodies endowed with sentiency the qualities of external objects affect the sense-organs, and the activity of mind is preceded by a bodily affection which calls forth the mind's action upon itself, and stimulates the forms till that moment lying inactive within, yet, I say, if in these bodies endowed with sentiency the mind is not inscribed by mere passive affection, but of its own efficacy discriminates the impressions furnished to the body, how much more do intelligences free from all bodily affections employ in their discrimination their own mental activities instead of conforming to external objects? So on these principles various modes of cognition belong to distinct and different substances. For to creatures void of motive power—shell-fish and other such creatures which cling to rocks and grow there—belongs Sense alone, void of all other modes of gaining knowledge; to beasts endowed with movement, in whom some capacity of seeking and shunning seems to have arisen, Imagination also. Thought pertains only to the human race, as Intelligence to Divinity alone; hence it follows that that form of knowledge exceeds the rest which of its own nature cognizes not only its proper object, but the objects of the other forms of knowledge also. ⟨But what if Sense and Imagination were to gainsay Thought, and declare that universal which Thought deems itself to behold to be nothing? For the object of Sense and Imagination cannot be universal; so that either the judgment of Reason is true and there is no sense-object, or, since they know full well that many objects are presented to Sense and Imagination, the conception of Reason, which looks on that which is perceived by Sense and particular as if it were a something "universal," is empty of content. Suppose, further, that Reason maintains in reply that it does indeed contemplate the object of both Sense and Imagination under the form of universality, while Sense and Imagination cannot aspire to the knowledge of the universal, since their cognizance cannot go beyond bodily figures, and that in the cognition of reality we ought rather to trust the stronger and more perfect faculty of judgment. In a dispute of this sort, should not we, in whom is planted the faculty of reasoning as well as of imagining and perceiving, espouse the cause of Reason?

'In like manner is it that human reason thinks that Divine Intelligence cannot see the future except after the fashion in which its own knowledge is obtained. For thy contention is, if events do not appear to involve certain and necessary issues, they cannot be foreseen as certainly about to come to pass. There is, then, no foreknowledge of such events; or, if we can ever bring ourselves to believe that there is, there can be nothing which does not happen of necessity. If, however, we could have some part in the judgment of the Divine mind, even as we participate in Reason, we should think it perfectly just that human Reason should submit itself to the Divine mind, no less than we judged that Imagination and Sense ought to yield to Reason. Wherefore let us soar, if we can, to the heights of that Supreme Intelligence; for there Reason will see what in itself it cannot look upon; and that is in what way things whose occurrence is not certain may yet be seen in a sure and definite foreknowledge; and

Notis applicat exteris
Introrsumque reconditis
Formis miscet imagines.

Prosa V

Quodsi in corporibus sentiendis, quamuis afficiant instrumenta sensuum forinsecus obiectae qualitates animique agentis uigorem passio corporis antecedat, quae in se actum mentis prouocet excitetque interim quiescentes intrinsecus formas, si in sentiendis, inquam, corporibus animus non passione insignitur, sed ex sua ui subiectam corpori iudicat passionem, quanto magis ea quae cunctis corporum affectionibus absoluta sunt in discernendo non obiecta extrinsecus sequuntur, sed actum suae mentis expediunt! Hac itaque ratione multiplices cognitiones diuersis ac differentibus cessere substantiis. Sensus enim solus cunctis aliis cognitionibus destitutus immobilibus animantibus cessit, quales sunt conchae maris quaeque alia saxis haerentia nutriuntur; imaginatio uero mobilibus beluis, quibus iam inesse fugiendi appetendiue aliquis uidetur affectus. Ratio uero humani tantum generis est sicut intellegentia sola diuini: quo fit ut ea notitia ceteris praestet quae suapte natura non modo proprium sed ceterarum quoque notitiarum subiecta cognoscit.

Quid igitur, si ratiocinationi sensus imaginatioque refragentur nihil esse illud uniuersale dicentes quod sese intueri ratio putet? Quod enim sensibile uel imaginabile est id uniuersum esse non posse; aut igitur rationis uerum esse iudicium nec quicquam esse sensibile aut, quoniam sibi notum sit plura sensibus et imaginationi esse subiecta, inanem conceptionem esse rationis, quae quod sensibile sit ac singulare quasi quiddam uniuersale consideret. Ad haec si ratio contra respondeat se quidem et quod sensibile et quod imaginabile sit in uniuersitatis ratione conspicere, illa uero ad uniuersitatis cognitionem aspirare non posse quoniam eorum notio corporales figuras non posset excedere, de rerum uero cognitione firmiori potius perfectiorique iudicio esse credendum: in huius modi igitur lite nos, quibus tam ratiocinandi quam imaginandi etiam sentiendique uis inest, nonne rationis potius causam probaremus?

Simile est quod humana ratio diuinam intellegentiam futura nisi ut ipsa cognoscit non putat intueri. Nam ita disseris: si qua certos ac necessarios habere non uideantur euentus ea certo euentura praesciri nequeunt. Harum igitur rerum nulla est praescientia; quam si etiam in his esse credamus, nihil erit quod non ex necessitate proueniat. Si igitur uti rationis participes sumus ita diuinae iudicium mentis habere possemus, sicut imaginationem sensumque rationi cedere oportere iudicauimus sic diuinae sese menti humanam summittere rationem iustissimum censeremus. Quare in illius summae intellegentiae cacumen si possumus erigamur; illic enim ratio uidebit quod in se non potest intueri: id autem est, quonam modo

that this foreknowledge is not conjecture, but rather knowledge in its supreme simplicity, free of all limits and restrictions.'

Song V — The Upward Look.

In what divers shapes and fashions do the creatures great and small
Over wide earth's teeming surface skim, or scud, or walk, or crawl!
Some with elongated body sweep the ground, and, as they move,
Trail perforce with writhing belly in the dust a sinuous groove;
Some, on light wing upward soaring, swiftly do the winds divide,
And through heaven's ample spaces in free motion smoothly glide;
These earth's solid surface pressing, with firm paces onward rove,
Ranging through the verdant meadows, crouching in the woodland grove.
Great and wondrous is their variance! Yet in all the head low-bent
Dulls the soul and blunts the senses, though their forms be different.
Man alone, erect, aspiring, lifts his forehead to the skies,
And in upright posture steadfast seems earth's baseness to despise.
If with earth not all besotted, to this parable give ear,
Thou whose gaze is fixed on heaven, who thy face on high dost rear:
Lift thy soul, too, heavenward; haply lest it stain its heavenly worth,
And thine eyes alone look upward, while thy mind cleaves to the earth!

VI.

'Since, then, as we lately proved, everything that is known is cognized not in accordance with its own nature, but in accordance with the nature of the faculty that comprehends it, let us now contemplate, as far as lawful, the character of the Divine essence, that we may be able to understand also the nature of its knowledge.

'God is eternal; in this judgment all rational beings agree. Let us, then, consider what eternity is. For this word carries with it a revelation alike of the Divine nature and of the Divine knowledge. Now, eternity is the possession of endless life whole and perfect at a single moment. What this is becomes more clear and manifest from a comparison with things temporal. For whatever lives in time is a present proceeding from the past to the future, and there is nothing set in time which can embrace the whole space of its life together. To-morrow's state it grasps not yet, while it has already lost yesterday's; nay, even in the life of to-day ye live no longer than one brief transitory moment. Whatever, therefore, is subject to the condition of time, although, as Aristotle deemed of the world, it never have either beginning or end, and its life be stretched to the whole extent of time's infinity, it yet is not such as rightly to be thought eternal. For it does not include and embrace the whole space of infinite life at once, but has no present hold on things to come, not yet accomplished. Accordingly, that which includes and possesses the whole fulness of unending life at once, from which nothing future is absent, from which nothing past has escaped, this is rightly called eternal; this must of necessity be ever present to itself in full self-possession, and hold the infinity of

etiam quae certos exitus non habent certa tamen uideat ac definita praenotio, neque id sit opinio sed summae potius scientiae nullis terminis inclusa simplicitas.

Metrum V

Quam uariis terras animalia permeant figuris!
Namque alia extento sunt corpore pulueremque uerrunt
Continuumque trahunt ui pectoris incitata sulcum;
Sunt quibus alarum leuitas uaga uerberetque uentos
Et liquido longi spatia aetheris uolatu;
Haec pressisse solo uestigia gressibusque gaudent
Vel uirides campos transmittere uel subire siluas.
Quae uariis uideas licet omnia discrepare formis,
Prona tamen facies hebetes ualet ingrauare sensus;
Vnica gens hominum celsum leuat altius cacumen
Atque leuis recto stat corpore despicitque terras.
Haec, nisi terrenus male desipis, ammonet figura:
Qui recto caelum uultu petis exserisque frontem,
In sublime feras animum quoque, ne grauata pessum
Inferior sidat mens corpore celsius leuato.

Prosa VI

Quoniam igitur, uti paulo ante monstratum est, omne quod scitur non ex sua sed ex comprehendentium natura cognoscitur, intueamur nunc quantum fas est quis sit diuinae substantiae status, ut quaenam etiam scientia eius sit possimus agnoscere.

Deum igitur aeternum esse cunctorum ratione degentium commune iudicium est. Quid sit igitur aeternitas consideremus; haec enim nobis naturam pariter diuinam scientiamque patefacit. Aeternitas igitur est interminabilis uitae tota simul et perfecta possessio. Quod ex collatione temporalium clarius liquet. Nam quicquid uiuit in tempore id praesens a praeteritis in futura procedit nihilque est in tempore constitutum quod totum uitae suae spatium pariter possit amplecti, sed crastinum quidem nondum apprehendit hesternum uero iam perdidit; in hodierna quoque uita non amplius uiuitis quam in illo mobili transitorioque momento. Quod igitur temporis patitur condicionem, licet illud, sicuti de mundo censuit Aristoteles, nec coeperit umquam esse nec desinat uitaque eius cum temporis infinitate tendatur, nondum tamen tale est ut aeternum esse iure credatur. Non enim totum simul infinitae licet uitae spatium comprehendit atque complectitur, sed futura nondum, transacta iam non habet. Quod igitur interminabilis uitae plenitudinem totam pariter comprehendit ac possidet, cui neque futuri quicquam absit nec praeteriti fluxerit, id aeternum esse iure perhibetur idque necesse est et sui compos praesens sibi semper assistere et infinitatem mobilis temporis habere praesentem.

movable time in an abiding present. ℂWherefore they deem not rightly who imagine that on Plato's principles the created world is made co-eternal with the Creator, because they are told that he believed the world to have had no beginning in time,[9] and to be destined never to come to an end. For it is one thing for existence to be endlessly prolonged, which was what Plato ascribed to the world, another for the whole of an endless life to be embraced in the present, which is manifestly a property peculiar to the Divine mind. Nor need God appear earlier in mere duration of time to created things, but only prior in the unique simplicity of His nature. For the infinite progression of things in time copies this immediate existence in the present of the changeless life, and when it cannot succeed in equalling it, declines from movelessness into motion, and falls away from the simplicity of a perpetual present to the infinite duration of the future and the past; and since it cannot possess the whole fulness of its life together, for the very reason that in a manner it never ceases to be, it seems, up to a certain point, to rival that which it cannot complete and express by attaching itself indifferently to any present moment of time, however swift and brief; and since this bears some resemblance to that ever-abiding present, it bestows on everything to which it is assigned the semblance of existence. But since it cannot abide, it hurries along the infinite path of time, and the result has been that it continues by ceaseless movement the life the completeness of which it could not embrace while it stood still. So, if we are minded to give things their right names, we shall follow Plato in saying that God indeed is eternal, but the world everlasting.

'Since, then, every mode of judgment comprehends its objects conformably to its own nature, and since God abides for ever in an eternal present, His knowledge, also transcending all movement of time, dwells in the simplicity of its own changeless present, and, embracing the whole infinite sweep of the past and of the future, contemplates all that falls within its simple cognition as if it were now taking place. And therefore, if thou wilt carefully consider that immediate presentment whereby it discriminates all things, thou wilt more rightly deem it not foreknowledge as of something future, but knowledge of a moment that never passes. For this cause the name chosen to describe it is not prevision, but providence, because, since utterly removed in nature from things mean and trivial, its outlook embraces all things as from some lofty height. Why, then, dost thou insist that the things which are surveyed by the Divine eye are involved in necessity, whereas clearly men impose no necessity on things which they see? Does the act of vision add any necessity to the things which thou seest before thy eyes?'

'Assuredly not.'

'And yet, if we may without unfitness compare God's present and man's, just as ye see certain things in this your temporary present, so does He see all things in His eternal present. Wherefore this Divine anticipation changes not the natures and properties of things, and it beholds things present before it, just as they will hereafter come to pass in time. Nor does it confound things in its judgment, but in the one mental view distinguishes alike what will come necessarily and what without necessity. For even as ye, when at one and the same time ye see a man walking on the earth and the sun rising in the sky, distinguish between the two, though one glance embraces both, and judge the former voluntary, the latter necessary action:

---

9   Plato expressly states the opposite in the 'Timæus' (28B), though possibly there the account of the beginning
     of the world in time is to be understood figuratively, not literally. See Jowett, vol. iii., pp. 448, 449 (3rd ed..).

Vnde non recte quidam, qui cum audiunt uisum Platoni mundum hunc nec habuisse ini‐
tium temporis nec habiturum esse defectum hoc modo conditori mundum fieri coaeternum
putant. Aliud est enim per interminabilem duci uitam, quod mundo Plato tribuit, aliud inter‐
minabilis uitae totam pariter complexum esse praesentiam, quod diuinae mentis proprium
esse manifestum est. Neque deus conditis rebus antiquior uideri debet temporis quantitate
sed simplicis potius proprietate naturae. Hunc enim uitae immobilis praesentarium statum
infinitus ille temporalium rerum motus imitatur, cumque eum effingere atque aequare non
possit, ex immobilitate deficit in motum, ex simplicitate praesentiae decrescit in infinitam
futuri ac praeteriti quantitatem, et cum totam pariter uitae suae plenitudinem nequeat pos‐
sidere, hoc ipso quod aliquo modo numquam esse desinit illud quod implere atque exprimere
non potest aliquatenus uidetur aemulari alligans se ad qualemcumque praesentiam huius
exigui uolucrisque momenti, quae quoniam manentis illius praesentiae quandam gestat ima‐
ginem, quibuscumque contigerit id praestat ut esse uideantur. Quoniam uero manere non
potuit, infinitum temporis iter arripuit eoque modo factum est ut continuaret eundo uitam
cuius plenitudinem complecti non ualuit permanendo. Itaque si digna rebus nomina uelimus
imponere, Platonem sequentes deum quidem aeternum, mundum uero dicamus esse
perpetuum.

Quoniam igitur omne iudicium secundum sui naturam quae sibi subiecta sunt compre‐
hendit, est autem deo semper aeternus ac praesentarius status, scientia quoque eius omnem
temporis supergressa motionem in suae manet simplicitate praesentiae infinitaque praeteriti
ac futuri spatia complectens omnia quasi iam gerantur in sua simplici cognitione considerat.
Itaque si praeuidentiam pensare uelis qua cuncta dinoscit, non esse praescientiam quasi futuri
sed scientiam numquam deficientis instantiae rectius aestimabis. Vnde non praeuidentia sed
prouidentia potius dicitur, quod porro a rebus infimis, constituta quasi ab excelso rerum
cacumine cuncta prospiciat. Quid igitur postulas ut necessaria fiant quae diuino lumine
lustrentur, cum ne homines quidem necessaria faciant esse quae uideant? Num enim quae
praesentia cernis aliquam eis necessitatem tuus addit intuitus?

Minime.

Atqui si est diuini humanique praesentis digna collatio, uti uos uestro hoc temporario
praesenti quaedam uidetis ita ille omnia suo cernit aeterno. Quare haec diuina praenotio nat‐
uram rerum proprietatemque non mutat taliaque apud se praesentia spectat qualia in tempore
olim futura prouenient. Nec rerum iudicia confundit unoque suae mentis intuitu tam neces‐
sarie quam non necessarie uentura dinoscit, sicuti uos cum pariter ambulare in terra hominem
et oriri in caelo solem uidetis, quamquam simul utrumque conspectum tamen discernitis et

so also the Divine vision in its universal range of view does in no wise confuse the characters of the things which are present to its regard, though future in respect of time. Whence it follows that when it perceives that something will come into existence, and yet is perfectly aware that this is unbound by any necessity, its apprehension is not opinion, but rather knowledge based on truth. ⸫And if to this thou sayest that what God sees to be about to come to pass cannot fail to come to pass, and that what cannot fail to come to pass happens of necessity, and wilt tie me down to this word necessity, I will acknowledge that thou affirmest a most solid truth, but one which scarcely anyone can approach to who has not made the Divine his special study. For my answer would be that the same future event is necessary from the standpoint of Divine knowledge, but when considered in its own nature it seems absolutely free and unfettered. So, then, there are two necessities—one simple, as that men are necessarily mortal; the other conditioned, as that, if you know that someone is walking, he must necessarily be walking. For that which is known cannot indeed be otherwise than as it is known to be, and yet this fact by no means carries with it that other simple necessity. For the former necessity is not imposed by the thing's own proper nature, but by the addition of a condition. No necessity compels one who is voluntarily walking to go forward, although it is necessary for him to go forward at the moment of walking. In the same way, then, if Providence sees anything as present, that must necessarily be, though it is bound by no necessity of nature. Now, God views as present those coming events which happen of free will. These, accordingly, from the standpoint of the Divine vision are made necessary conditionally on the Divine cognizance; viewed, however, in themselves, they desist not from the absolute freedom naturally theirs. Accordingly, without doubt, all things will come to pass which God foreknows as about to happen, but of these certain proceed of free will; and though these happen, yet by the fact of their existence they do not lose their proper nature, in virtue of which before they happened it was really possible that they might not have come to pass.

'What difference, then, does the denial of necessity make, since, through their being conditioned by Divine knowledge, they come to pass as if they were in all respects under the compulsion of necessity? This difference, surely, which we saw in the case of the instances I formerly took, the sun's rising and the man's walking; which at the moment of their occurrence could not but be taking place, and yet one of them before it took place was necessarily obliged to be, while the other was not so at all. So likewise the things which to God are present without doubt exist, but some of them come from the necessity of things, others from the power of the agent. Quite rightly, then, have we said that these things are necessary if viewed from the standpoint of the Divine knowledge; but if they are considered in themselves, they are free from the bonds of necessity, even as everything which is accessible to sense, regarded from the standpoint of Thought, is universal, but viewed in its own nature particular. "But," thou wilt say, "if it is in my power to change my purpose, I shall make void providence, since I shall perchance change something which comes within its foreknowledge." My answer is: Thou canst indeed turn aside thy purpose; but since the truth of providence is ever at hand to see that thou canst, and whether thou dost, and whither thou turnest thyself, thou canst not avoid the Divine foreknowledge, even as thou canst not escape the sight of a present spectator, although of thy free will thou turn thyself to various actions.

hoc uoluntarium illud esse necessarium iudicatis. Ita igitur cuncta dispiciens diuinus intuitus qualitatem rerum minime perturbat apud se quidem praesentium ad condicionem uero temporis futurarum. Quo fit, ut hoc non sit opinio sed ueritate potius nixa cognitio, cum exstaturum quid esse conoscit quod idem exsistendi necessitate carere non nesciat.

Hic si dicas quod euenturum deus uidet id non euenire non posse, quod autem non potest non euenire id ex necessitate contingere, meque ad hoc nomen necessitatis adstringas, fatebor rem quidem solidissimae ueritatis sed cui uix aliquis nisi diuini speculator accesserit. Respondebo namque idem futurum cum ad diuinam notionem refertur necessarium, cum uero in sua natura perpenditur liberum prorsus atque absolutum uideri. Duae sunt etenim necessitates, simplex una, ueluti quod necesse est omnes homines esse mortales, altera condicionis, ut si aliquem ambulare scias eum ambulare necesse est. Quod enim quisque nouit id esse aliter ac notum est nequit, sed haec condicio minime se cum illam simplicem trahit. Hanc enim necessitatem non propria facit natura sed condicionis adiectio; nulla enim necessitas cogit incedere uoluntate gradientem, quamuis eum tum cum graditur incedere necessarium sit. Eodem igitur modo, si quid prouidentia praesens uidet, id esse necesse est tametsi nullam naturae habeat necessitatem. Atqui deus ea futura quae ex arbitrii libertate proueniunt praesentia contuetur; haec igitur ad intuitum relata diuinum necessaria fiunt per condicionem diuinae notionis, per se uero considerata ab absoluta naturae suae libertate non desinunt. Fient igitur procul dubio cuncta quae futura deus esse praenoscit, sed eorum quaedam de libero proficiscuntur arbitrio, quae quamuis eueniant exsistendo tamen naturam propriam non amittunt qua prius quam fierent etiam non euenire potuissent.

Quid igitur refert non esse necessaria, cum propter diuinae scientiae condicionem modis omnibus necessitatis instar eueniet? Hoc scilicet quod ea quae paulo ante proposui, sol oriens et gradiens homo, quae dum fiunt non fieri non possunt, eorum tamen unum prius quoque quam fieret necesse erat exsistere, alterum uero minime. Ita etiam, quae praesentia deus habet dubio procul exsistent, sed eorum hoc quidem de rerum necessitate descendit illud uero de potestate facientium. Haud igitur iniuria diximus haec si ad diuinam notitiam referantur necessaria, si per se considerentur necessitatis esse nexibus absoluta, sicuti omne quod sensibus patet si ad rationem referas uniuersale est, si ad se ipsa respicias singulare. Sed si in mea, inquies, potestate situm est mutare propositum, euacuabo prouidentiam, cum quae illa praenoscit forte mutauero. Respondebo propositum te quidem tuum posse deflectere, sed quoniam et id te posse et an facias quoque conuertas praesens prouidentiae ueritas intuetur diuinam te praescientiam non posse uitare, sicuti praesentis oculi effugere non possis intuitum quamuis te in uarias actiones libera uoluntate conuerteris. Quid igitur, inquies, ex

Wilt thou, then, say: "Shall the Divine knowledge be changed at my discretion, so that, when I will this or that, providence changes its knowledge correspondingly?"

'Surely not.'

'True, for the Divine vision anticipates all that is coming, and transforms and reduces it to the form of its own present knowledge, and varies not, as thou deemest, in its foreknowledge, alternating to this or that, but in a single flash it forestalls and includes thy mutations without altering. And this ever-present comprehension and survey of all things God has received, not from the issue of future events, but from the simplicity of His own nature. Hereby also is resolved the objection which a little while ago gave thee offence—that our doings in the future were spoken of as if supplying the cause of God's knowledge. For this faculty of knowledge, embracing all things in its immediate cognizance, has itself fixed the bounds of all things, yet itself owes nothing to what comes after.

'And all this being so, the freedom of man's will stands unshaken, and laws are not unrighteous, since their rewards and punishments are held forth to wills unbound by any necessity. God, who foreknoweth all things, still looks down from above, and the ever-present eternity of His vision concurs with the future character of all our acts, and dispenseth to the good rewards, to the bad punishments. Our hopes and prayers also are not fixed on God in vain, and when they are rightly directed cannot fail of effect. Therefore, withstand vice, practise virtue, lift up your souls to right hopes, offer humble prayers to Heaven. Great is the necessity of righteousness laid upon you if ye will not hide it from yourselves, seeing that all your actions are done before the eyes of a Judge who seeth all things.'

meane dispositione scientia diuina mutabitur, ut cum ego nunc hoc nunc illud uelim illa quoque noscendi uices alternare uideatur?

Minime.

Omne namque futurum diuinus praecurrit intuitus et ad praesentiam propriae cognitionis retorquet ac reuocat; nec alternat, ut aestimas, nunc hoc nunc aliud praenoscendi uice, sed uno ictu mutationes tuas manens praeuenit atque complectitur. Quam comprehendendi omnia uisendique praesentiam non ex futurarum prouentu rerum sed ex propria deus simplicitate sortitus est. Ex quo illud quoque resoluitur quod paulo ante posuisti, indignum esse si scientiae dei causam futura nostra praestare dicantur. Haec enim scientiae uis praesentaria notione cuncta complectens rebus modum omnibus ipsa constituit, nihil uero posterioribus debet.

Quae cum ita sint, manet intemerata mortalibus arbitrii libertas nec iniquae leges solutis omni necessitate uoluntatibus praemia poenasque proponunt. Manet etiam spectator desuper cunctorum praescius deus uisionisque eius praesens semper aeternitas cum nostrorum actuum futura qualitate concurrit bonis praemia malis supplicia dispensans. Nec frustra sunt in deo positae spes preces que, quae cum rectae sunt inefficaces esse non possunt. Auersamini igitur uitia, colite uirtutes, ad rectas spes animum subleuate, humiles preces in excelsa porrigite. Magna uobis est, si dissimulare non uultis, necessitas indicta probitatis cum ante oculos agitis iudicis cuncta cernentis.

Credit where it is due

A project like this cannot come together without a variety of help. Since every step of the way is open source, public domain or freely available, I would like to give credit for the tools I have used.

Open Office – openoffice.org – I used the word processor for the body of the book. Truly the best on-computer office suite available.

GIMP – gimp.org – Any of the graphics editing needed for this book was done with GIMP. It is not Adobe Photoshop, but what it lacks there is makes up for in being open source.

Scribus – scribus.net – An open source page design software, which I used for the cover.

Linden Hill – theleagueofmoveabletype.com – The book is set in Linden Hill. Finding fonts that are both freely available and beautiful can be tricky. This foundry manages both.

Wheel of fortune graphic – This is one of those graphics you find online for which the source has been stripped clean. It's pretty clearly English and no earlier than Henry VII's reign, as both Henry VII and Richard III are depicted at 10 and 2, respectively, on the wheel. Past that, I cannot say and reverse image searches turn up other copies of the image, but also without source.

There might be a few other groups I have forgotten, but I think I have covered every organization whose work I have used to put this book together.

There are also many people who deserve a bit of credit, even if they did not know it: Lou Bolchazy, *requiesce in pace mi patrone*, taught me that you can make whatever books you want and that you shouldn't listen to naysayers. Laura Gibbs and Geoffrey Steadman have shown the way on semi-academic self-publishing. Nina Paley has shown the way on copyright. Stephen Duncombe has shown that academics and open source go together. Alexander Arguelles has created an amazing list of Great Books, which I plan to mine for future editions of the Open Source Classics (http://bit.ly/1dgSzeZ). Thank you to all of you.

All of the flaws in this book are wholly my own. If you find any, please e-mail me at pete@pluteopleno.com with the subject line: corrigenda so I can incorporate corrections as they need to be incorporated.